KEY THEMES IN SOCIAL POLICY

Key Themes in Social Policy provides an accessible and authoritative introduction to the key concepts used in social policy, from autonomy to well-being.

With over 100 ideas discussed, this is a comprehensive student guide and is designed to help readers to gain a deeper understanding of major debates and issues. Each entry:

- explores the background of the concept
- discusses its relationship to the social sciences
- describes its relevance to social policy and how widespread its use is
- outlines some of the key thinkers and research on the topic and gives suggestions for further reading.

Making it easy to understand and use the most important ideas in the area, this is an essential companion for all students taking social policy courses.

Patricia Kennedy is a Senior Lecturer in Social Policy in the School of Applied Social Science at University College Dublin, Ireland. She has taught social policy since 1993 and co-founded the Irish Social Policy Association in 1997.

KEY THEMES IN SOCIAL POLICY

Patricia Kennedy

Routledge
Taylor & Francis Group

LONDON AND NEW YORK

First published 2013
by Routledge
2 Park Square, Milton Park, Abingdon, Oxon, OX14 4RN

Simultaneously published in the USA and Canada
by Routledge
711 Third Avenue, New York, NY 10017

Routledge is an imprint of the Taylor & Francis Group, an informa business

British Library Cataloguing in Publication Data
A catalogue record for this book is available from the British Library

Library of Congress Cataloging in Publication Data
Kennedy, Patricia, 1963–
Key themes in social policy / Patricia Kennedy.
p. cm.
1. Social policy. I. Title.
HN18.3.K46 2013
361.2'5—dc23
2012033397

ISBN: 978-0-415-52096-6 (hbk)
ISBN: 978-0-415-52097-3 (pbk)
ISBN: 978-0-203-59418-6 (ebk)

Typeset in Sabon
by Prepress Projects Ltd, Perth, UK

This book is dedicated to my wonderful daughter Millie.

And a special thank you to Conor, Dylan and Fionn for their love, patience and support.

CONTENTS

INTRODUCTION

Key Themes in Social Policy introduces students to some of the themes which come to the fore again and again in social policy studies. Social Policy as a subject evolved from the subject of Social Administration, whose beginnings can be traced back to the end of the nineteenth century. Some of the early empirical studies were carried out in Britain at the end of the nineteenth century and focused on poverty. However, if we look at policies we see examples as far back as the Elizabethan Poor Law of 1604. Social insurance was introduced by Otto von Bismarck in the nineteenth century. If one reads the classic texts in Social Policy associated with such writers as Richard Titmuss and Amartya Sen, more recent classic feminist approaches by Fiona Williams, or comparative studies such as those associated with Esping-Andersen, one recognizes themes emerging. If one reads government reports, pieces of legislation, for example the Poor Law, the Beveridge Report, Obama's Patient Protection and Affordable Care Act, or reports published by the World Health Organization (WHO), the Organisation for Economic Co-operation and Development (OECD), the International Monetary Fund (IMF), the European Union (EU), the International Labour Organization (ILO) and the World Bank, similar themes emerge. Even though different views are evident and a range of explanations and empirical evidence is presented, themes exist. After a while, one may begin to recognize these, but, when starting out as a student of Social Policy, it is useful to have signposts to help in grasping these themes, identifying and managing them so that when they are encountered one has a working knowledge and adequate understanding to progress.

This is the aim of this book. It is concerned with equipping students with a basic knowledge when they are engaging with social policy literature and documents in various guises. It is a reference book which introduces a broad range of concepts and theories, which need to be identifiable, accessible and comprehensible to students as they launch an investigation into social policy at third level. It is a guide to a more comprehensive treatment of the topic. The types of themes which emerge are in relation to defining welfare, welfare states, systems and regimes, redistribution and what it involves. Broader philosophical ideas on justice, equality, needs and rights are introduced in an accessible way. They are presented alphabetically as a useful, accessible resource for students.

This book is based on over thirty years of reading social policy in various forms, and over sixteen years introducing key concepts and theories in social policy to undergraduate Social Policy students. Any two people will choose different themes; however, there are many viewed as central. Concepts are abstract and so can be difficult to grasp. In my teaching I have drawn on a broad range of writing on a multitude of topics.

They come from a range of social sciences, including sociology, philosophy, economics, politics and social psychology. This book is aimed at undergraduate students. In explaining the themes, concepts are presented and explained. Concepts enable us to ask intelligent questions. We need consensus on the possible meaning of the concept to ensure we have a shared understanding. That is not to say that a concept cannot have a variety of meanings and standpoints, but we need to know this. To make sense of the empirical evidence in social policy we need tools to understand and analyse. To do this we need concepts. Concepts are words, abstract ideas which we use daily to explain, understand and analyse. Many of them are the common everyday words used in conversation. Even the youngest children claim they have rights: 'that's not fair', 'he got more than me'. When we start to interrogate the world as policy analysts, we need clarity. Social policy analysis employs concepts to understand, explain, construct and deconstruct empirical evidence. This is the task of this book. It is concerned with clarifying the true definition of the words used in social policy debates. Defining concepts will help us to use them precisely, to understand their theoretical underpinnings. Some words have lost meaning through overuse; for example power, exclusion and equality. What do these mean? Many of the concepts presented in this book are contested. They are also interconnected. Although each section ends with suggestions for further reading, each will contain references that can be found in the extensive bibliography, which is a resource. There will be cross-referencing when useful. I have incorporated texts stretching back over several decades, which are the foundation stones of social policy. I draw on recent material from relevant journals and organizations and introduce examples of policy from around the globe. It is my hope that this book will serve as a launch pad for Social Policy students and help them on their journey of discovery of this very important academic subject.

ABBREVIATIONS

European Union (EU)
Gross Domestic Product (GDP)
International Labour Conference (ILC)
International Labour Organization (ILO)
International Monetary Fund (IMF)
Organisation for Economic Co-operation and Development (OECD)
World Health Organization (WHO)

KEY THEMES IN SOCIAL POLICY

ACTIVE WELFARE

> Related entries: Labour

Active welfare is an approach to welfare which is concerned with encouraging welfare participants to take action which will move them towards employment. The corollary is passive and raises assumptions about what it means to be active in society. For example, those involved in caring work and in voluntary work participate actively in society but, because they are not engaged in paid work, are often perceived as inactive. The active welfare subject is often described as a citizen, customer, stakeholder or consumer whose responsibilities rather than entitlement are emphasized. Active welfare is associated with active labour market policies (ALMPs), which consist of a range of strategies which involve assistance, training and employment initiatives to support the unemployed to enter/re-enter the labour market. In its *Jobs Strategy* the OECD (1994) states: 'A progressive shift of resources is needed from passive income support to active measures. Active labour market policies improve access to the labour market and jobs; develop job-related skills; and promote more efficient labour markets' (http://www1.oecd.org/sge/min/job94/part2d.htm (2 of 4), accessed 15 March 2012).

The European Commission adopted the concept of active welfare in its *European Employment Strategy* (1997). This was promoted and reiterated by the OECD in its revised *Jobs Strategy* in 2007. Active welfare stresses that payments are conditional on participation in some kind of programme generally associated with training and/ or work. Conditions regulating income protection schemes are linked to stronger work incentives and to labour and targeted at specific groups of unemployed people. Welfare recipients have to show they are trying to obtain work or are taking steps to retrain and improve their employment opportunities by up-skilling. The key components of such a strategy are as follows: registration for placement and assessment of work availability as preconditions for benefit payment; regular and intense interventions in the period of unemployment; explicit regulations regarding job search requirements; direct referrals to vacant jobs; referrals to ALMPs (including education, training and employment programmes), with compulsory participation for some job-seekers (OECD, 2007). The OECD is an important source of information on ongoing developments in this area.

Van Berkel (2009), in a comparative study of the UK, the Netherlands, Denmark and Germany, indicates that active welfare is an international phenomenon and, although it can take different forms, it always involves a stronger integration of income protection and activation programmes alongside increased conditionality criteria. Such strategies demand greater cooperation between income protection agencies and those responsible for activation programmes. Van Berkel argues that:

> the shift from income protection to activation as the core objective of policy interventions targeted at unemployed people implies that the agencies involved in

the provision of services for the unemployed have to change their 'core business' and introduce new technologies for social interventions.

(Van Berkel, 2009: 29)

Van Berkel differentiates between services involved in 'people-sustaining' activities, concerned with the well-being of clients, and activation, which is concerned with 'people-changing' (Van Berkel, 2009: 9). He indicates that with active labour market policies a more individual response is required, which means making room for discretion.

Kelly and colleagues (2011) indicate that, although research on the impact of active labour market programmes is far from conclusive, it is possible to identify types of programmes that have been found to enhance employment prospects of participants. Kelly and colleagues (2011) present a useful typology for understanding ALMPs. On the one hand they identify strategies to assist jobseekers to reintegrate into the labour market which are encouraging and supportive and can include personal development-type activities such as counselling, vocational guidance and individual action plans, as well as job search programmes. On the other hand, a more punitive approach involves monitoring attempts to seek work and these can include forfeiting a portion of income for non-compliance. Sometimes programmes are targeted at specific groups, including early school leavers or lone parents. Kelly identifies different types of training programmes in the public and private sectors. In the former, job creation programmes focus on public jobs that produce public goods and services. These can be traced back as far as public work programmes in the nineteenth century. Private-sector schemes are concerned with providing incentives for employers to maintain or create jobs and include such measures as wage subsidies and/or start-up grants. Such subsidies can be given directly to the employer or employee, tend to be for a fixed period of time and are often targeted at more disadvantaged individuals. Start-up incentives, which are provided to unemployed individuals who want to establish their own businesses, are another type of private-sector incentive programme. However, Kelly and colleagues advise that a strict classification of an ALMP is not always feasible, as some countries have schemes that contain elements of more than one programme (Kelly *et al.*, 2011: 8).

Kenworthy (2010: 435) suggests that 'activation is by no means novel' but 'what is new is the centrality of activation to modern welfare states', and identifies several reasons for their adoption, including funding the welfare state; fairness; poverty reduction; social inclusion; promoting women's independence and fulfilment; and sometimes external encouragement. Kenworthy, like Van Berkel (2009) and Kelly and colleagues (2011), outlines how activation can be pursued through restrictions and conditionality; assistance with job search and placement; assistance with transportation; in-work subsidy; employer subsidy; public employment; the promotion of part-time and flexible work schedules; reduction of tax disincentives to second earners; reduction of real wages; reduction of non-wage labour costs; easing of employment protection regulations; the introduction of family-friendly policies; human capital measures; and definite career ladders. Interestingly, Kenworthy concludes that there is:

more than one route to rising employment and to a high employment rate. There may be elective affinities among certain activation policies, but countries as diverse as Denmark, the Netherlands, and the United States have (at least until 2008) secured comparatively high rates of employment with very different sets of policies and institutions.

(Kenworthy, 2010: 446)

Van Berkel and colleagues (2011) explore such different policies in *The Governance of Active Welfare States in Europe*, in which they compare reforms in a diverse range of countries including the UK, France, Germany, Italy, the Netherlands, the Czech Republic, Sweden and Finland. The book is a result of a European research network on reconciling work and welfare in Europe (RECWOVE).

Further reading

Kelly, E., McGuinness, S. and O'Connell, P.J. (2011) *What Can Active Labour Market Policies Do?* Renewal Series Paper 1, Economic and Social Research Institute, Dublin, November.

Kenworthy, L. (2010) 'Labour Market Activation', in Castles, F., Leibfried, S., Lewis, J., Obinger, H. and Pierson, C. (eds.), *The Oxford Handbook of the Welfare State*. Oxford: Oxford University Press, pp. 435–447.

Van Berkel, R. (2009) 'The Provision of Income Protection and Activation Services for the Unemployed in "Active" Welfare States: An International Comparison', *Journal of Social Policy*, 39(1): 17–34.

Van Berkel, R., De Graaf, W. and Sirovátka, T. (eds.) (2011) *The Governance of Active Welfare States in Europe*. London: Palgrave Macmillan.

AGENCY

Related entries: Autonomy

Agency refers to the capacity of an individual to act, to make their own free choice. It is often discussed in relation to structure, which refers to the context such as social class, gender, race, ethnicity within which individuals operate. Deacon and Mann (1999: 413) define agency as: 'actions, activities, decisions, and behaviours that represent some measure of meaningful choice. That does not mean that such choices are free floating of any structural constraints, but rather that some other option also existed, albeit also restrained'. They argue in favour of agency as an analytical concept in welfare scholarship.

Giddens (1976: 161) refers to knowledgeable and enabled agents. He argues that reflexivity is important and that people are engaging with the structures in which they live, which in turn influences how they act. Sewell (1992: 20) suggests: 'To be an agent means to be capable of exerting some degree of control over the social relations in which one is enmeshed, which in turn implies the ability to transform those social relations to some degree'. Agency is linked to one's relationship to resources. Hays (1994: 62) argues that people 'are *not* mere automatons habitually following a precise and all-encompassing pattern dictated by social structure'. She suggests: 'agency always implies that an array of alternative forms of behavior are possible, and that people make (conscious or unconscious) *choices* among those alternatives' (Hays, 1992: 62).

Williams (1999: 689) refers to the welfare subject 'as an active element in the social relations of welfare, rather than the passive recipient of (benevolent or controlling) welfare'. While welfare systems exist, individuals retain the power to choose how to behave within the constraints of such systems. Williams acknowledges the importance of identity in relation to exercising agency and that recognition of identity can lead to political action in relation to demands for redistribution of resources. She links this to demands for resources from groups/movements which have become more vocal in line with the emergence of new social risks, for example: 'domestic violence, racial violence, forms of discrimination, child sexual abuse, lack of autonomy, rights circumscribed according to sexual preference, environmental risks from pollution' (Williams, 1999: 673). She argues that, as needs have been voiced, policy responses have developed accordingly. Thus, rather than being passive citizens who are recipients/beneficiaries of welfare, citizens can actively engage with and shape welfare.

Further reading

Giddens, A. (1976) *New Rules of Sociological Method: A Positive Critique of Interpretive Sociologies.* London: Hutchinson.
Hays, S. (1994) 'Structure and Agency and the Sticky Problem of Culture', *Sociological Theory,* 12(1): 57–72.
Sewell, W.H. (1992) 'A Theory of Structure: Duality, Agency and Transformation', *American Journal of Sociology,* 98(1): 1–29.
Williams, F. (1999) 'Good Enough Principles for Welfare', *Journal of Social Policy,* 28(4): 667–687.

ALTRUISM

Related entries: Community; Sustainable development; Welfare/well-being

Altruism is usually expressed as unselfish behaviour. Studies of altruism have been conducted in many disciplines including economics and psychology. Heywood (2007: 55) defines altruism as 'concern for the interests and welfare of others, based either upon enlightened self-interest or a belief in a common humanity'. Adam Smith wrote: 'how selfish so-ever man may be supposed, there are evidently some principles in his nature, which interest him to the fortune of others, and render their happiness necessary to him, though he deserves nothing from it except the pleasure of seeing it' (quoted by Collard, 1978: 52).

Altruism has been the focus of many social policy scholars since the 1960s. Titmuss's (1970) book *The Gift Relationship* is a seminal work in which he concentrates on altruism in relation to blood donation. He asks the question: 'why give to strangers?' For Titmuss (1968: 22) altruism is central to social policy:

the grant, or the gift of unilateral transfer – whether it takes the form of cash, time, energy, satisfaction, blood or even life itself – is the distinguishing mark of the social (in policy and administration) just as exchange or bilateral transfer is the mark of the economic.

Pinker (1971: 211) refers to the 'altruistic potentialities of ordinary citizens' and suggests:

> the welfare institutions of a society symbolise an unstable compromise between compassion and indifference, between altruism and self-interest. If men were predominantly altruistic, compulsory forms of social service would not be necessary; and if men were exclusively self-regarding such compulsion would be impossible. The spirit of altruism, far from being a natural flowering of human nature, must be seen as the product of the rigorous discipline of injunction to self-denial and the repression of the grosser form of self-love.

Writing on people's motivation in relation to welfare, Julian Le Grand (1997) suggests that the market turned knights into knaves, knights being more altruistic than knaves, who are self-interested. He suggests:

> a welfare state constructed on the assumption that people are motivated primarily by their own self interest – that they are . . . *knaves,* would be quite different from one constructed on the assumption that people are predominantly public spirited or altruistic – that they are what we might term *knights* in contrast to knaves. Similarly, if policy-makers work on the assumption that people are essentially passive or unresponsive – neither knights or knaves, but *pawns* – then again the policy concerned would be quite different from one designed on the assumption that human beings respond actively to the incentive structures with which they are faced.
>
> (Le Grand, 1997: 154)

Land (2008: 50) suggests: 'the collective obligations which underpin social policy are based on a mixture of altruism and self-interest'. She quotes Beveridge on altruism meaning 'a sense of Divine vocation', referring to women's 'Serving, exhausting oneself without thought of personal reward – isn't that what most women do most of their lives in peace or war?' and 'women's altruism within the family was therefore more accurately described as "compulsory"' (Land, 2008: 54). A similar sentiment was echoed by the economist Becker (1991: 303), who argues:

> families in all societies, including market oriented societies, have been responsible for a sizeable part of economic activity – half or more – for they have produced much of the consumption, education, health and other human capital of members. If I am correct that altruism dominates family behaviour, perhaps to the same extent as selfishness dominates market transactions, then altruism is much more important in economic life than is generally understood.

Land (2008: 50) suggests 'support for altruism and reciprocity in the future may require a fundamental review of the obligations and rights of citizenship'.

Altruism has become prominent in discourse on the environment and sustainable development. The *World Commission on Environment and Development Report* (WCED, 1987) states sustainable development 'meets the needs of the present without compromising the ability of future generations to meet their own needs' (WCED, 1987: 43). It was concerned with equity, within and between generations, and it focused on participation in decision making. It referred to the environment as 'where we all live' and development as 'what we all do in attempting to improve our lot' (WCED, 1987: xi).

Further reading

Collard, D. (1978) *Altruism and Economy: A Study in Non-Selfish Economics*. Oxford: Martin Robertson.

Land, H. (2008) 'Altruism, Reciprocity, and Obligation', in Alcock, P., May, M. and Rowlingson, K. (eds.), *The Student's Companion to Social Policy*, 3rd edn. Oxford: Blackwell, pp. 50–57.

Le Grand, J. (1997) 'Knights, Knaves or Pawns? Human Behaviour and Social Policy', *Journal of Social Policy*, 26: 149–169.

Titmuss, R. (1970) *The Gift Relationship*. London: Allen and Unwin.

ASSISTANCE PAYMENTS

> Related entries: Deserving/undeserving; Discretion; Means test; Selectivity; Stigma

Assistance payments are cash payments to individuals and families. They are usually based on assessed need. They are targeted non-contributory means-tested payments. They are selectivist. They are judged as being less wasteful than universal payments, yet there is a cost associated with such payments. This can be a financial cost associated with administration and a personal cost of stigmatizing the recipient. They are financed from taxation and are vertical, as they usually involve redistribution from the better-off to the less well-off. They are associated with poverty traps and unemployment traps. Assistance payments are associated with a residual model of welfare, as identified by Titmuss (1974: 30), as a system which assumes the family is responsible for its own welfare and the state will only intervene as a last resort when families and individuals are incapable of providing for themselves. Such payments can be traced back to the Poor Law. In a similar vein, Esping-Andersen (1990) uses 'liberal' to describe a welfare regime in which assistance payments are favoured and are targeted at low-income people who are dependent on the state for welfare. He suggests 'in this model the progress of social reform has been severely circumscribed by traditional, liberal, work-ethic norms: it is one where the limits of welfare equal the marginal propensity to opt for welfare instead of work' (Esping-Andersen, 1999:

26). Generally there are strict entitlement rules, payments are modest and stigma is associated with their receipt. The ILO (1942: 84) defines social assistance as 'benefits to persons of small means as of right in amounts sufficient to meet minimum standards of need and financed from taxation'. Gough and colleagues (1997) present a typology of social assistance. They caution that social assistance does not have a fixed or universal meaning (Gough *et al.*, 1997: 18). However, they define it as 'means tested or income-related benefits where eligibility is dependent upon current or recent resources, though other categorical conditions may also apply' (Gough *et al.*, 1997: 19). These they refer to as 'resource-tested benefits'. Bahle and colleagues (2010) suggest that the first comprehensive study on social assistance in OECD countries was that undertaken by Eardley and colleagues (1996) and remains the major reference. Eardley and colleagues develop a taxonomy of benefits and introduce three major dimensions: poverty-tested versus means-tested; cash versus tied (i.e. earmarked for specific purposes); and general versus categorical, targeted at a specific group. Assistance payments remain an important part of welfare provision and this is likely to endure in the context of a global economic downturn. There is a trend towards active labour market policies which emphasize personal responsibility and focus on shifting the recipient from welfare to work.

Further reading

Bahle, T., Pfeifer, M. and Wendt, C. (2010) 'Social Assistance', in Castles, F., Leibfried, S., Lewis, J., Obinger, H. and Pierson, C. (eds.), *The Oxford Handbook of the Welfare State*. Oxford: Oxford University Press, pp. 448–461.

Eardley, T., Bradshaw, J., Ditch, J., Gough, I. and Whiteford, P. (1996) *Social Assistance in OECD Countries: Synthesis Report*, Research Report 46. London. HMSO: Department of Social Security. Available at http://research.dwp.gov.uk/aasd/asd5/rrepo46.pdf

Gough, I., Bradshaw, J., Ditch, J., Eardley, T. and Whiteford, P. (1997) 'Social Assistance in OECD Countries', *Journal of European Social Policy*, 7(1): 17–43.

ASYLUM SEEKER

Related entries: Citizenship; Deserving/undeserving; Ethnicity; Migration; Needs; Race; Stigma

Asylum seeker is a term which has appeared more noticeably in policy documents since the end of the 1990s. Many national and international debates have evolved in relation to rights and needs of asylum seekers and appropriate policy responses. The International Organization for Migration (IOM, 2012) defines an asylum seeker as:

A person who seeks safety from persecution or serious harm in a country other than his or her own and awaits a decision on the application for refugee status under relevant international and national instruments. In case of a negative decision, the person must leave the country and may be expelled, as may any non-national in an irregular or unlawful situation, unless permission to stay is provided on humanitarian or other related grounds.

(http://www.iom.int/jahia/Jahia/about-migration/key-migration-terms/lang/en#Asylum-Seeker, accessed 20 March 2012)

Further reading

Bloch, A. (2008) 'Migrants and Asylum-Seekers', in Alcock, P., May, M. and Rowlingson, K. (eds.), *The Student's Companion to Social Policy*. Oxford: Blackwell, pp. 410–417.

IOM (International Organization for Migration) (2004) *IOM Glossary on Migration*, International Migration Law Series No. 25. Available at http://www.iom.int/jahia/Jahia/about-migration/key-migration-terms/lang/en#Immigration

AUTONOMY

> **Related entries: Agency; Capabilities; Citizenship; Feminism; Liberty; Power**

Autonomy is generally understood to mean self-government. Doyal and Gough (1991: 59) in their classic text *A Theory of Human Need* suggest: 'individuals express their autonomy with reference to their capacity to formulate consistent aims and strategies which they believe to be in their interests and their attempts to put them into practice in the activities in which they engage'. They identify key variables which affect levels of individual autonomy. These are the level of understanding a person has about herself, the culture and what is expected of her as an individual within it; the psychological capacity she has to formulate opinions for herself; and the objective opportunities enabling her to act accordingly. They quote Raz (1986: 154), who argues that significant autonomy is a matter of degree:

> A person may be more or less autonomous . . . autonomous persons are those who can shape their life and determine its course. They are not merely rational agents who can choose between options after evaluating relevant information, but agents who can in addition adopt personal projects, develop relationships, and accept commitments to causes, through which their personal integrity and sense of dignity and self-respect are made concrete. In a word, significantly autonomous agents are part creators of their own moral world.
>
> (Doyal and Gough, 1991: 67–68)

Friedman discusses feminist scholarship on autonomy. Whereas feminist writing in the 1970s perceived autonomy as having a liberating potential for women, in the 1980s and 1990s this was challenged by some feminists as too individualistic. The critique has continued into more recent times with a focus on relational autonomy (Friedman, 1997: 40). Friedman argues that feminist writers have criticized the notion of autonomy because it ignores the social nature of the self and the importance of social relations. It is a problematic term as it is too closely linked with individual liberalism. The most prominent critics are Nancy Chodorow (1978) and Carol Gilligan (1982).

For the philosopher Gerald Dworkin (1988: 30–31), autonomy is concerned with achieving meaning in one's life 'in all kinds of ways: from stamp collecting to taking care of one's invalid parents'. For Dworkin:

> autonomy is conceived as a second-order capacity of persons to reflect critically upon their first-order preferences, desires, wishes, and so forth and the capacity to accept or attempt to change these in light of higher-order preferences and values. By exercising such a capacity persons define their nature, give meaning and coherence to their lives and take responsibility for the kind of person they are.
>
> (Dworkin, 1988: 20)

In *The Three Worlds of Welfare Capitalism*, Esping-Andersen (1990) employs the concept of decommodification, which is closely related to autonomy as it is related to one's ability to choose not to engage with the labour market. Lister argues that, without social citizenship, political and civil status will be undermined. She states that social citizenship rights 'promote the "de-commodification of labour" by decoupling the living standards of individual citizens from their "market value" so that they are not totally dependent on selling their labour power on the market' (Lister, 1997: 17). She stresses the importance of linking social citizenship rights with human need, and adopts Doyal and Gough's (1991: 54) model of human need, which stresses the importance of personal autonomy.

Writing on gender and welfare regimes, Sainsbury (1999: 1) states: 'the bases of entitlement differ in their emancipatory or regulatory potential for women'. She refers to the extension of the concept of rights by feminist writers to include personal autonomy, going beyond the ability to form an autonomous household to incorporate personhood and bodily integrity. This is endorsed by Williams (1999: 680), who refers to 'the right of the individual to protect his/her body against external or internal risk. The body is a site of control, resistance, and pleasure; it is inscribed in the social relations of power in which it exists'. She continues: 'our bodies mark the physical boundaries of our sense of self, our own dignity and self-respect. Respect for the integrity of the body is fundamental to the maintenance of the autonomy of the welfare citizen' (Williams, 1999: 680). O'Connor (1993) suggests that the incorporation of gender into writing on welfare regimes demands a reassessment of the conventional definitions of political mobilization and participation and a modification of the concept of decommodification, which she says 'must be supplemented by the concept of personal autonomy or insulation from personal and/or public dependence' (O'Connor, 1993: 501). She suggests that personal autonomy 'is central to unravelling the complexity of the relationships amongst state, market and family' (O'Connor, 1993: 513).

Further reading

Doyal, L. and Gough, I. (1991) *A Theory of Human Need*. London: Macmillan.
Dworkin, G. (1988) *The Theory and Practice of Autonomy*. Cambridge: Cambridge University Press.
Friedman, M. (1997) 'Autonomy and Social Relationships: Rethinking the Feminist Critique', in Meyers, D.T. (ed.), *Feminists Rethink the Self*. Boulder, CO: Westview Press, pp. 40–61.

BASIC INCOME

Related entries: Citizenship; Entitlement; Needs; Poverty; Wages

Basic income is an income maintenance strategy which guarantees every citizen an amount of money on a regular basis as a right. Lister (2008: 238) refers to a *citizen's income* or *basic income*: 'Under which every individual would receive a tax-free benefit without any conditions attached. Access would be on the basis of citizenship rights alone'. Debates about basic income are a part of social policy discourse. *Basic Income Studies,* an academic journal, was established in 2010 as a response to the increased interest in basic income as a strategy. De Wispelaere and Stirton (2004: 266) argue that 'one of the intriguing aspects of basic income is precisely its capacity to secure support across the ideological spectrum'. They argue that debates on basic income have reached maturity and suggest that any basic income strategy must be designed with context in mind. They suggest that universalist strategies can take a myriad of forms. They explore the many dimensions of basic income, including universality, individuality, conditionality, uniformity, frequency and duration, modality and adequacy. They suggest that a bottom-up approach is preferred and that it can take different shapes in different welfare systems.

An example of basic income can be seen in Alaska, where an annual dividend is paid to Alaskan residents from investment earnings on mineral royalties. Alaskans receive a share in a portion of the state minerals revenue in the form of a dividend. The Permanent Fund Dividend (PFD) is based on the number of eligible Alaskan applicants in a dividend year and half of the statutory net income averaged over the five most recent fiscal years. The available funds are also reduced by prior-year dividend obligations, PFD operation expenses and other state agency programme appropriations. The Alaska Department of Revenue, PFD Division, is responsible for determining applications (http://www.pfd.state.ak.us/AboutUs.aspx).

Further reading

Basic Income Studies, http://www.degruyter.com/view/j/bis
De Wispelaere, J. and Stirton, L. (2004) 'The Many Faces of Universal Basic Income', *Political Quarterly*, 75(3): 266–274.
Lister, R. (2008) 'Citizenship and Access to Welfare', in Alcock, P., May, M. and Rowlingson, K. (eds.), *The Student's Companion to Social Policy*. Oxford: Blackwell, pp. 234–240.

BENEFIT

> Related entries: Bismarckian; Selectivity; Universality

A benefit is usually perceived as something positive. In relation to welfare it is associated with the receipt of resources, usually monetary. There are contributory and non-contributory benefits. Non-contributory benefits are allocated based on criteria other than financial need. They are financed out of the general taxation system and include payments to certain categories; for example, in Ireland child benefit is paid to families with children, regardless of means, and is non-contributory. On the other hand, contributory benefits are based on previous contributions and are paid out of a special social insurance fund. One has an entitlement based on one's previous contributions; for example, contributory unemployment, disability and old age benefits belong to these categories. Sometimes benefits are paid by the state, the employer, the private sector or a combination of all three. Benefits are perceived as less stigmatizing than assistance payments as they are usually based on right rather than financial need.

Benefit schemes are associated with the Bismarckian model of welfare. Otto von Bismarck (1815–98), Chancellor of the German Empire from 1887 to 1890, is credited with introducing benefit payments. They are based on the principle of social insurance, with an important role for employers. In 1883 he introduced health insurance and in 1884 accident insurance, followed by old age and disability pensions in 1889. Benefit schemes are related to previous earnings and occupation and are a middle way between more socialist and residual models of welfare. Titmuss (1974), in his three-pronged model of welfare, referred to the industrial-achievement model, a system in which entitlements are earned based on contributory payments associated with one's employment. The schemes are earnings related, and are concerned with maintaining one's standard of living if one has to exit the labour market.

Those who study social policy from a comparative perspective often examine how welfare systems have very different ways of organizing benefits. They are often presented as models of welfare or welfare regimes in attempts to explore difference.

Benefit in kind refers to benefits provided in the form of goods or services. In terms of welfare these can be resources such as education, housing or health care. In terms of payment for labour, payment in kind is a reward to complement a wage, which may include accommodation, transport or parking facilities, for example.

Benefit fraud is the term used to describe when people claim welfare payments to which they are not entitled.

Further reading

Bochel, H., Bochel, C., Page, R. and Sykes, R. (2009) *Social Policy: Themes, Issues and Debates*, 2nd edn. Harlow: Pearson.

BEVERIDGIAN WELFARE

Related entries: Bismarckian; Citizenship; Male breadwinner; Models of welfare

Beveridgian is a term used to describe a particular model of welfare which emerged after the publication of *Social Insurance and Allied Services* (The Beveridge Report; Beveridge 1942). It was the blueprint for the modern British welfare state and is commonly referred to by the name of its author, William Beveridge (1879–1963), who has been described as the founding father of the welfare state. The Committee on Social Insurance and Allied Services was established in June 1941 by the British Minister of Labour to inquire into the social security system. During the Second World War an interest in welfare reform developed alongside a concern that the current system was inefficient, as a number of government departments were engaged in the administration of welfare.

The Beveridge Report proposed a 'cradle to the grave' system for all British citizens. It formed the basis of the Labour government's (1945–51) programme for reform. It presented proposals for a national health service, family allowance, full employment and a comprehensive system of social insurance. It was seen as progress against the *five giants* of Want, Ignorance, Squalor, Idleness and Disease. It was based on three guiding principles: blending of experience of the past, comprehensive social planning, and cooperation between voluntary and public action and between the individual and the state. It designed a social insurance scheme which would provide a safety net in times when earning was interrupted, and for special events such as childbirth, marriage and death. It proposed flat rate contributions and benefits, simplification of administrative responsibility, and comprehensive coverage. It proposed guiding principles for social insurance policy. In times of sickness, retirement, unemployment and widowhood, benefits would be paid to those who had contributed. The report advocated a male-breadwinner model (Lewis, 1993: 61), which assumed the husband would participate in the labour market and earn a family wage and the wife/mother would be a carer/dependent. Colwill refers to the 'remarkably enduring influence of the Beveridge Report' and 'its spectacularly successful construction of womanhood in particular' (Colwill, 1994: 53).

Harris (1977) suggests that the report was used by the Ministry of Information as a means of fostering wartime morale. The report was viewed as revolutionary and on publication sold 100,000 copies within a month, and a special cheap edition was printed for circulation in the armed forces. Harris indicates that it was circulated among underground movements in Nazi-occupied countries and was viewed as propagandist in Germany. Beveridge was the Director of the London School of Economics from 1911 until 1937 and was an associate of the Fabians Sidney and Beatrice Webb.

Further reading

Beveridge, W. (1942) *Social Insurance and Allied Services* (Beveridge Report). London: HMSO.
Colwill, J. (1994) 'Beveridge, Women and the Welfare State', *Critical Social Policy*, 41: 53–78.
Harris, J. (1977) *William Beveridge, a Biography*. Oxford: Clarendon Press.

BISMARCKIAN MODEL

> Related entries: Benefit; Citizenship; Comparative social policy; Earnings;
> Entitlement; Models of welfare; Social insurance

The Bismarckian model of social policy is mostly associated with Germany; however, it was developed in other countries including Austria, France, Italy and the Netherlands. Hinrichs and Lynch (2010) note that the United States introduced a light version in the 1930s and southern European countries followed suit between the 1960s and 1970s. Otto von Bismarck (1815–98) became Prime Minister of Prussia in 1862 and was Chancellor of the German Empire from 1887 to 1890. He is credited with introducing social insurance legislation which is based on the principle of social insurance, with an important role for employers. In 1883 he introduced health insurance and in 1884 accident insurance, followed by old age and disability pensions in 1889. Benefit schemes are related to previous earnings and occupation, and the benefit system is a middle way between more socialist and residual models of welfare. The schemes are earnings related, and are concerned with maintaining one's standard of living if one has to exit the labour market. It embraces the principle of subsidiarity, which advocates that the state should intervene only as a last resort once individual and family resources are inadequate. The state, employers and trade unions are viewed as partners. It is based on consensus and has been judged as being gender biased in favour of men, as women have more broken relationships with the labour market owing to family responsibilities.

Scholarship on welfare regimes and models of welfare have focused on the Bismarckian model. Titmuss (1974), in his three-pronged model of welfare, referred to the industrial-achievement model, a system in which entitlements are earned based on contributory payments associated with one's employment. Esping-Andersen (1999: 24) refers to the social insurance model, which

> is a form of class politics. It sought, in fact, to achieve two simultaneous results in terms of stratification. The first was to consolidate divisions among wage-earners by legislating distinct programs for different class and status groups, each with its own conspicuously unique set of rights and privileges which was designed to accentuate the individual's appropriate station in life. The second objective was to tie the loyalties of the individual directly to the monarch or the central state authority. It allowed for a privileged welfare provision for the civil service.

Further reading

Esping-Andersen, G. (1990) *The Three Worlds of Welfare Capitalism*. Cambridge, UK: Polity Press.

Hinrichs, K. and Lynch, J.F. (2010) 'Old-Age Pensions', in Castles, F., Leibfried, S., Lewis, J., Obinger, H. and Pierson, C. (eds.), *The Oxford Handbook of the Welfare State*. Oxford: Oxford University Press, pp. 353–366.

Titmuss, R. (1974) *Social Policy: An Introduction*. London: Allen & Unwin.

BLACK ECONOMY

> Related entries: Labour

The black economy, shadow economy or informal economy refers to the exchange of goods or services which operates outside the formal economy. It is difficult to assess what occurs in the black economy because it is unofficial and hidden. Statistics are not gathered and usually the payment of tax is evaded. It can relate to illegal employment practices. It is often referred to as the informal economy. Black economies exist throughout the world. Feld and Schneider (2010: 111) suggest:

> The shadow economy includes all market-based legal production of goods and services that are deliberately concealed from public authorities for one or more reasons:
> (1) to avoid payment of income, value added or other taxes,
> (2) to avoid payment of social security contributions,
> (3) to avoid certain legal labour market standards, such as minimum wages, maximum working hours, safety standards, etc., and
> (4) to avoid certain administrative obligations, such as completing statistical questionnaires or other administrative forms.

They exclude both illegal underground economic activities (drug dealing etc.) and all household services and production.

The International Labour Conference (ILC) noted that, although there is 'no universally accurate or accepted description or definition' of the term informal economy, it may be taken to refer to 'all economic activities by workers and economic units that are – in law or in practice – not covered, or insufficiently covered, by formal arrangements' (ILC, 2002: 26). They are operating outside the law. The informal economy accounts for about half of the workers in the world and includes workers who are self-employed, work in a family-run business and work in informal enterprises. In most societies there is a growing divide between a formal global economy and the expansion of an informal local economy. Social protection and employment issues are interwoven owing to the manifold related risks.

Further reading

Feld, L.P. and Schneider, F. (2010) 'Survey on the Shadow Economy and Undeclared Earnings in OECD Countries', *German Economic Review*, 11(2): 109–149.

ILC (International Labour Conference) (2002) *Provisional Record: The Informal Economy (General Discussion)*, Committee on the Informal Economy, 90th Session, Geneva, June, paragraph 3. Available at http://www.ilo.org/public/english/standards/relm/ilc/ilc90/pdf/pr-25.pdf

BODY

> **Related entries: Autonomy; Care; Citizenship; Equality; Gender; Needs; Power; Race; Sexuality; Social justice**

The body is defined in anatomical, physiological terms, yet in the social sciences it is often discussed in a social context. Turner suggests that humans are perceived as having needs because they have bodies: 'Our basic needs are thus typically seen as physical; the need to eat, sleep and drink is a basic feature of people or organic systems. It is also used in social philosophy to recognize needs which are not overtly physical, for example the need for companionship and self-respect' (Turner, 2008: 19). We see how this has been interpreted in the social policy literature in different theories of need, for example those proposed by Maslow (1943) and Doyal and Gough (1991). The body is also central to debates on citizenship, for example in relation to bodily integrity and personal autonomy as discussed by Williams (1999). Twigg (2000a: 132) asserts: 'so far there has been no social policy of the body – though, as we shall see, one may be in the process of forming'. Twigg has contributed greatly to the literature on social policy and the body which has developed since then.

Several writers (Coffey, 2004; Twigg, 2000a, 2000b, 2002, 2006, 2008; Ellis and Dean, 1999) perceive that social policy has not concerned itself with the body as have other disciplines, yet the body is at the centre of most welfare needs, and social policy is concerned with bodies which are challenged for one reason or another. Twigg (2002) offers important insights when she presents six ways in which the body is relevant to social policy. These are (1) health; (2) community care; (3) areas where the body has been ignored in the name of 'good practice', giving old age and disability as examples; (4) bio-power in relation to institutions and professions; (5) consumptionist orientations to the body; and (6) finally, what she describes as cross-cutting categories of social policy, including gender, race, age and sexuality.

Coffey (2004: 83) draws our attention to the relevance of social policies, for example in relation to ageing bodies, and those that have been harmed physically or emotionally and may be in need of physical or emotional repair. This includes those that may have experienced abuse or addiction. She refers also to institutions in which bodies are housed, contained, restrained and manipulated. Coffey calls for a more embodied perspective within social policy and looks at three specific categories. The first is 'body work', focusing on the body in the everyday tasks of social policy, which include moving, tending, cleaning, caring and sheltering of the physical and emotional. Second, she refers to 'body organization': the way in which the institutions and spaces of social policy manage the body. These include schools, hospitals, prisons, residential homes and others involved in the management and organization of bodies. Finally, Coffey refers to 'body discourse': the construction of bodies through social policy discursive practices and talk. This involves talk, images, documents, regulations and professional codes (Coffey, 2004: 86). She talks of refocusing social policy through a 'body lens' which will add to the analytical scope of social policy (Coffey, 2004: 86).

Further reading

Coffey, A. (2004) 'Social Policy and the Body', in *Reconceptualising Social Policy, Sociological Perspectives on Contemporary Social Policy.* Maidenhead: Open University Press, pp. 77–94.
Turner, B.S. (2008) *The Body and Society*, 3rd edn. London: Sage.
Twigg, J. (2000a) 'Social Policy and the Body', in Lewis, G., Gewirtz, S. and Clarke, J. (eds.), *Rethinking Social Policy.* London: Sage, pp. 127–140.
Twigg, J. (2000b) *Bathing – The Body and Community Care.* London: Routledge.
Twigg, J. (2002) 'The Body in Social Policy: Mapping a Territory', *Journal of Social Policy*, 31(3): 421–439.
Twigg, J. (2006) *The Body in Health and Social Care.* London: Palgrave Macmillan.

BUREAUCRACY

Related entries: Deserving/undeserving; Discretion; Entitlement; Means testing; Power; Social administration

Bureaucracy refers to a form of organization which is hierarchical and complex. The term was introduced in 1745 by Monsieur de Gournay. It unites the Greek word *cracy* (to rule) with the French word *bureau* (office or writing table) (Giddens, 2006: 639). It was introduced to describe the development of organizations and within them administrative roles and functions. Thus, it is very important for social policy where there is an emphasis on the administration of welfare, often through or by the state.

Bureaucracy is usually associated with the sociologist Max Weber (1864–1920). He developed an ideal type which was characterized by people having specific tasks with associated knowledge and skills. There is a clear hierarchy of authority and a clear set of rules. It is based on the idea of building an impersonal system. Rules and guidelines are written down and adhered to. A feature of bureaucracies is the functional division of labour, with differential roles and tasks for individual bureaucrats. Within bureaucracies people have different skills and qualifications. There are professionals and semi-professionals who have a different range of skills and are empowered to make decisions based on professional guidelines. Management is usually concerned with performance criteria. Although structures are important in terms of achieving transparency and accountability, bureaucracies can be seen as unresponsive and distant. Bureaucracies are often perceived as inefficient, for example in relation to debates on the public service.

Bureaucracies are very much part of the complex delivery of welfare. If we look at the health service, for example, there are administrators, a broad range of medical professionals such as nurses and surgeons, and semi-professionals such as play workers. If we look at housing, we see a range of workers including planners, engineers, architects, housing officers and administrators. In the current economic recession there is an increasing emphasis on streamlining public services in countries including Ireland, Greece, Spain and Portugal, with part of the discourse arguing that existing structures are too wasteful and bureaucratic.

Street-level bureaucracy is a concept introduced by Michael Lipsky (1980). He argues that street-level bureaucrats, as front line workers, have to balance meeting their clients' needs with adhering to procedures. As a result, they sometimes develop reactionary strategies including rationing resources and screening and routinizing clients. Such strategies become a form of decision making. This could be applied to some welfare systems, for example when there are discretionary payments which are determined by an official having met a client face-to-face. Such a system exists in Ireland, where there is an Exceptional Needs Payment which stems from the Poor Law (www.welfare.ie).

Further reading

Giddens, A. (2006) *Sociology*, 5th edn. Cambridge, UK: Polity Press.
Lipsky, M. (1980) *Street Level Bureaucracy*. New York: Russell Sage Foundation.
Spicker, P. (2008) *Social Policy Themes and Approaches*, 2nd edn. Bristol: Policy Press.

CAPABILITIES

Related entries: Autonomy; Functionings; Needs; Poverty; Quality of life

Capability is ability: the potential to do something. In Social Policy the concept is associated with the writing of the Nobel laureate Amartya Sen (2009), who suggests that well-being is to do with what people can do (capabilities) and what people can be (functionings). Capabilities are to do with potential, and functionings are to do with realizing that potential and having achieved status, being part of something and being able to do something. This is a substantive approach in which outcomes are measurable and is closely linked to social justice. Sen states: 'Individual advantage is judged in the capability approach by a person's capability to do things he or she has reasons to value . . . The focus here is on the freedom that a person actually has to do this or be that thing that he or she may value doing or being' (Sen, 2009: 231–232). Sen argues that policies should focus on the expansion of capabilities.

The philosopher Martha Nussbaum, like Sen, links capabilities to well-being and argues for this approach as a constitutional guarantee. Nussbaum, in *Creating Capabilities* (Nussbaum, 2011), asks what each person is able to do and what opportunities are available to him or her. She argues that, to date, dominant theories of development have led to policies that ignore people's most basic human needs for

19

dignity and self-respect. She argues that if a country's Gross Domestic Product (GDP) increases each year, and there is a parallel increase in the numbers of people deprived of basic education, health care, and other opportunities, then it is questionable whether that country is really making progress. Thus, conventional economic indicators do not reflect the reality of people's lives.

The *capabilities approach* was adopted by the United Nations Development Programme (UNDP) in the Human Development Index (HDI) in 1990 (www.undp.com). This is a composite index that measures a country's average achievements in three basic aspects of human development: health, knowledge and income. It was first developed by the economist Mahbub ul Haq with the collaboration of Amartya Sen for the first Human Development Report in 1990. It was introduced as an alternative to conventional measures of national development, such as level of income and the rate of economic growth.

The British Equality and Human Rights Commission (EHRC) has adopted the capabilities approach. It lists those things that people need in order to thrive and identifies capabilities for adults grouped under ten headings or domains. These are life; physical security; health; education; standard of living; productive and valued activities; individual, family and social life; decision making, influence and voice; identity, expression and self-respect; and legal security (www.equalityhumanrights.com).

The EHRC (2009) also presents a children's list, which applies to 0- to 17-year-olds. It includes the capability to be alive; to live in physical security; to be healthy; to be knowledgeable, to understand and reason, and to have the skills to participate in society; to enjoy a comfortable standard of living, with independence and security; to engage in productive and valued activities; to enjoy individual, family and social life; to participate in decision making, have a voice and influence; the capability of being and expressing one's self, and having self-respect; and the capability of knowing that one will be protected and treated fairly by the law (www.equalityhumanrights.com).

In 2008, French President Sarkozy established *The Commission on the Measurement of Economic Performance and Social Progress* to explore the adequacy of current measures of economic performance, in particular those based on GDP figures, and to address broader concerns about the measurement of societal well-being and economic, environmental and social sustainability. The Commission was chaired by Professor Joseph E. Stiglitz, Columbia University. Professor Amartya Sen, Harvard University, was Chair Adviser. Professor Jean-Paul Fitoussi, Institut d'Etudes Politiques de Paris, President of the Observatoire Français des Conjonctures Economiques (OFCE), was Coordinator of the Commission. Its final report was published in September 2009 (Stiglitz *et al.*, 2009). Stiglitz and colleagues argue that the capabilities approach 'conceives a person's life as a combination of various "doings and beings" (functionings) and of his or her freedom to choose among these functionings (capabilities). Some of these capabilities may be quite elementary, such as being adequately nourished and escaping premature mortality, whereas others may be more complex, such as having the literacy required to participate actively in political life' (Stiglitz *et al.*, 2009: 42).

Walby (2012) explores in great detail the interpretations and implications of the work of Sen in theoretical and practical contexts. She reviews and clarifies the range of meaning of Sen's concepts in their philosophical and economic contexts; reviews the development of justice frameworks in the UNDP and the British EHRC and the

Government Equalities Office in its Equality Measurement Framework; and explores whether the use of Sen's capabilities approach makes any difference to the measurement of justice, fairness, equality and progress.

The Human Development and Capability Association was launched in September 2004. Amartya Sen was the founding President and remained President until 2006, when Martha Nussbaum became President. It now has members from over seventy countries and its aim is to promote research from many disciplines on problems related to impoverishment, justice and well-being (http://www.capabilityapproach.com).

Further reading

Burchardt, T. and Vizard, P. (2009) *Research Report 18: Developing an Equality Measurement Framework: A List of Substantive Freedoms for Adults and Children.* Centre for Analysis of Social Exclusion, London School of Economics. Available at http://www.equalityhuman-rights.com

Nussbaum, M. (2011) *Creating Capabilities: The Human Development Approach.* Cambridge, MA: Harvard University Press.

Sen, A. (2009) *The Idea of Justice.* London: Allen Lane.

Stiglitz, J., Sen, A. and Fitoussi, J. (2009) *Report by the Commission on the Measurement of Economic Performance and Social Progress.* Available at http://www.stiglitz-sen-fitoussi.fr

Walby, S. (2012) 'Sen and the Measurement of Justice and Capabilities: A Problem in Theory and Practice', *Theory, Culture & Society*, 29(1): 99–118.

CAPITALISM

> **Related entries: Bureaucracy; Class; Commodification and decommodification; Equality; Labour; Welfare**

Capitalism is a term used to describe modern economic systems of production and exchange. It can present in different guises but is widespread throughout the modern world. We can speak of capitalism in a national context, or in a global context as global capitalism. Capitalism is a system of wage labour and commodity production for sale or exchange for profit rather than for the use of those who produce it. Welfare capitalism refers to the organization of welfare within capitalist systems.

Karl Marx (1818–83) and Max Weber (1864–1920) developed theories of capitalism. Marx identified two elements in capitalism: capital and wage labour. Capital is any money, machines or factories which are used to make profit. Wage labour is used to refer to people who sell their labour. Marx argues that capitalism is a relationship between people, and in particular between two classes: the bourgeoisie who own the means of production, the non-labour elements, and the proletariat who own labour power. Herein lies the conflict which is central to Marxist analysis. Marx focused on production and social class, the relationship between those who owned the means of production and those who sell their labour. Spicker (2008: 94) acknowledges that 'Marxism is not a unified doctrine; it has come to stand for a wide range of opinions within an analytical framework that is critical of capitalist society'.

Max Weber (1864–1920) focused on economic issues but he also focused on religion, science and bureaucracy. He held that religious outlook was important in creating a capitalist outlook (Giddens, 2006: 113). As science shapes technology it impacts on economic growth and on political growth. Within capitalist societies, bureaucracies are one way of organizing people. Weber allowed for a number of classes. He was concerned with class, status and party. Unlike Marx, conflict was not Weber's central focus.

Welfare capitalism refers to the relationship between capitalist societies and the organization of welfare. This is the focus of comparative social policy literature; for example, in *The Three Worlds of Welfare Capitalism*, Esping-Andersen (1990) classifies three regimes as liberal, conservative corporatist and social democratic according to their welfare systems, and he employs the concept of decommodification to explain one's ability to survive outside the labour market.

Further reading

Esping-Andersen, G. (1990) *The Three Worlds of Welfare Capitalism*. Cambridge, UK: Polity Press.
Giddens, A. (2006) *Sociology*, 5th edn. Cambridge, UK: Polity Press.

CARE/CARER/CARING

Related entries: Community; Dependency; Gender; Welfare/well-being

Grahame (1983: 23) refers to caring as both an 'identity and activity'. Lynch and McLaughlin, writing on care, refer to 'love labour', which involves reciprocity and suggest: 'one cannot provide love on a rational contractual basis like one provides other services' (Lynch and McLaughlin, 1995: 261). The very nature of love labour renders both parties vulnerable. The vulnerability of the recipient of care is an issue which became increasingly visible in feminist writing in the 1990s (Morris, 1991). Williams (1999: 677–678) suggests:

> One important way in which welfare states construct a boundary between public rights and responsibilities and private duties is the extent to which they recognise, remunerate or socialise the work involved in caring for and/or supporting children, older frail or sick people, people who are disabled and require support, for, on the whole, this has been assumed to be the unpaid responsibility of women in the home.

She suggests that care requires recognition but also careful negotiation of the different interests caught up in its discourse and practice.

Tronto (2008) writes of an ethics of care which has four elements: caring about, which demands attentiveness; taking care, which demands responsibility; giving care, which demands skills and competencies; and care-receiving, which demands a relational dynamic between the carer and the cared-for, that is a responsiveness. It stresses interdependence and relational autonomy and relates it to citizenship. Care work involves power relations and there is a clear gender division.

Community care is a concept used in social policy to describe non-residential or non-institutional care in the community which is usually supported by the informal sector, family and friends, usually women. Sharkey (2000: 1) defines community care as care in the community which is concerned with three elements: first, care of people who were previously in long-stay institutions; second, efforts to support vulnerable people within the community rather than have them go into institutions; and, finally, considerable unpaid support by informal carers, family, relations and neighbours. Sharkey suggest that most of us will have had first-hand experience of informal caring in the community so will be aware of some of the issues. It is an emotive topic. He identifies key questions for social scientists (Sharkey, 2000: 22–23): who is doing the caring – friends, neighbours or relatives (informal care); what proportion of the care is formal (state); has the balance between these two sectors changed; and in what way will changing demographic factors have implications for the future? He refers to the notion of 'interweaving' as used by Bayley (1973). He presents Twigg and Atkin's (1994) typology of carer as resource, carer as co-worker, carer as co-client and the superseded carer.

Global care chains is a term devised by Arlie Hochschild to describe 'a series of personal links between people across the globe based on the paid or unpaid work of caring' (Hochschild, 2000: 13).

Further reading

Grahame, H. (1983) 'Caring, a Labour of Love', in Finch, J. and Groves, D. (eds), *A Labour of Love*. London: Routledge and Kegan Paul, p. 23.
Hochschild, A.R. (2000) 'Global Care Chains and Emotional Surplus Value', in Hutton, W. and Giddens, A. (eds.), *On the Edge: Living with Global Capitalism*. London: Jonathan Cape, pp. 130–146.
Lynch, K. and McLaughlin, E. (1995) 'Caring Labour and Love Labour', in Clancy, P., Drudy, S., Lynch, K. and O'Dowd, L. (eds.), *Irish Society: Sociological Perspectives*. Dublin: Institute of Public Administration, pp. 250–292.
Sharkey, P. (2000) *The Essentials of Community Care, a Guide for Practitioners*. London: Macmillan.
Tronto, J. (1993) *Moral Boundaries: A Political Argument for an Ethics of Care*. New York: Routledge.
Williams, F. (1999) 'Good Enough Principles for Welfare', *Journal of Social Policy*, 28(4): 667–687.

CATEGORICAL BENEFITS

> Related entries: Deserving/undeserving; Needs; Stigma; Universal; Selectivity

These payments are made to people who belong to an identifiable group or category, for example families or the elderly. It is a way of targeting resources. It can be traced back to the Poor Law and the notion of deserving and undeserving. It involves differentiating between groups of people and involves normative judgements.

In the literature, categorical benefits appear under different headings. Gal (1998), in his study of categorical payments in Britain and Israel, remarks that categorical benefits have received less attention than other benefit types in the social policy literature. He refers to the many terms that have been employed to describe such benefits as:

> 'demogrants', 'universal benefits', 'social allowances', 'basic incomes', 'universal benefits', 'contingency benefits', 'citizenship benefits' and 'categorical entitlements'. They refer to a variety of social security programmes to be found in many welfare states, among them child benefits, universal basic pensions, disability benefits, war pensions, maternity grants, industrial injury benefits and burial grants.
>
> (Gal, 1998: 74)

Gal offers his own definition of categorical benefits: 'Categorical benefits are state-administered cash benefits paid to individuals who belong to socially defined categories, regardless of their specific income status or prior contribution to a social insurance system' (Gal, 1998: 77). This, he suggests, shows that such benefits are always dependent upon an individual's membership of a specific category of people that has been socially defined. This will be as a result of a political decision in which a 'deserving' category of individuals will be established and eligibility criteria will be outlined.

Gal distinguishes between the different functions of categorical payments which result in different types of payments: a compensatory function, which employs compensatory categorical benefits to provide compensation for individuals in the case of job loss, death or loss of faculty; an income maintenance function, which employs an income maintenance categorical benefit to provide a minimum income to those individuals who, for a variety of reasons, are unable to support themselves through paid work (however, unlike compensatory categorical benefits, this inability is not because of circumstances that are regarded as justifying compensation); and an income supplement function, which will employ an income supplement categorical benefit to cover the expenses incurred by specific groups within the population who are regarded as having additional needs and expenses.

Further reading

Gal, J. (1998) 'Categorical Benefits in Welfare States: Findings from Great Britain and Israel', *International Social Security Review*, 1: 73–101.

CHILD ALLOWANCES

Related entries: Deserving/undeserving; Family; Equality

These are benefits given to families with children and are usually conditional on the age of the child and residency requirements. They are direct payments paid to families through either cash transfers or tax allowances. They are viewed as important in targeting resources at families, avoiding child poverty and in some cases guaranteeing mothers an income. They are often viewed as part of an equality strategy, either for children or for mothers. In some welfare systems, payments are paid to all families with children of a certain age. There may be conditions in relation to the number of children, parental income and residency requirements. Specific child allowances are sometimes targeted at lone parents.

Child allowances can include birth grants, back to school allowances and childcare allowances. Benefits in kind can refer to such resources as childcare places and school meals. Blumkin and colleagues (2010) explore fiscal measures and argue that preferential tax treatment of families with children is associated with four factors. These are, first of all, concerns with horizontal equality in relation to those with and without children. Second is a concern with demographic factors: that fertility is at or below replacement level and incentives for childbearing and rearing are introduced as part of a pro-natalist policy. Third, child allowances can be used to encourage female participation in the labour market. Finally, use of child allowances can be used in the redistribution of resources to those that are financially less well-off.

Further reading

Blumkin, T., Margalioth, Y. and Sadka, E. (2010) *Taxing Children: The Re-distributive Role of Child Benefits – Revisited*. CESIFO Working Paper No. 2970. Available at http://www.cesifo-group.org/wptpapers.ssrn.com/sol3/papers.cfm?abstract_id=1564044

CITIZENSHIP

Related entries: Commodification and decommodification; Community; Equality; Rights; Social exclusion

Citizenship is central to debates in social policy. Basically, it means rights and responsibilities associated with belonging to a particular group. Therefore, it is concerned with exclusion and inclusion and with equality of status. The concept is associated with T.H. Marshall's *On Citizenship and Social Class* (Marshall, 1950). Scholarship on citizenship has gathered momentum since then with some noteworthy books including those of Ruth Lister, who was instrumental in addressing citizenship from a feminist perspective (Lister, 1997, 2003) and exploring it in depth in relation to social policy (Lister, 2010), as did Peter Dwyer (2003).

Citizenship is linked to need and equality in social policy debates. Dean (2010) outlines the historical link between needs and rights. He refers to Thomas Paine's (1791) *The Rights of Man*, proposing the abolition of the Poor Law and instead the granting of relief as a right (Dean, 2010: 141). Dean suggests inherent needs may be translated into 'doctrinal' rights and interpreted needs into claim-based rights (Dean, 2010: 141). Dean distinguishes between thin (formal) and thick (substantive) rights.

Marshall (1950) argued that citizenship consists of three parts or elements: civil, political and social. Civil/legal rights are concerned with individual freedom, including free speech, thought and faith, the right to own property and to conclude valid contracts, and the right to justice. Political/democratic rights relate to the right to participate in the exercise of political power, as a member of a body invested with political authority or as an elector of the members of such a body, for example parliament and local government. Social/welfare citizenship relates to economic welfare and security and 'the right to share to the full in the social heritage and to live the life of a civilized being according to the standards prevailing in the society' (Marshall, 1950: 10–11). Marshall explains citizenship in evolutionary terms, with civil, political and social rights emerging in the eighteenth, nineteenth and twentieth centuries respectively.

Citizenship as a concept is central to the debate on redistribution; some benefits are rights based, others are needs based. Esping-Andersen's (1990) use of decommodification is linked to this. Decommodification is one's ability to survive financially outside the labour market. The ability to survive outside the labour market can be viewed in terms of access to social rights. As Lister (2008: 234) suggests: 'the principle of social citizenship overrides . . . that of the market, in that it is argued that every member of society has a right to be able to participate fully in that society'.

In recent years, with public concern about immigration and movement of people, there is an increased emphasis on citizenship. Lister has highlighted differential citizenship, addressing citizenship in relation to age, social class, gender, ethnicity, sexuality and (dis)ability. Lister (2010: 198) is concerned with how citizenship can be a force of exclusion. She looks beyond nation as used by Marshall (2010: 199). She remarks that in Britain citizenship tends to emphasize relationships between the state and the individual, whereas in Scandinavia the relationship between citizens is emphasized, reflecting dominant ideologies (2010: 195). Lister refers to 'lived citizenship' as people's experiences of citizenship. On membership of a community, she differentiates between thin and thick, the former meaning that membership can have little significance for one's identity and actions, whereas thick can have meanings associated with belonging (2010: 197). She defines thick as:

> membership of a citizenship community . . . [which] involves a set of social and political relationships, practices and identities that together can be described as a sense of belonging. Belonging is not a fixed state, nor just a material one; it involves also emotional and psychological dimensions.
>
> (Lister *et al.*, 2007: 9)

Fitzpatrick (2011a) presents a taxonomy in an attempt to explain perspectives on the relationship between rights and responsibilities and the extent to which people should be coerced into performing such responsibilities. Whereas Marshall is concerned with rights within nations, Dower (2003) refers to *global citizenship* involving an ethical and an institutional component and having three aspects. First, a normative claim in relation to moral duties: 'we have certain duties that in principle extend to all human beings anywhere in the world and that all human beings have a certain moral status of being worthy of moral respect' (Dower, 2003: 7). Second, an existential claim: 'a global citizen is the bearer of human rights' (Dower, 2003: 54). Third, 'an "aspirational claim" in which basic values are more fully realized which requires the strengthening of institutions of global governance' (Dower, 2003: 70).

Intimate citizenship is a term used by Plummer (2003: 38–39):

> this speaks to an array of concerns too often neglected in past debates over citizenship, and which extended notions of rights and responsibilities. I call this 'Intimate Citizenship' because it is concerned with all those matters linked to our most intimate desires, pleasures and ways of being in the world. Some of this must feed back into traditional citizenship; but equally, much of it is concerned with new spheres, new debates, and new stories. For many people in the late modern world there are many decisions that can, and increasingly have to, be made about a life; making decisions around *the control (or not)* over one's body, feelings, relationships; *access (or not) to* representations, relationships, public spaces, etc.; and *socially grounded choices (or not) about* identities, gender experiences, erotic experiences.

In a similar vein, Weeks (1998) refers to the 'sexual citizen', a term also used by Richardson (2000: 105) differentiating between conduct-based, identity-based and relationship-based rights claims.

Further reading

Dower, N. (2003) *An Introduction to Global Citizenship*. Edinburgh: Edinburgh University Press.
Dwyer, P. (2003) *Understanding Social Citizenship*, 2nd edn. Bristol: Policy Press.
Lister, R. (2010) *Understanding Theories and Concepts in Social Policy*. Bristol: Policy Press.
Marshall, M.H. (ed.) (1950) *On Citizenship and Social Class and Other Essays*. Cambridge: Cambridge University Press.

CLASS

> **Related entries: Equality; Power; Stratification**

Class is a way of explaining how people in society are stratified into different levels or layers. Mooney (2000: 158) defines class as 'a way of making sense of a person's economic position and the inequalities that this may generate'. He suggests, 'class divisions refer to people's socioeconomic circumstances, whether in the labour market or in the production process. Although material/economic factors are crucial in the structuring of class inequalities, class also refers to wider differences in power, social position and life chances in general' (*ibid.*). He says that in the social policy literature class tends to be understood 'as emerging from exploitative production relations; as economic position and as occupational status' (*ibid.*).

Mooney states: 'class is both central and marginal to social policy' (Mooney, 2000: 156). He calls for class to be used not merely as a descriptive category but, additionally, 'as an analytical category, and as a means to explore unequal class relations' (Mooney, 2000: 156–157). This, he argues, will help us to understand the inequalities in society, but also how inequalities are reproduced through social policy.

Sociologists have tended to use the term in relation to economic divisions and inequalities, rooted in property and employment relations. People are stratified into class/strata of a social hierarchy because of their economic relations. For Karl Marx (1818–83), class is one's relationship to the means of production. The bourgeoisie/capitalist own the means of production and the proletariat workers sell their labour power, the mode of production.

Max Weber (1864–1920) discussed class in relation to a shared set of economic circumstances. However, his focus was broader than that of Marx because he recognized that class was also related to status and party. This allowed for a broader range of classes than those described by Marx (Giddens, 2006: 302–303). It also acknowledged differences within classes, for example differences in qualifications and professional status.

Class is sometimes defined according to occupational status; for example, as in a population census where one is defined in relation to occupational status, or the occupational status of the head of household. This is controversial, as aggregates such as households can mask inequalities within them.

Class mobilization is a concept employed by Esping-Andersen (1990: 16) in *The Three Worlds of Welfare Capitalism*, when he examines class in the context of mobilization for change.

Underclass is a concept introduced by Gunnar Myrdal (1963: 10): 'class of unemployed, unemployables, and underemployed who are more and more hopelessly set apart from the nation at large and do not share in its life, its ambitions and its achievements'. This was taken up by Charles Murray (1990, 1994). For a spirited debate on Murray's work see Lister (1996). Karl Marx used the term *lumpenproletariat* in a similar vein.

Further reading

Giddens, A. (2006) *Sociology*, 5th edn. Cambridge, UK: Polity Press.

Mooney, G. (2000) 'Class and Social Policy', in Lewis, G., Gewirtz, S. and Clarke, J. (eds.), *Rethinking Social Policy*. Basingstoke, UK: Open University Press, pp. 156–170.

Myrdal, G. (1963) *Challenge to Affluence*. New York: Random House.

CLAW-BACK

Related entries: Basic income; Means testing; Redistribution; Selectivity; Universality

Claw-back refers to money or benefits that are distributed, a portion of which is taken back as a result of special circumstances. This applies to situations in which benefits are viewed as part of a person's income and they are taxed accordingly. Claw-back is often discussed in relation to debates on basic income or in relation to universal payments when it is suggested that the payment be included in overall income and taxed.

COLLECTIVISM

Related entries: Communitarian; Ideology

Collectivism, in terms of social policy, means shared responsibility, and it is central to welfare provision. Collectivism is the corollary of individualism. Individualism is associated with right-wing ideologies which view individuals as responsible for their own and their family's welfare; the state intervenes only as a last resort in the residual model (Titmuss, 1974), or in the liberal model, as described by Esping-Andersen (1999).

Although the individualist perceives welfare as wasteful and individuals as likely to become dependent, unmotivated and a burden as a result, the collectivist approach views welfare as a necessary part of striving for an equal society and recognizes the need to compensate citizens for the diswelfares of capitalist societies. A collectivist approach emphasizes shared responsibility for welfare. This is associated with more left-wing ideologies, for example as in the institutional-redistributive model (Titmuss, 1974) and the social democratic model (Esping-Andersen, 1999).

Further reading

George, V. and Wilding, P. (1994) *Welfare and Ideology*. London: Harvester Wheatsheaf.

COMMODIFICATION AND DECOMMODIFICATION

Related entries: Citizenship; Labour; Stratification; Welfare regimes

A commodity is an item exchanged in the market. Commodification relates to a person becoming a commodity. Within Marxist theory this refers to the production of commodities for exchange. People can be considered subject to commodification in contexts such as slavery, in which human beings themselves become a commodity to be bought and sold. There is increasing emphasis on the trafficking of people for labour, including sex work. However, there is a distinction between selling people as workers and people selling their labour.

In Social Policy literature, commodification came to the fore in Esping-Andersen's *Three Worlds of Welfare Capitalism*. He writes:

> workers are not commodities like others because they must survive and reproduce both themselves and the society they live in. It is possible to withhold washing machines from the market until the price is agreeable; but labour is unable to withhold itself for long without recourse to alternative means of subsistence.
>
> (Esping-Andersen, 1990: 37)

He refers to decommodification occurring when a service is rendered as a matter of right, and when a person can maintain a livelihood without reliance on the market. He argues that decommodification 'has been a hugely contested issue in welfare state development' (Esping-Andersen, 1990: 22) He suggests that 'de-commodification strengthens the workers rights and weakens the absolute authority of the employer' (*ibid.*). Such rights can relate to needs or rights in different welfare systems. Esping-Andersen (1990: 23) states that 'a minimal definition must entail that citizens can freely, and without potential loss of job, income or general welfare, opt out of work when they themselves consider it necessary'.

Stephens (2010) builds on the writing of Esping-Andersen and concludes that 'the conception of social rights of citizenship should include a right to satisfying work and human self development and not just "a modicum of economic welfare and security"' (Stephens, 2010: 514). He continues: 'Thus, social rights should include the whole range of public human investment policies from early childhood education to higher education, adult education, active labour market policy and health care as well as work and family reconciliation policies such as public day care and maternity and parental leave' (*ibid.*). O'Connor (1993) suggests that the incorporation of gender into writing on welfare regimes demands a reassessment of the conventional definitions of political mobilization and participation and a modification of the concept of decommodification, which she says 'must be supplemented by the concept of personal autonomy or insulation from personal and/or public dependence' (O'Connor, 1993: 501). She suggests that personal autonomy 'is central to unravelling the complexity of the relationships amongst state, market and family' (O'Connor, 1993: 513).

Further reading

Esping-Andersen, G. (1990) *The Three Worlds of Welfare Capitalism*. Cambridge, UK: Polity Press.

Stephens, J.D. (2010) 'Social Rights of Citizenship', in Castles, F., Leibfried, S., Lewis, J., Obinger, H. and Pierson, C. (eds.), *The Oxford Handbook of the Welfare State*. Oxford: Oxford University Press, pp. 511–525.

COMMUNITARIAN

Related entries: Collectivism; Community; Individual

Communitarians prioritize community over the individual. *Communitarianism* is concerned with the common good. Communitarians draw on ideas of civic republicanism. Originating in ancient Greece, citizenship imposed a civic duty on individuals to participate in political life. Etzioni (1996), who is associated with the term, was concerned that individuals had too much freedom and not enough responsibilities. He and others advocated greater responsibilities and fewer rights, focusing on the common good. In the 1980s, communitarianism was associated with Charles Taylor, Michael Sandel and Michael Walzer, who were critical of liberalism's self-interested individualism. In the 1990s, Etzioni formed the school of 'responsive communitarianism', which was concerned with balancing the common good with individual rights.

Lister (2010: 3) indicates that the common good is central to communitarianism, arguing: 'individuals are social beings, embedded in national and local communities. As such their responsibilities towards fellow members of the community are emphasized over their rights and it is proper for community members to judge each other's behaviour'. Dean (2000: 73) refers to the normative tone of communitarianism, which views community in a positive light and those individuals who are socially excluded and behaving inappropriately as emerging from dysfunctional communities. Social cohesion and morality are valued.

In the United States the Institute for Communitarian Policy Studies at The George Washington University is a research institute which is concerned with communitarian policy research (http://icps.gwu.edu/).

Further reading

Dean, H. (2000) 'Managing Risk by Controlling Behaviour: Social Security Administration and the Erosion of Welfare Citizenship', in Taylor-Gooby, P. (ed.), *Risk, Trust and Welfare*. London: Macmillan, pp. 71–92.

Etzioni, A. (1996) *The New Golden Rule: Community and Morality in a Democratic Society*. New York: Basic Books.

Lister, R. (2010) 'Citizenship and Community', in Lister, R., *Understanding Theories and Concepts in Social Policy*. Bristol: Policy Press, pp. 195–222.

COMMUNITY

Related entries: Care; Citizenship; Communitarianism

Community is generally understood as something which unites a group of people, be it place, religion, interest, or ethnicity, for example New Yorkers, Jews, Travellers. Communities are to do with boundaries: there are insiders and there are outsiders. The concept of community has different meanings in different contexts; it suggests some sort of relationship between people and implies a sense of togetherness and cooperation. It implies living together in close proximity. It can refer to a geographical setting or to people with a common interest. The idea of community has been a central issue in sociology right from its foundation as a discipline. Tönnies (1885–1936), Marx (1818–83), Weber (1864–1920), Durkheim (1858–1917) and Comte (1798–1857) all wrote on community and presented ideas and theories of what the term represented.

Tönnies differentiated between *gemeinschaft* and *gesellschaft*. The former refers to the affective, spontaneous, close-knit, familial relationships, an essential part of identity and kinship relations. The latter is more of an association between individuals that bear a transitory, instrumental relationship. Tönnies saw this as a feature of modern societies linked to the division of labour.

Durkheim's theory focused on the disintegration of social relations into 'anomie': a state of normlessness. He perceived that there was a transition, from a community based on one type of social relations to another: from 'mechanical' to 'organic' solidarity. For Durkheim, social relations were changing as society progressed towards industrialization. Mechanical solidarity is characteristic of small-scale communities where relations are based on family and community ties that involve enduring relations, and in such communities division of labour is based on gender and position within the community, rather than ability or achievement. Organic solidarity, on the other hand, is characteristic of larger societies, where division of labour is based on achievement and ability and social relations based on diversity, rather than similarity. Durkheim saw society as becoming one big community.

Marx equated the decline of community with the development of capitalism. According to Marx, as societies became increasingly capitalistic, two groups emerged: the bourgeoisie, who represented the elitist ruling class, and the proletariat, who represented the working class and who were exploited by the ruling class. Marx saw the decline of community as occurring as the ruling class gained more power over the working class, and social relations become based more on money and capital gain. The common theme running throughout the writings of all the nineteenth-century theorists is the fact that community declines as industrialization and capitalism develop.

Multiple uses surround the term community, and, although the term usually refers to a local, small-scale setting, it also refers to social issues such as religion, culture, kin, work and the economy. Community can be defined in four ways. First, it can be a geographical setting in which people are identified as being part of a community when they live in the same area. In this respect, the term community represents merely a geographical location and does not suggest any sort of cooperation or relationships between people except that they are part of the same community, as they share an address.

Second, a community may represent a social network, which comes about through a set of interactions between people. This does not have to be geographical. Social networks may develop as a result of common interests. Membership of communities, such as those based on religious beliefs, defines the patterns of social contact.

Third, common culture may define a community. The term 'culture' refers to a set of behaviour patterns including language, attitudes, values and beliefs. Subcultures within the dominant culture can also be described as forming a community based on their common experiences. The ties in this respect are cultural and relate to beliefs and values.

Fourth, people with common interests may form a community, for example the Islamic community or the gay community. However, the fact that they have common interests does not necessarily mean they will have social contact.

Weeks (1996: 72), on *sexual community*, argues 'the social relations of a community are repositories of meaning for its members, not sets of mechanical linkages between isolated individuals. A community offers a "vocabulary of values" through which individuals construct their understanding of the social world and of their sense of identity and belonging'. He identifies four elements of a sexual community (Weeks, 1996: 73): community as a focus of identity; as ethos of repository values; as social capital; and as politics.

Community care is a concept used in social policy to describe non-residential or non-institutional care in the community which is usually supported by the informal sector, family and friends, usually women. For a full discussion of community care see Sharkey (2001).

Further reading

Sharkey, P. (2000) *The Essentials of Community Care: A Guide for Practitioners*. London: Macmillan.
Weeks, J. (1996) 'The Idea of a Sexual Community', *Soundings*, 2: 71–84.
Weeks, J. (1998) 'The Sexual Citizen', *Theory, Culture & Society*, 15(3): 35–52.

COMPARATIVE SOCIAL POLICY

Related entries: Families of nations; Models of welfare; Path dependency; Welfare regimes

Comparative social policy is the practice of comparing welfare systems or elements of welfare and has gained momentum in universities and research centres since the 1960s. Clasen (2004: 99) suggests that 'attempting to define comparative social policy seems somewhat fruitless'. Nevertheless, he concludes: 'there are several parallel discourses and analytical frames of reference, aims and approaches which can broadly be subsumed under the rubric of comparative social policy and which have emerged and evolved over time' (Clasen, 2004: 100).

The publication of *The Three Worlds of Welfare Capitalism* in 1990 brought renewed vigour to the debates and there has been a plethora of publications in the field since then. Some have highlighted gender (Lewis, 1993; Orloff, 1993; Sainsbury, 1994) whereas others have added ethnicity to the debate (Morrisens and Sainsbury, 2005), or have focused on specific areas such as health (Bambra, 2005a). Comparative social policy is concerned with comparing different/similar patterns in welfare system development in different countries. It is concerned with identifying both commonalities and differences and trying to explain these. It is worth going back to Titmuss's work in 1974, which identified models of welfare, and subsequently Mishra (1977), who identified the value of models in clarifying explanation and understanding, and how such a route would be cumulative and lead to the universal development of social policy as a subject. Comparative social policy therefore provides us with a wide range of concepts and theoretical approaches to explain the development of welfare regimes in the past and in the future. Gathering and comparing empirical information on policies and services in one country can help signpost possible trajectories for other countries. Different states may find similar or different solutions to similar problems: we can learn what works or does not work.

There is a variety of approaches and, as Mayo (2008) suggests, policy analysts operate at different levels of abstraction. Whereas some policy analysts conduct country-specific studies, others compare programmes; whereas some focus on legislation and regulation, others focus on provision, users and pressures for change. Other studies compare and characterize whole systems over time and look at the welfare mix. Thus, comparative social policy is a complex field. There is increasingly a wide availability of data from such sources as the Organisation for Economic Co-operation and Development, Eurostat and Luxembourg Income Studies. Some of the problems can relate to use/misuse of terminology.

Further reading

Clasen, J. (2004) 'Defining Comparative Social Policy', in Kennett, P. (ed.), *A Handbook of Comparative Social Policy*. Cheltenham: Edward Elgar, pp. 91–102.

Esping-Andersen, G. (1990) *The Three Worlds of Welfare Capitalism*. Cambridge, UK: Polity Press.

Mayo, M. (2008) 'The Role of Comparative Study in Social Policy', in Alcock, P., May, M. and Rowlingson, K. (eds.), *The Student's Companion to Social Policy*, 3rd edn. Oxford: Blackwell, pp. 421–429.

CONDITIONALITY

Related entries: Deserving/undeserving; Entitlement; Equality; Means testing; Stigma

Access to resources through the welfare system is usually dependent on meeting certain criteria or conditions. This is conditionality and it refers to criteria of eligibility. It can stigmatize people or create normative divisions, for example between the deserving and undeserving poor as developed in the Poor Law. Conditions generally exclude rather than include people. Conditions can be related to such criteria as residency, age, marital status and co-habitation.

Further reading

Lister, R. (2008) 'Citizenship and Access to Welfare', in Alcock, P., May, M. and Rowlingson, K. (eds.), *The Student's Companion to Social Policy*, 3rd edn. Oxford: Blackwell, pp. 234–240.
Sen, A. (1991) *Poverty and Fairness: An Essay on Entitlement and Deprivation*. Oxford: Clarendon Press.

CONVERGENCE

Related entries: Comparative social policy; Models; Welfare regimes

Convergence means meeting or coming together. In Social Policy the term is generally associated with comparing welfare systems. It proposes that as nations achieve similar levels of economic development they will become more alike. It is associated with modernization theories and theories of social change. The term is accredited to Wilensky (1975), who argued that all countries are placed on a similar development track and are converging towards a similar social and economic future. This was further developed by Castles (1999). In his study of twenty-one OECD countries he concludes that in the second half of the twentieth century all have undergone major changes in economic growth and policy planning. There has been much variation between countries due to political circumstances, changes in economic growth and policy planning. Convergence is associated with the term 'logic of industrialism', which suggests that welfare systems develop along a path as societies become more industrialized. Knill (2005: 768) defines policy convergence as 'any increase in the similarity between one or more characteristics of a certain policy . . . across a given set of political jurisdictions'. Convergence downwards is referred to as the race to the bottom, a notion Mishra (1999) associates with globalization.

Spicker (2008: 125–126) outlines four reasons for convergence: common problems, common approaches, common methods and common policy. He suggests that as societies industrialize they may experience common problems; for example, as developing countries experience industrialization they may experience certain common problems, such as housing shortages and issues associated with worker protection. Common approaches can be adopted by people in different countries to address social problems. Thus there can develop common methods. He refers to common policy developing as those countries imitate each other.

Further reading

Knill, C. (2005) 'Introduction: Cross-National Policy Convergence: Concepts, Approaches and Explanatory Factors', *Journal of European Public Policy*, 12(5): 764–774.
Wilensky, H.L. (1975) *The Welfare State and Equality: Structural and Ideological Roots of Public Expenditures*. Berkeley: University of California Press.

CORPORATISM

Related entries: Comparative social policy; Welfare regimes

Corporatism has been described as a system of interest representation in which

> the constituent units are organised into a limited number of singular, compulsory, non-competitive, hierarchically ordered and functionally differentiated categories, recognised or licensed (if not created) by the state and granted a deliberate representational monopoly within their respective categories in exchange for observing certain controls on their selection of leaders and articulation of demand and supports.
>
> (Schmitter, 1974: 93–94)

Esping-Andersen (1990) drew attention to corporatism in *The Three Worlds of Welfare Capitalism* when he referred to conservative corporatism as one of the three welfare regimes, along with liberal and social democratic regimes. He argued that Austria, France, Germany and Italy belong to this category. He referred to them as conservative and strongly corporatist, characterized by preservation of status differentials with rights attached to class and status and by private insurance, and with occupational fringe benefits playing a marginal role. In such regimes, there is a strong Church influence, a concern with the preservation of traditional family values and structures; social insurance excludes working wives and family benefits encourage motherhood. Women tend to be under-represented in the labour market and are more concentrated in part-time work. Day care and other family services are underdeveloped and the principle of subsidiarity is strong. Subsidiarity is defined by Esping-Andersen as 'the idea that higher and larger levels of social collectivity should only intervene when the family's capacity for mutual protection was rendered impossible' (Esping-Andersen, 1990: 61). The principle of subsidiarity is associated with Catholic social teaching and particularly with *Rerum Novarum*, an 1891 papal encyclical.

Further reading

Esping-Andersen, G. (1990) *The Three Worlds of Welfare Capitalism*. Cambridge, UK: Polity Press.
Schmitter, P. (1974) 'Still the Century of Corporatism', *Review of Politics*, 36: 85–131.

CRISIS OF WELFARE

Related entries: Capitalism; Globalization; Welfare state

The idea of a crisis in the welfare state emerged in the 1970s, following economic crisis. It has been described as the end of the 'consensus' which had existed following the Second World War. Ramesh Mishra in *The Welfare State in Crisis* wrote: 'in varying degrees and forms, the welfare state throughout the industrialized West is in disarray' (Mishra, 1984: xiii). He pointed to the reduced resource base to fund welfare and a perception that it was a barrier to economic growth. For many commentators, the welfare state was viewed as undermining the market and individual responsibility, competitiveness and growth. Pierson (2006: 145) refers to four aspects of crisis: as turning point, as external shock, as longstanding contradiction and as any large-scale problem.

Marxists argue that crisis is inevitable in capitalism. The Organisation for Economic Co-operation and Development (OECD, 1981) in *Crisis in the Welfare State* suggested welfare states need to reform in order to survive. Alcock and colleagues (2000) summarize the crisis as a concern with expenditure getting out of control and that demographic pressures would break the welfare state. They suggest that there was an economic crisis of welfare that suggested economies could no longer support high levels of welfare. It would lead to political crisis as the state was too large and bureaucratic, a social crisis referring to the role of welfare in undermining family values, and internal failures in that the welfare state had failed to achieve its own goals. Thus, the legitimacy of the welfare state is at risk. Even though welfare systems have survived since 'crisis' was first perceived in the 1970s, the current economic crisis is once again drawing attention to the cost of welfare and the functioning of public services throughout Europe.

Further reading

Alcock, C., Payne, S. and Sullivan, M. (2000) 'The Welfare State in Crisis', in Alcock, C., Payne, S. and Sullivan, M., *Introducing Social Policy*. Harlow: Prentice Hall, pp. 42–57.
Pierson, C. (2006) *Beyond the Welfare State*, 3rd edn. Cambridge, UK: Polity Press.

CRITICAL JUNCTURES

> Related entries: Comparative social policy; Models of welfare; Path dependency

Critical junctures is a term employed in explanations of social change. It implies that policy change occurs when an important 'juncture' or a choice of pathways is encountered, like a junction on a road or path. Paul Pierson's writing on path dependency suggests that following on from a critical juncture, a new institutional arrangement emerges that continues to reproduce itself in a path-dependent process (Pierson, 2004). Critical juncture refers to a change in trajectory. Things are going in a particular direction and then things go in a different direction.

Collier and Collier (2002: 27) suggest that 'a critical juncture may be defined as a period of significant change, which typically occurs in distinct ways in different countries (or in other units of analysis) and which is hypothesized to produce distinct legacies'. This turning point is a way of explaining and analysing a change in trajectory. Critical junctures have been described in the literature as 'turning points' (Doran, 1980), and as 'contingent' (Lebow, 2000).

Changes and continuities in social policy have been discussed widely by 'path dependency' theorists, emphasizing the historicity of policy making (Room, 2008a), that is that the historical context needs to be considered. Present policies have emerged from a historical context whose structures influence present resources and prospects for shaping future strategies. Greer (2008) looks at health policy in the European Union, drawing attention to such developments as the EU Working Time Directive as a potential critical juncture. Kennedy and Einasto (2010) explore maternity policy legislation in Ireland and Estonia, discussing membership of the EU as a critical juncture for both countries.

The start of a path, taking place in a specific type of situation, often called a 'critical juncture' or breakage point, or 'explosion', is often crucially important for subsequent policies. In these critical junctures or explosive moments the development curve transforms into a new trajectory. These moments are likely in periods when the very structure of the state is at issue and is undergoing transformation. Particular policies may be advocated or opposed for reasons other than their perceived relevance to socioeconomic needs or cultural ideas (Orloff and Skocpol, 1984). Despite change, certain values of the previous period are maintained and co-exist. Pfau-Effinger (2005) suggests it is possible that actors voluntarily take the risk that they may be creating inefficiencies in the present, for they think that such steps are required to create new futures.

Further reading

Doran, C.F. (1980) 'Modes, Mechanisms, and Turning Points: Perspectives on the Transformation of the International System', *International Political Science Review*, 1(1): 35–61.

Greer, S.L. (2008) 'Choosing Paths in European Health Services Policy: A Political Analysis of a Critical Juncture', *Journal of European Social Policy*, 18(3): 219–231.

Pierson, P. (2004) *Politics in Time, History, Institutions and Social Analysis*. Princeton, NJ: Princeton University Press.

DEMOCRACY

Related entries: Capitalism; Ideology; Power

Democracy is a term used in a positive way to imply inclusion and participation. It derives from the Greek word δημοκρατία (dēmokratía) 'rule of the people', which was coined from δῆμος (dēmos) 'people' and κράτος (kratos) 'power', which denotes the political systems then existing in some Greek city-states, notably Athens following a popular uprising in 508 BC. Democracy is defined as rule by the people; it is representative of people and for people. Spicker (2008: 88) says it can relate to a system of government, a system of decision making and a society in which people have rights. Heywood (2007: 44) explains different types of democracy and distinguishes between six different understandings of democracy, which he classifies as liberal, conservative, socialist, anarchist, fascist and ecologist.

Democratic socialism and social democratic are terms which explain left-of-centre politics. The focus is on equality, and within that substantive equality, that is equality of outcome or real equality as opposed to equal rights and formal equality. George and Wilding (1994) identify the social democratic vision of welfare as abolition of poverty; promoting economic growth; fulfilment of individual abilities; promoting social integration; encouraging altruism; compensating for diswelfares in society; a welfare state that reduces both horizontal and vertical inequalities; and a belief in universal services. Social democracy is a strand of socialism which demands a balance between the market and state rather than the abolition of capitalism.

In *The Three Worlds of Welfare Capitalism*, Esping-Andersen (1990) in his analysis of welfare regimes describes the social democratic model alongside liberal and conservative corporatist models as three distinct types. The social democratic model he views as forming the smallest of the three regime types. It is characterized by a commitment to universalism and decommodification of social rights. He argues that in such regimes social democracy was the dominant force in social reform. Such regimes are committed to equality of the highest standard and that levels of services and benefits be of the standard expected by the 'new middle classes', that workers are guaranteed 'full participation in the quality of rights enjoyed by the better-off' (Esping-Andersen, 1990: 27). Esping-Andersen concludes: 'this model crowds out the market and consequently constructs an essentially universal solidarity in favour of the welfare state. All benefit; all are dependent; and all will presumably feel obliged to pay' (Esping-Andersen, 1990: 28).

Further reading

Esping-Andersen, G. (1990) *The Three Worlds of Welfare Capitalism*. Cambridge, UK: Polity Press.
George, V. and Wilding, P. (1994) *Welfare and Ideology*. London: Harvester Wheatsheaf.
Heywood, A. (2007) *Political Ideologies: An Introduction*, 4th edn. London: Palgrave Macmillan.

DEPENDENCY

> Related entries: Male breadwinner

To be dependent means to rely on or to lean on someone else. In social policy terms it can mean one is dependent on the state for resources, or within a household it is often assumed that one is *dependent* on another, one is a *dependant*. Thus, the state of being dependent, or *dependency*, is central to social policy. Titmuss referred to 'states of dependency' which can arise for many people when they are not in a position to earn an income. He suggests that in industrialized societies there can be many causes; for example, he differentiates between 'natural dependencies' associated with childhood, old age or physical and psychological ill health, and those caused by social and cultural factors, which he refers to as 'manmade' dependencies (Titmuss, 2001: 64). These include unemployment and underemployment, protective and preventative legislation and compulsory retirement. These, he suggests, may 'involve to some degree the destruction, curtailment, interruption or frustration of earning power in the individual, and more pronounced secondary dependencies when they further involve the wives, children and other relatives' (*ibid.*).

Dependency raises issues in relation to gender, age and ability, and can be associated with stigma. It relates to one individual relying on another for income or services. Similarly, it can refer to an individual's or household's dependency on the state for income or services. It is a concept that has been contested by some writers who argue that the concept should be replaced with interdependency. Williams (2000: 342) defines it as the principle 'which brings into play all those emotional, material, physical networks of unequal reciprocity, and creates the basis for autonomy'. It emphasizes a collective commitment to individual welfare and vice versa. Williams argues that we are all dependent on others in some spheres and she challenges the social relations which render some groups unnecessarily dependent. She also relates dependency to care.

Williams looks at the way welfare institutions, policies and professionals construct certain social groups as dependent and thus unable to exercise autonomy in certain areas of their lives. Furthermore, she asserts that the construction of women as financially dependent on their partners limits their access to certain benefits and assumes their subordinate position to male partners in relation to other areas of personal relationships: in decision making, in relation to sexual relationships or in spending power.

Williams (1999: 676) also writes about the creation of dependency of disabled people through their dependency on carers.

Further reading

Titmuss, R. (2001) 'The Social Division of Welfare: Some Reflections on the Search for Equity, Lecture at the University of Birmingham in honour of Eleanor Rathbone (1955), in Alcock, P., Glennester, H., Oakley, A. and Sinfield, A. (eds.), *Welfare and Wellbeing: Richard Titmuss's Contribution to Social Policy*. Bristol: Policy Press, pp. 59–70.

Williams, F. (1999) 'Good Enough Principles for Welfare', *Journal of Social Policy*, 28(4): 667–687.

Williams, F. (2000) 'Principles of Recognition and Respect in Welfare', in Lewis, G., Gewirtz, S. and Clarke, J. (eds.), *Rethinking Social Policy*. London: Open University Press, pp. 338–352.

DESERVING/UNDESERVING

Related entries: Discretion; Needs; Stigma

Desert, merit and reward are associated with moral judgements. We are not born deserving; it is decided that we are so. In terms of social policy it means that a decision is made that one is deserving of welfare. The distinction between the deserving and undeserving which still exists today can be traced back to the Elizabethan Poor Laws. It introduced a residency qualification which linked eligibility to parish boundaries. Titmuss (1967: 121) distinguishes between 'faults in the individual' and 'faults in society'. The former refer to moral, psychological and social faults which may render one undeserving. For example, a widow is judged as a victim and thus deserving whereas a divorced woman may be judged to have created her own situation. Deserving and undeserving are associated with residual welfare and again can be associated with stigma as individuals are judged and labelled.

Further reading

Lister, R. (2008) 'Citizenship and Access to Welfare', in Alcock, P., May, M. and Rowlingson, K. (eds.), *The Student's Companion to Social Policy*, 3rd edn. Oxford: Blackwell, pp. 234–240.

DISABILITY

Related entries: Autonomy; Citizenship; Deserving/undeserving; Discrimination; Equality; Needs

Although 'disability' and 'disabled' are words commonly used, like other concepts they are contested. 'Dis' is associated with a lack of something, in this case 'ability', which means capacity. Thus, disability is concerned with lacking capacity in some way. The World Health Organization (WHO, 2011) indicates that:

more than one billion people in the world live with some form of disability, of whom nearly 200 million experience considerable difficulties in functioning. In the years ahead, disability will be an even greater concern because its prevalence is on the rise. This is because of ageing populations and the higher risk of disability in older people as well as the global increase in chronic health conditions such as diabetes, cardiovascular disease, cancer and mental health disorders.

(2011: xi)

The *International Classification of Functioning, Disability and Health* (ICF) defines disability as an umbrella term for impairments, activity limitations and participation restrictions. It states that 'Disability is the interaction between individuals with a health condition (e.g. cerebral palsy, Down syndrome and depression) and personal and environmental factors (e.g. negative attitudes, inaccessible transportation and public buildings, and limited social supports)' (WHO, 2001). This is an important definition because it includes both physical impairment and environmental factors.
The World Health Organization reports that:

Across the world, people with disabilities have poorer health outcomes, lower education achievements, less economic participation and higher rates of poverty than people without disabilities. This is partly because people with disabilities experience barriers in accessing services that many of us have long taken for granted, including health, education, employment, and transport as well as information. These difficulties are exacerbated in less advantaged communities.

(WHO, 2011: xi)

Thus, disability is an important aspect of social policy. Despite this it has been noted that 'not only has the welfare state failed disabled people but that the academic discipline of social policy has added insult to injury' (Shakespeare, 2000: 52) in that discourses of dependency employed in social policy scholarship have been inadequate in facilitating an understanding of lived experience and have led to inadequate responses. There have, however, been developments in the literature in the interim led by the independent living movement and feminist writers (Lister, 2010).
Scholarship on disability differentiates between the social and medical model of disability. The *medical* or *personal tragedy model* views disability in terms of impairment and how such an impairment impacts on one's life. The social model, on the other hand, views disability in a social context and the extent to which society disables people. Michel Oliver coined the term 'social model of disability', which he explains 'involves nothing more or less fundamental than a switch away from focusing on the physical limitations of particular individuals to the way the physical and social environment impose limitations upon certain categories of people' (Oliver, 1981: 28). Barnes (2011: 63) outlines the usefulness of the social model of disability: 'In short, the social model of disability is a tool with which to provide insights into the disabling tendencies of contemporary society in order to generate policies and practices to facilitate their eradication'.
Oliver (1996: 63) recognizes that the welfare state 'has failed disabled people among others'. The problem he asserts is that of placing need rather than rights as

central to debates on welfare. He suggests that welfare is 'an essential ingredient for the development of a truly inclusionary society. That is to say, a society in which both disabled and non-disabled people can participate and realize their full potential and where the notion of disability and all its associated deprivations are little more than a dim and distant memory' (Oliver and Barnes, 2009; quoted in Morris, 2011: 4). Oliver refers to the shift from needs- to rights-based policies. The independent living movement promotes a rights-based approach to care and advocates supports to facilitate independent living. Shakespeare (2000: 59) outlines its claims: that there is not a major distinction between the needs of disabled and non-disabled people; that dependency has to be deconstructed; that disabled people need personal assistance in order to achieve goals; and that disabled people want social independence.

Lister (2010: 259) reviews the literature on disability and citizenship. She comments on the emergence of scholarship on disability movements, as opposed to 'movement', which she suggests 'have been in the vanguard of contemporary social welfare movements'. Lister draws attention to the fact that people with disabilities are not a homogeneous group. Shildrick (2004: 124) refers to the reductive use of the term disabled and offers as an example the wheelchair sign representing disability, which has no meaning for those with disabilities that are without mobility problems. This is also recognized by the WHO (2011: 7): 'Generalizations about "disability" or "people with disabilities" can mislead. Persons with disabilities have diverse personal factors with differences in gender, age, socioeconomic status, sexuality, ethnicity, or cultural heritage. Each has his or her personal preferences and responses to disability. Furthermore, although disability correlates with disadvantage, not all people with disabilities are equally disadvantaged'.

Disability is increasingly understood as a human rights issue. *Article 25 of the UN Convention on the Rights of Persons with Disabilities* (CRPD) reinforces the right of persons with disabilities to attain the highest standard of health care, without discrimination:

> Parties recognize that persons with disabilities have the right to the enjoyment of the highest attainable standard of health without discrimination on the basis of disability. Parties shall take all appropriate measures to ensure access for persons with disabilities to health services that are gender-sensitive, including health-related rehabilitation. In particular, Parties shall:
> (a) Provide persons with disabilities with the same range, quality and standard of free or affordable health care and programmes as provided to other persons, including in the area of sexual and reproductive health and population-based public health programmes;
> (b) Provide those health services needed by persons with disabilities specifically because of their disabilities, including early identification and intervention as appropriate, and services designed to minimize and prevent further disabilities, including among children and older persons;
> (c) Provide these health services as close as possible to people's own communities, including in rural areas;
> (d) Require health professionals to provide care of the same quality to persons with disabilities as to others, including on the basis of free and informed

consent by, inter alia, raising awareness of the human rights, dignity, autonomy and needs of persons with disabilities through training and the promulgation of ethical standards for public and private health care;

(e) Prohibit discrimination against persons with disabilities in the provision of health insurance, and life insurance where such insurance is permitted by national law, which shall be provided in a fair and reasonable manner;

(f) Prevent discriminatory denial of health care or health services or food and fluids on the basis of disability.

(http://www2.ohchr.org/english/law/disabilities-convention.htm#II)

Priestly (2010: 411) traces the relationship between welfare provision and disability in Britain back to the 1601 Poor Law and in Germany to the Bismarckian model. He suggests that, although there has been harmonization of disability policies, there remains scope for diversity at a national level. Such differences can be seen in cash payments and expenditure, work-centred eligibility criteria and employment measures. Morris (2011: 17) argues that 'Disabled people need the kind of welfare state which is not a mere "safety net" but which invests in tackling disabling barriers and in providing resources to meet the additional costs related to impairment'. She strongly argues that we need to challenge the argument that welfare payments are a drain on the economy and that they should be seen as an indicator of social responsibility and social justice (Morris, 2011: 16). She also argues that we need to promote a wider concept of social security, striving for social responsibility and social justice. 'In order to experience equal access to full citizenship, disabled people require some kind of collective and redistributive mechanism. Such redistribution needs to be in the context of a value system which values diversity and in which disabled people are treated as belonging and contributing to the communities in which they live' (ibid.). She calls for more radical changes in disability policy, arguing that it is time to revisit underlying concepts and engage in wider social and economic debates, and suggests: 'A key part of placing social justice at the heart of the welfare state is the need to defend and extend the principle of universalism' (Morris, 2011: 17).

The *World Report on Disability* charts the steps that are required to improve participation and inclusion of people with disabilities and suggests:

steps for all stakeholders – including governments, civil society organizations and disabled people's organizations – to create enabling environments, develop rehabilitation and support services, ensure adequate social protection, create inclusive policies and programmes, and enforce new and existing standards and legislation, to the benefit of people with disabilities and the wider community. People with disabilities should be central to these endeavors.

(WHO, 2011: xi)

Further reading

Barnes, C. (2011) 'Understanding Disability and the Importance of Design for All', *Journal of Accessibility and Design for All*, 1(1): 54–79.

Morris, J. (2011) 'Rethinking Disability Policy', York: Joseph Rowntree Foundation, 15 November. Available at http://www.jrf.org.uk/publications/rethinking-disability-policy

Oliver, M. (1990) *The Politics of Disablement*. London: Macmillan.
Oliver, M. (1996) *Understanding Disability: From Theory to Practice*. London: Palgrave.
WHO (World Health Organization) (2001) *International Classification of Functioning, Disability and Health*. Geneva: WHO. Available at http://www.who.int/classifications/icf/en/
WHO (2011) *World Report on Disability*. Geneva: WHO. Available at http://whqlibdoc.who.int/publications/2011/9789240685215_eng.pdf

DISCRETION

Related entries: Assistance payments; Deserving/undeserving; Needs; Stigma

Discretion means having the authority to make a decision. It is an important aspect of redistribution through state welfare. It is associated, on the one hand, with flexibility, being able to respond to the merits of individual cases, but this in itself brings values and judgements into play and distinguishes between the deserving and undeserving.

Lister (2008: 235) explains that the roots of the discretionary approach can be traced to charity, where ideas of desert and merit were implicated as much as need. It is associated with residual welfare and with needs-based social assistance schemes, and thus can be stigmatizing for individuals. Lister refers to the superiority of the rights-based approach as 'it gives greater power to users by providing them with (more or less) clear, enforceable entitlements' (Lister, 2008: 236).

In Ireland, Exceptional Needs Payments administered by Community Welfare Officers are discretionary payments, a throwback to the Poor Law which are designed to assist with emergencies and special needs (www.socialprotection.ie).

Further reading

Lister, R. (2008) 'Citizenship and Access to Welfare', in Alcock, P., May, M. and Rowlingson, K. (eds.), *The Student's Companion to Social Policy*, 3rd edn. Oxford: Blackwell, pp. 234–240.

DISCRIMINATION

Related entries: Equality; Social divisions; Social justice

To discriminate against a person or group is to treat them unfairly. There are two types of discrimination: direct and indirect. The former is overt and the latter is hidden. With overt discrimination, the intent is obvious and reasons are often stated; for example 'No Dogs. No Blacks. No Irish': a sign which could be seen in places of employment and accommodation in Britain prior to the introduction of equality legislation. Indirect discrimination, however, can be more difficult to address, as it is hidden and more insidious, for example telling a person that they cannot enter a premises because it is full, when it clearly is not full. Indirect discrimination can be when one cannot enter a building because there is no suitable access for an individual with a wheelchair or pram. Thus, discrimination occurs when a person or group is treated differently from others primarily because they belong to a particular social category, for example on grounds of age, gender, disability, sexuality or ethnicity. They are seen no longer as individuals but as members of a group who share common characteristics and attributes.

Law suggests:

> discrimination refers to the differential, and often unequal, treatment of people who have been either formally or informally grouped into a particular class of persons. There are many forms of discrimination that are specified according to the ways in which particular groups are identified, including race, ethnicity, gender, marital status, class, age, disability, nationality, religion, or language.
>
> (Law, 2010: 167)

There are different strategies aimed at combating discrimination. There is a spectrum which ranges from minimalist to maximalist strategies. These include affirmative/positive action and positive discrimination. Titmuss (1967: 22) was an advocate for positive discrimination, viewing it as a solution when universal services were judged as too expensive and selectivist services as too stigmatizing. Positive discrimination could be a solution in relation to groups living in specific geographical areas. Edwards (1987) wrote at length about the morality of positive discrimination. He focused his attention on affirmative/positive action, positive discrimination and reverse discrimination.

Affirmative action is concerned with positive measures introduced with the aim of remedying the effects of past discrimination. They are targeted at specific groups, for example based on race, ethnicity or gender, who are currently under-represented in significant positions in society. These strategies explicitly take into account the characteristics which have been the basis for discrimination and are attempts at making progress towards achieving substantive equality; thus, functionings (Sen, 2009) are relevant here. There is criticism of such programmes, in that they are sometimes viewed as discriminatory in themselves and also in relation to whether or not they work or are necessary. If successful, they should eliminate societal barriers and lead to substantive equality and become redundant in the future for that particular group.

Further reading

Edwards, J. (1987) *Positive Discrimination: Social Justice and Social Policy*. London: Tavistock.
Law, I. (2010) *Racism and Ethnicity: Global Debates, Dilemmas, Directions*. Harlow: Pearson.

DISWELFARES

Related entries: Capitalism; Collectivism; Welfare/well-being

The term 'diswelfares' was introduced by Titmuss to describe how

> They are part of the price we pay to some people for bearing part of the costs of other people's progress; the obsolescence of skills, redundancies, premature retirements, accidents and many categories of disease and handicap, urban blight and slum clearance, smoke pollution, and, a hundred-and-one other socially generated disservices. They are socially caused diswelfares, the losses involved in aggregate welfare gains.
>
> (Alcock *et al.*, 2001: 120–121)

He notes that the agents of diswelfares are more difficult to identify and he says that 'we have therefore as societies to make other choices: either to provide social services or to allow the social costs of the system to lie where they fall' (Alcock *et al.*, 2001: 121).

Reisman (2001) gives a detailed analysis of Titmuss's concern with diswelfares. He explains that businesses and individuals bear some of the cost of development and change. However, in many cases the costs fall on third parties. He gives an example: 'A opens a railway and B makes a trip – but C loses his forest as a consequence of the sparks. D opens a factory and E buys his goods – but, the river polluted, F as a result can neither fish nor swim' (Reisman, 2001: 159).

Thus, diswelfare is linked to a commitment to collective responsibility. Welfare systems adopt different approaches to deal with diswelfares on a spectrum from individualist to collectivist approaches.

Further reading

Reisman, D. (2001) *Richard Titmuss: Welfare and Society*, 2nd edn. London: Palgrave.

DIVISION OF LABOUR

Related entries: Equality; Labour

Division of labour is the term first used by Adam Smith (1776) in *An Inquiry into the Nature and Causes of the Wealth of Nations*. He was concerned with increasing productivity. His work was based on a pin factory where, if the task was broken down into a number of tasks and workers specialized, productivity increased.

Adam Smith suggested the increased productivity of labour after division was because workers became more dexterous and effective from concentrating on a single task. This can lead to increased speed and accuracy and a higher quality of work. In this method, time is saved and machinery can work constantly.

In another context, division of labour is used to describe the gendered nature of domestic labour. The term was employed in feminist debates in the 1970s and began to define women's work in the home, similar to men's work in the labour market, as 'labour'. Hartmann (1982) wrote on the hierarchical division of labour and how this was linked to the division of labour in the home. She suggested that low wages kept women in a place of dependency on men: 'domestic division of labour, in turn, acts to weaken women's position in the labour market. Thus, the hierarchical domestic division of labour is perpetuated by the labour market, and vice versa' (Hartmann, 1982: 448).

Double shift is a term which refers to the situation where women carry the dual burden of labour. They work outside the home in paid employment and then perform the 'double shift' when they have to perform the usual domestic chores such as cleaning, cooking, shopping and caring. A comparative study of 400 men and women with dependent children in Ireland, France, Italy and Denmark on work–life balance indicates that in all four countries mothers are still bearing the main responsibility and carrying out significantly more of the domestic and childcare tasks in the home than fathers (Fine-Davis, 2005).

Further reading

Fine-Davis, M. (2005) 'Work–Life Balance of Irish Parents: A Cross-National Comparative Study', in Boucher, G. and Collins, G. (eds.), *The New World of Work: Labour Markets in Contemporary Ireland*. Dublin: Liffey Press, pp. 17–41.

Hartmann, H. (1982) 'Capitalism, Patriarchy and Job Segregation by Sex', in Giddens, A. and Held, D. (eds.), *Classes, Power and Conflict*. London: Macmillan, pp. 446–469.

Smith, A. (1776/1976) *An Inquiry into the Nature and Causes of the Wealth of Nations* (ed. by Campbell, R.H. and Skinner, A.S.). Oxford: Clarendon Press.

EARNINGS

Related entries: Benefit; Employment; Labour; Wages

Earnings is the reward a worker receives for work. It includes cash and non-cash benefits. There are different ways of measuring earnings. *Gross earning* is the amount of all wages, salaries, allowances, commissions, bonuses, holiday pay and so on that is paid to employees (i.e. before deduction of income tax, employee contributions to social security, employee contributions to pension schemes, etc.). *Net earnings* is the amount the employee receives after deductions and allowances.

The International Labour Organization (ILO) defines earnings (wages and salaries) as the remuneration in cash and in kind paid to employees for time worked or work done together with remuneration for time not worked, such as annual vacation and other paid leave or holidays. Earnings exclude employers' contributions in respect of their employees paid to social security and pension schemes and also the benefits received by employees under these schemes. Earnings also exclude severance and termination pay (ILO, 1973).

Earnings-related benefits are non-wage benefits enjoyed by some workers, also known as fringe benefits. These include employers' statutory compulsory payments, for example in relation to pension and health insurance. They include non-payment benefits, for example paid leave for holidays, sickness and parental leave. Some companies provide other 'perks' such as subsidized meals, access to leisure facilities or subsidized housing. Sometimes these benefits are not taxed and so they are attractive to employees. From the employer's viewpoint they are an incentive (ILO, 1973).

Earnings inequality is an important measurement of inequality. Earnings are affected by age, education, qualifications, experience, gender, race and other social divisions (ILO, 1973).

Further reading

ILO (International Labour Organization) (1973) *Resolutions Concerning an Integrated System of Wages: Statistics Adopted by the 12th International Conference of Labour Statisticians*, October, paragraph 8. Geneva: ILO.

ELIGIBILITY

Related entries: Deserving/undeserving; Needs; Rights; Stigma

Eligibility involves meeting certain criteria. This can be determined by means testing or by establishing rights. In social policy, eligibility criteria are used to decide who can access resources, be they money or services. Titmuss (1967) suggests that the fundamental tests of eligibility are to keep people out. Therefore, they are treated as applicants or supplicants and not beneficiaries or consumers. Welfare systems differentiate between individuals and groups of people in this way.

Less eligibility was a condition of the Poor Law Amendment Act 1834. It was intended to make workhouses a deterrent, guaranteeing that conditions in the workhouse had to be worse than the worst job possible outside the workhouse. The intention was to deter the able-bodied unemployed from claiming poor relief.

Further reading

Lister, R. (2008) 'Citizenship and Access to Welfare', in Alcock, P., May, M. and Rowlingson, K. (eds.), *The Student's Companion to Social Policy*, 3rd edn. Oxford: Blackwell, pp. 234–240.
Sen, A. (1991) *Poverty and Fairness: An Essay on Entitlement and Deprivation*. Oxford: Clarendon Press.

EMPLOYMENT

> Related entries: Active welfare; Earnings; Labour; Occupational welfare; Welfare regimes

Employment means working for money in a formal way. It is an important concept in social policy as there is a relationship between welfare systems and employment. Often citizens gain access to welfare based on their employment status and history. As employment is gendered this is reflected in the gendering of welfare payments. Keynesianism after the Second World War emphasized full employment. Esping-Andersen's (1990) work on welfare regimes emphasizes the importance of employment in different welfare regimes.

Further reading

Kenworthy, L. (2010) 'Labour Market Activation', in Castles, F., Leibfried, S., Lewis, J., Obinger, H. and Pierson, C. (eds.), *The Oxford Handbook of the Welfare State*. Oxford: Oxford University Press, pp. 435–447.

ENTITLEMENT

> Related entries: Citizenship; Eligibility; Universality

To be entitled to something means one has a right to it. In social policy it relates to one's right to welfare provision. It is related to citizenship, as individuals have different entitlements based on their citizenship status; for example, migrants often have differential rights to welfare from citizens of the host country.

Sen (1991) in *Poverty and Famines* uses entitlement to describe the means of access to resources in society. Nozick (1974) in *Anarchy, State and Utopia* wrote of the entitlement theory of distributive justice, which argues that there are two sources of entitlement. Individuals have rights over their own bodies and they have property rights over what they have produced or acquired through exchange. He encourages a 'night watchman state' which limits government intervention to protecting such entitlements.

Further reading

Nozick, R. (1974) *Anarchy, State and Utopia*. New York: Basic Books.
Sen, A. (1991) *Poverty and Famines: An Essay on Entitlement and Deprivation*. Oxford: Clarendon Press.

ENVIRONMENTALISM

> Related entries: Ideology; Sustainable development

Environmentalism or green ideology has become more central to social policy debates since its appearance as a marginal topic in the 1970s. Despite this, Fitzpatrick (2011b: 2) remarks, 'the literature that encompasses both subjects remains thin on the ground' and he explains 'books, articles, reports and so on dealing with the environment, green politics ecological economics and so forth have usually neglected social policies' (Fitzpatrick, 2011b: 3). He writes of the 'enormous amount of work to do in understanding the relationship between environmentalism and social policy – in all its positive and negative aspects' (Fitzpatrick, 2011b: 5).

Huby (2002) identifies some similarities in scholarship on social policy and scholarship on the environment. They both draw on theoretical frameworks developed in other disciplines for analytical purposes. 'Just as there is no specifically taught "theory of social policy", so neither is there a particular "theory of environmental study"'. She suggests that both areas have a concern with practical problems and she identifies a shared concern with inequality, sustainability and responsibility (Huby, 2002: 4).

An interest in environmentalism emerged in the 1970s in the context of an oil crisis and a search for new technologies. In general, the slogan adopted by environmentalists is 'think globally, act locally', emphasizing that what we occurs at a local level has global implications and this relates to both solutions and problems. Green ideology has gained prominence as interest in sustainable development has grown (WCED, 1987). Sustainable development argues that the social, economic and environmental aspects of society are interlinked.

There are different strands of environmentalism or *Greenism* as identified by George and Wilding (1994). They differentiate between social ecologists and radical activists. Social ecology is the idea that humans operate according to ecological principles and there is a need for balance between humans and nature. Deep green/deep ecology, on the other hand, gives priority to nature. They elaborate:

> the weak side of Greenism accepts the current world order with its emphasis on constantly rising rates of economic growth and consumption; all it asks for is that economic growth and consumption should be environmentally friendly. It puts faith in complex forms of technology to achieve the economic miracle and to deal with any environmental problems that may arise in the process.
>
> (George and Wilding, 1994: 162)

In contrast, strong Greenism

> stands for exactly the opposite: technological fixes cannot solve the current environmental problems: only reductions in economic growth and consumption stand any chance of achieving this; species egalitarianism means that humans are not

superior to other life – they are simply one of many species on the planet; and a new world order is needed to save mankind from ecological disaster that is neither capitalist nor socialist but Green.

(George and Wilding, 1994: 163)

Fitzpatrick (2011b: 202) identifies six schools of thought within environmentalism but warns that this list is 'far from exhaustive'. He identifies libertarians and free markets; conservatives; centrists/liberals; social democrats; socialists/Marxists; and feminists. He explores the principal challenges that all welfare systems face and reviews the main criticisms of environmentalists towards existing social policies. He discusses the relationship between poverty and the environment and examines some 'environmental pioneers'. He explores several global warming targets and strategies and the broad parameters of a green economy. He also outlines basic questions for an 'eco-social policy' agenda.

Fitzpatrick (2011b: 9–10) identifies some of the key perspectives in environmental scholarship. These are survivalists, 'those who anticipate the worse' and as a result seek drastic action; ecological modernisers, who are 'generally optimistic about environmental problems' and believe in the existing structures as adequate to cope as necessary; social radicals, who are 'concerned with the social causes and impacts of climate change', and who focus on the socio-economic, cultural and moral origins of the problem; deep ecologists, who 'argue that only through a fundamental break with excising moral values and social philosophies can we cope with the challenges ahead'; democratic pragmatists, who believe in 'democratic reform possesses the necessary resources'; market liberals, who believe that 'unregulated markets will enable us to cope with ecological risks'; and conservationist conservatives, which 'describes those who combine a love of nature and the land, often in patriotic and nationalistic terms, with an "organic politics of limits and stewardship"'.

Fitzpatrick (2011a) identifies four basic critiques of social policy from an environmental perspective. First of all, social policies are dependent upon levels of and forms of growth which are unacceptable. Second, there are issues in relation to time and social policy having to think long term and globally. Third, social policy may need to reflect on its assumptions regarding labour and employment and types of work. Fourth, there are issue with existing forms of organization and participation.

Green ideologies tend to emphasize non-hierarchical, devolved ways of working and more localized administration. Green ideology emphasizes active participation and citizenship. In relation to welfare, George and Wilding (1994) suggest that the Green focus is critical of the state for dealing with the symptoms rather than causes of societies' problems: its costs, the role of professionals and reliance on technology and large units of organization. They suggest that Green social policy has added another dimension to welfare in that it embraces broader terms than other ideologies and stresses environmental criteria as well as social and economic criteria.

This is reflected in some of the policies promoted, for example a guaranteed basic income. It encourages a more holistic approach in terms of health, education, housing and employment. It is committed to organizing at local level, for example in relation to education and work occurring at local community level. Greens are committed to power sharing and cooperation with education for life. They support working from home and living near the workplace. They take a holistic approach to health care, with a focus on rights and a universal healthcare system, emphasizing prevention and complementary medicines, healthy food and lifestyle. They focus on an effective public transport system with options to include cycle lanes and the needs of pedestrians. They recognize that a healthy environment is a prerequisite for personal health. They encourage the development of inner-city green houses, allotments and farms. In relation to housing and environment they advocate sustainable communities and the use of renewable building materials and renewable forms of energy, and they consider that housing should be a right for all.

Further reading

Fitzpatrick, T. (2011a) *Welfare Theory: An Introduction to the Theoretical Debates in Social Policy*, 2nd edn. London: Palgrave Macmillan.
Fitzpatrick, T. (2011b) *Understanding the Environment and Social Policy*. Bristol: Policy Press.
George, V. and Wilding, P. (1994) *Welfare and Ideology*. London: Harvester Wheatsheaf.
Huby, M. (2002) *Social Policy and the Environment*. Buckingham: Open University Press.

EQUALITY

Related entries: Citizenship; Discrimination; Social justice

Equality means sameness. It is an important concept in social policy, as social policies are often understood as strategies to combat inequality and to promote equality. Equality can relate to individuals and groups. There is a continuum from minimalist to maximalist definitions of equality. Minimalist involves formal equality, generally associated with equal opportunities and equal rights. Equality of condition, on the other hand, refers to substantive equality, focusing on outcome. Egalitarianism is the desire to promote equality. Whereas equality emphasizes treating people the same, equity is concerned with fairness and treating people according to need.

Baker and colleagues (2004: 24), in discussing 'equality of what', link it to five dimension of well-being: respect and recognition; resources; love, care and solidarity; power; and working and learning. Liberal equality of opportunity, usually viewed as a minimalist approach to defining equality, is associated with formal equality. Debates on equality focus on freedom; formal equality is concerned with people having rights but not impinging on the freedoms of others. This is a negative approach to freedom and is associated with liberal ideology. Substantive accounts of equality would view inequalities as hampering peoples' freedoms. This is a positive approach to freedom and is associated with more left-wing approaches. It is equated with Sen's (2009) concept of functionings.

Baker and colleagues (2004) provide a framework for understanding equality which is particularly pertinent to social policy, as they are concerned with moving from theory to action, and policy is concerned with action. They identify basic equality as 'a cornerstone of all egalitarian thinking: the idea that at some very basic level all human beings have equal worth and importance, and are therefore equally worthy of concern and respect' (Baker *et al.*, 2004: 23). Baker and colleagues differentiate between liberal egalitarianism and equality of condition. In relation to the former they suggest that there is an acceptance that there will always be inequalities between people in relation to status, resources, work and power. The state has a role in managing these inequalities, through, for example, equal opportunities legislation. Some are committed to basic equality whereas others allow for more. Baker and colleagues refer to Rawls's difference principle as the most ambitious liberal principle (Baker *et al.*, 2004: 25).

Equality can relate to individuals or groups. Equality is relational. Equality of condition is usually viewed as a maximalist conception of equality, 'to eliminate major inequalities altogether, or at least massively to reduce the current scale of inequality. The key to this much more ambitious agenda is to recognize that inequality is rooted in changing and changeable social structures and particularly in structures of domination and oppression' (Baker *et al.*, 2004: 33).

Social policy writers have drawn on Le Grand's (1982) taxonomy of equality, which includes five types of equality: equality of public expenditure; equality of final outcome; equality of use; equality of cost; and equality of outcome.

An alternative taxonomy is presented by the National Economic and Social Forum (NESF) in *Equality Proofing Issues* (NESF, 1996). It presents a ladder in which one progresses from one rung to a higher one en route from a minimalist definition of equality to a maximalist one. The first rung represents formal rights or equality of access and opportunity. This includes equality legislation. The second rung relates to equality of participation, which assumes that formal equality exists. This relates not only to rights but also to access, ability, and access to resources to exercise the right to formal equality. This may necessitate the introduction of positive action strategies to enable and encourage people, and these may include educational and psychological support. The next rung relates to equality of outcome, achieving tangible results which achieve overall equality between the targeted group and the non-targeted group in relation to the distribution of educational, cultural, political and other benefits. A series of strategies may be necessary, for example positive action programmes and quota systems.

The final rung is equality of condition, which focuses on the development of an egalitarian society by striving for the equal status of all citizens. This embraces a commitment to equality in all aspects of the lives of all citizens taking account of difference. This demands a fundamental change in social, cultural, economic and political infrastructures and in constitutional and legislative frameworks. The privileged in society would have to support such aims, which NESF indicates would demand compassion and enlightened self-interest. Equality is also related to citizenship in that it guarantees members of a particular group equal rights and responsibilities.

Further reading

Baker, J., Lynch, K., Cantillon, S. and Walsh J. (2004) *Equality from Theory to Action*. London: Palgrave.

Le Grand, J. (1982) *The Strategy of Equality*. London: Allen & Unwin.

NESF (National Economic and Social Forum) (1996) *Equality Proofing Issues: Forum Report Number 10*, February. Available at www.nesf.ie

ETHNICITY

> Related entries: Discrimination; Equality; Social divisions

'Ethnic' comes from the Greek word *ethno*, which means a tribe or a people with distinct cultural features. It refers to people with a distinct cultural identity and distinct cultural features such as language, religion and history. It is often erroneously associated with minority groups. There are different approaches to studying ethnicity. Law (2010) reviews the various approaches to studying ethnicity and distinguishes between primordial and instrumental ethnicity. The former, associated with Edward Shils (1957), refers to ethnicity as something one is born into, an identity which is static and unchangeable. The latter, associated with Michael Banton (1993), views ethnicity as social, political and cultural and can be drawn on in competition for resources or motivation for conflict. Law is critical of both: the first for not allowing for change over time and the second for underplaying unchanging ethnicities over time (Law, 2010: 79).

Banton draws on the work of Fredrik Barth's (1969) 'transactionalist' approach to ethnic boundaries, which distinguishes between culture and ethnicity, as Law (2010: 79) suggests: 'ethnic groups are not hermeneutically sealed cultural entities, boundaries are porous and subject to negotiation. Ethnic boundaries are established through social interaction and may for example become fixed whilst cultural patterns within those boundaries may be rapidly converging'. This is acknowledged by Callister (2005): 'Ethnicity is a key variable in social science research and policy making. Yet, for many individuals in New Zealand society ethnicity is a fluid characteristic' (http://www.msd.govt.nz/about-msd-and-our-work/publications-resources/journals-and-magazines/social-policyjournal/spj23/index.html).

Law identifies four questions which he says remain unanswered and are useful here for understanding the relationship between welfare and ethnicity. These are the significance of ethnicity in differing everyday contexts, such as the home, work or education; the significance of ethnicity for social identities; the significance of ethnicity for governance and citizenship; and racism and ethnicity in global and comparative context.

Further reading

Banton, M. (1993) *Racial and Ethnic Competition*. Cambridge, UK: Cambridge University Press.

Barth, F. (ed.) (1969) *Ethnic Groups and Boundaries: The Social Organisation of Cultural Difference*. London: Allen & Unwin.

Callister, P. (2005) 'Ethnicity Measures, Intermarriage and Social Policy', *Social Policy Journal of New Zealand Te Puna Whakaaro*. Available at http://www.msd.govt.nz/about-msd-and-our-work/publications-resources/journals-and-magazines/social-policyjournal/spj23/index.html

Law, I. (2010) *Racism and Ethnicity: Global Debates, Dilemmas, Directions*. Harlow: Pearson.

Shils, E. (1957) 'Primordial, Personal, Sacred and Civil Ties', *British Journal of Sociology*, 8(2): 130–145.

FABIANISM

Related entries: Social administration

Fabianism refers to the ideas of the Fabian Society, which was founded in 1884 by Sidney and Beatrice Webb. It was fuelled by the belief that social democracy could be a reality in Britain. Fabianism took a social scientific approach and criticized capitalism for being wasteful and inefficient. Its focus on scientific principles was an important link to the development of Social Policy as a subject area closely associated with the Webbs and the London School of Economics. Fabians believed that the state could promote welfare for the collective good. Their ideas were very influential in informing the labour movement and the development of social administration as a subject in the London School of Economics.

The Fabian Society

> is Britain's oldest political think tank. Since 1884 the society has played a central role in developing political ideas and public policy on the left. It aims to promote: greater equality of power, wealth and opportunity; the value of collective action and public service; an accountable, tolerant and active democracy; citizenship, liberty and human rights; sustainable development; and multilateral international cooperation. Through a wide range of publications and events the society influences political and public thinking, but also provides a space for broad and open-minded debate, drawing on an unrivalled external network and its own expert research and analysis. Its programme offers a unique breadth, encompassing national conferences and policy seminars; periodicals, books, reports and digital communications; and commissioned and in-house research and comment.
> (http://www.fabians.org.uk)

The Fabian Society has almost 7000 members. During its history the membership has included many of the key thinkers on the British left and every Labour Prime Minister. Currently, there are over 200 parliamentarians in the Fabian Society. It consists of seventy local Fabian societies, the Scottish and Welsh Fabians, the Fabian Women's Network and the Young Fabians. The society was one of the original founders of the Labour Party and is constitutionally affiliated to the party.

Further reading

http://www.fabians.org.uk

FAMILIES OF NATIONS

> Related entries: Comparative social policy; Models of welfare; Welfare regimes

This term is associated with Francis Castles and Deborah Mitchell (Castles and Mitchell, 1993), and is an explanatory term that has become part of the discourse in comparative social policy. Certain welfare states share common and relevant social, demographic, cultural, structural characteristics and certain aspects of the structuring of their welfare states. Castles and Mitchell write in terms of consanguinity and question Esping-Andersen's (1990) *Three Worlds of Welfare Capitalism*:

> in our analysis, we question his conclusions, not because we doubt that the three worlds of Liberal, conservative or corporatist and Social Democratic welfare capitalism he identifies have strong empirical referents, but rather because our empirical analysis of the linkages between effort, instruments and outcomes suggests, in addition the existence of a fourth 'radical' world, the characteristics of which help to explain some of the puzzles arising from the welfare performance of English-speaking nations.
>
> (Castles and Mitchell, 1993: 103)

Castles and Mitchell identify four families of nations. These are an English-speaking family of nations including Australia, Canada, Ireland, New Zealand, the United Kingdom and the United States; a Continental family of nations consisting of Austria, Belgium, France, Germany, Italy and the Netherlands; a Scandinavian family of nations consisting of Denmark, Finland, Norway and Sweden; and a southern family of nations comprising Greece, Portugal and Spain. A vast scholarship on families, regimes and clusters has developed in the intervening years (Arts and Gelissen, 2010; Castles, 2010a; Ferrera, 2010; Huber and Bogliaccini, 2010; Peng and Wong, 2010).

Further reading

Castles, F. and Mitchell, D. (1993) 'Worlds of Welfare and Families of Nations', in Castles, F.G. (ed.), *Families of Nations: Patterns of Public Policy in Western Democracies*. Aldershot, UK: Dartmouth, pp. 93–128.

FAMILY

> Related entries: Dependency; Gender; Household; Male breadwinner

Although it may seem simple to define family, it is not so. A family is generally understood to consist of a number of people who share kinship ties. However, some people may claim to compose a family without such ties. The *nuclear family* and the *extended family* are two family forms long recognized. The former refers to a mother, father and children. The latter usually has some element of multiple generation composition. As societies have diversified, families take a variety of forms. *Families of choice*, or *friendship families*, refers to non-familial social networks, which have been highlighted as playing a larger role in the lives of lesbian, gay, bisexual and transgender (LGBT) people, and *civil partnership* is a term increasingly employed. Sociologists and anthropologists have studied 'families'. Land (2008: 50) notes that the family is important in all societies in relation to allocation of resources between genders and generations. Welfare resources are often distributed based on family membership, an issue criticized by feminist writers who argue that the concept of dependency is problematic.

Familialism focuses on the family in relation to welfare provision. What occurs within the family is welfare production, an issue highlighted by feminist writers since the 1970s. Ruth Lister (2010: 66) claims feminist scholarship 'has opened up what was the closed box of the family'. She suggests that feminism has drawn attention to the caring work and has 'revealed the importance of looking at how material resources – wages, social security benefits, goods and services and time – are distributed within families, between men, women and children, with implications for the incidence of poverty and hardship' (*ibid.*).

Gosta Esping-Andersen (1990) in *The Three Worlds of Welfare Capitalism*, an important book in comparative social policy literature, neglected the importance of the family, for which he was criticized by a series of writers including Peter Taylor-Gooby (1991), Ann Shola Orloff (1993) and Jane Lewis (1992, 1993), and he responded in 1999 by introducing concepts of *familialization* and *de-familialization*, stating: 'words like these will easily promote confusion' (Esping-Andersen, 1999: 45). He indicates that pro-family can be understood as restoring traditional family values or the promotion of a woman-friendly welfare state, dependent on interpretation. For his purpose, a familialistic welfare regime is one that 'assigns a maximum of welfare obligations to the household' (*ibid.*). 'De-famililiazation' he uses to refer to 'policies that lessen individuals' reliance on the family; that maximize the individuals' command of economic resources independently of familial or conjugal reciprocities' (*ibid.*). He distinguishes between welfare regimes in which households carry 'the principal responsibilities for members' welfare' and de-familializing regimes which seek 'to unburden the household and diminish individuals' welfare dependence on kinship' (Esping-Andersen, 1999: 51).

Family policy is a term used to describe policies directed at families. It is usually concerned with families with children. Alcock and colleagues (2008a: 381) suggest it is multidimensional and cross-cutting and involves many different policy areas. Interestingly, they suggest that the family is both the subject and object of policy in that it 'as a site for welfare intervention both gives and receives' (Alcock *et al.*, 2008a: 381). Mary Daly, who has written extensively on family and gender notes:

> many policies that actually affect gender and family functioning (whether intended or otherwise) are not titled as such. Hence, one has to range broader and include policies that relate to family as a sociological institution and family life as a set of

structures, relations, and practices. A number of policy domains are key in this respect: parental leaves, cash benefits, tax allowances (especially those relating to the care of children), and service provision for families with children.

(Daly, 2011: 3)

Family wage is associated with the traditional male breadwinner model, based on the assumption that the father will earn and the wife and children are dependants. Therefore, the wage he earns must be adequate for a family to live on. This was the bedrock of the Beveridge and Bismarckian welfare systems. Daly outlines how 'in the last thirty years family change has become a major factor driving policy change' (Daly, 2010: 138). She examines policy approaches to the inter-relations between family, state and market, suggesting there is 'a seeming consensus on the part of the European Union (EU) and the Organisation for Economic Co-operation and Development (OECD) about the appropriate focus and orientation of family and work life today' (Daly, 2010: 140). Daly introduces the main features of family policy, suggesting early family policies were based on the assumption of a male breadwinner, family caregiver and a family wage. She identifies a shift after the 1970s with the development of the service economy and the movement of women into the labour market. This, she suggests, 'turned the focus on the nature of family-related roles and functions and the interface between family and market' (Daly, 2010: 140). Critical of the traditional conceptualization of the family as 'static functionalist', Daly suggests a broader conceptualization which

views the interrelations between the family, state, and market in the following terms: looked at economically, the main functions of the family relate to income redistribution, labour supply, and consumption: looked at sociologically the family is a form of social organization that provides for care needs, arranges inter-generational and gender relations, and through these and other means plays a key role in the social organization of life; as an ideological entity the family affects continuity and change in value systems; looked at politically, the family is a site of control and a source of social order.

(Daly, 2010: 141)

Daly stresses the importance of feminist scholarship in highlighting the family in the comparative welfare literature. Daly identifies four concerns of the state in relation to family, which are demographic change, horizontal redistribution, poverty alleviation, and gender equality (Daly, 2010: 142).

Ferguson and colleagues (2002: 109) state that family-related policy is a central area of state social welfare activity. This includes the focus of social workers, public health workers and income support. They draw attention to the ideological role of family policies and suggest that there are ideas of an 'appropriate family'. In a review of scholarship on the family, Ferguson and colleagues suggest that, whereas feminist writers view families in terms of patriarchal oppression, left-wing writers, feminists among them, draw on Marxist concepts of reproduction and social reproduction and view the family as a site of oppression for women, which is a feature of capitalism. On the other hand, more conservative approaches would view the family as 'a haven in a heartless world' (Lasch, 1977). 'In one sense the family is a remarkably enduring institution' (Ferguson *et al.*, 2002: 115). Barrett and McIntosh write that the nineteenth-century ideal of the family still endures:

> has an orderly division of labour between husband and wife, and a firm but kindly style with the children that will be good for them in the long run. It is today's equivalent of the nineteenth-century bourgeois ideal. It appears in childcare manuals, in advertisements for cars and insurance policies, in the formal and the 'hidden' curricula of schools, in the catalogues of Mothercare and the brochures of travel agents.
>
> (Barrett and McIntosh, 1982: 29)

Alcock and colleagues (2008a) review scholarship on the family:

> for many utopian radicals, communists, anarchists and egalitarians from Plato to the present day, the family is naturally an object of suspicion, as the primary means for reproducing and transmitting class-based privilege and inequality from generation to generation through various forms of cultural and non-cultural capital. Radical utopians, viewing the family as selfish, inward-looking and antithetical to republican virtue, citizenship or society-wide communal attachments, have often proposed the abolition of the family and its replacement by collective forms of child-rearing and care-provision.
>
> (Alcock *et al.*, 2008a: 387)

Further reading

Alcock, C., Daly, G. and Griggs, E. (2008a) 'Family Policy', in Alcock, C., Daly, G. and Griggs, E., *Introducing Social Policy*, 2nd edn. Edinburgh: Pearson, pp. 381–402.

Barrett, M. and McIntosh, M. (1982) *The Anti-social Family*. London: Verso.

Daly, M. (2010) 'Families versus State and Market', in Castles, F., Leibfried, S., Lewis, J., Obinger, H. and Pierson, C. (eds.), *The Oxford Handbook of the Welfare State*. Oxford: Oxford University Press, pp. 139–151.

Ferguson, I., Lavalette, M. and Mooney, G. (2002) *Rethinking Welfare: A Critical Perspective*. London: Sage.

FEMINISM

> Related entries: Citizenship; Equality; Gender; Patriarchy; Power

Feminism comes from the French word *féminisme*. It is an ideology which embraces a spectrum, from right to left, from liberal to socialist and radical feminism, which focuses on women's reproductive capacities. It is concerned with women's inequality. There are two recognized waves of feminism: the first around the end of the nineteenth century; the second around the late 1960s and early 1970s. Feminists are concerned with ending women's oppression but have different views regarding how this may be achieved.

Mary McIntosh (1981) outlines the evolution of a feminist approach to social policy, indicating that there is not a single feminist social policy as there is not a single feminism. George and Wilding (1994) recognize feminism as an ideology: a view of the world which offers a critique of existing socio-economic systems, a vision of the future with some guidelines about how to achieve this ideal society. Feminist writers have questioned the subject of social policy, its theoretical basis and its services. Walby (1990: 20) defines patriarchy as 'A system of social structures and practices in which men dominate, oppress and exploit women'. Such structures are central to welfare provision.

Feminist critiques of the welfare state began in the 1970s and have become more mainstream since then. Fiona Williams (1989) produced a ground-breaking book, *Social Policy: A Critical Introduction, Issues of Race, Gender and Class*, in which she presents a framework for the study of social policy drawing on three perspectives: the political economy of welfare, feminism and work on race, class and imperialism. She outlines the marginalization of gender and social policy. Williams outlines six distinct strands of feminism. These are libertarian feminism, liberal feminism, welfare feminism, radical feminism, socialist feminism and black feminism. In her publication of 1997, Williams recognized the emergence of scholarship on identity politics 'especially around "race", disability, sexuality, and age' (Williams, 1997: 262).

Libertarian feminists, according to Williams (1989), view women's oppression as caused by state intervention and view liberty as achievable through the freedom of the market. They maintain the division between the public and the private and tend to be blind to class and racial differences. Liberal feminists view oppression as resulting from sex discrimination and sex-biased laws and look to the state to implement equality legislation as a means of achieving greater equality. They too maintain the separation between the public and private spheres and can tend to be blind to both race and class.

George and Wilding (1994) describe the focus of liberal feminists on the state and their concern with equal rights for women in all spheres of society, education, health and employment. Campaigns include the removal of discrimination and the promotion of equality legislation. George and Wilding highlight criticisms of the liberal feminist view, including the perception that the view of the state is simplistic, accepting the state as capitalist and patriarchal, restricting the analysis to the public sphere and perceiving equality of opportunity in male terms. It is viewed as a middle-class strategy.

Welfare feminists (Williams, 1989) view the institution of motherhood as devalued and see women's role as determined by biology. They view the welfare state as a potential vehicle of change and argue that the state should acknowledge the value of motherhood and introduce reforms for mothers and children; for example wages for housework and demands for child benefit.

Socialist feminism, associated with Mary McIntosh (1981), places the position of women within a socialist analysis of the state. Women's position must be looked at in terms of capitalism, but patriarchy is also crucial. Social reproduction is an important concept: women reproduce the working class on a daily basis and on a generational basis. Social reproduction involves the passing on of ideas, values and norms. Women form the reserve army of labour. Women's low pay reinforces women's dependency within marriage. Family has a central role in capitalist society.

Radical feminism views women's oppression as caused by patriarchy and capitalism, either together or separately. They argue that women's oppression is caused by patriarchy, in particular by men's power over women's reproduction and sexuality. They view the public and private as linked and stress that the personal is political (Firestone, 1979; Dworkin, 1981; Daly, 1978). Radical feminism focuses on biological determinism/biological essentialism. It suggests that men as a class oppress women as a class.

George and Wilding (1994) claim that feminism has added new insights and another dimension to our analysis of the welfare state. It has highlighted gender-specific consequences of social policy and has defined a range of social problems including domestic violence and rape. Feminism has emphasized that the personal is political and has put caring work on the public agenda. It has examined the social relations of welfare providers and users and it has added a gender dimension to socialist analysis, as well as to the equality debate in social policy, which traditionally focused on class.

Orloff (2010: 253) explores the important contribution of feminist scholars:

> rather than developing a new totalizing theory, they seek to understand men's and women's diverse gendered dispositions, capacities, resources, goals and modes of problem solving deployed in gendered political action. Conceptual innovations and reconceptualizations of foundational terms have been especially prominent in the comparative scholarship on welfare states, starting with gender, and including care, autonomy, citizenship, (in)dependence, political agency, and equality. It is impossible to see – much less to describe and understand – the mutually constitutive relation between gender and welfare states without these conceptual and theoretical innovations.

Orloff suggests that the relationship between mainstream and feminist scholars in welfare regime scholarship since the 1990s has been fruitful in that it has influenced the development of key themes and concepts such as 'defamilialization, the significance of unpaid care work in families and the difficulties of work–family reconciliation, gendered welfare institutions, the relation between fertility and women's employment, and the partisan correlates of different family and gender policy models'. Nevertheless, she suggests ' "gender mainstreaming" for the mainstream still resists the deeper implications of feminist work and has difficulties assimilating concepts of interdependency, care and gendered power' (Orloff, 2010: 254).

Further reading

Beasley, C. (1999) *What Is Feminism? An Introduction to Feminist Theory*. London: Sage.
McIntosh, M. (1981) 'Feminism and Social Policy', *Critical Social Policy*, 1: 32–42.
Orloff, A.S. (2010) 'Gender', in Castles, F. Leibfried, S., Lewis, J., Obinger, H. and Pierson, C. (eds.), *The Oxford Handbook of the Welfare State*. Oxford: Oxford University Press, pp. 252–264.
Williams, F. (1989) *Social Policy: A Critical Introduction, Issues of Race, Gender and Class*. Cambridge, UK: Polity Press.

FISCAL WELFARE

> Related entries: Models of welfare

Fiscal welfare is welfare provided through the tax system. Fiscal policy is concerned with government expenditure and revenue affecting employment and inflation in an economy. It directly affects people's incomes and firm's profits and thus expenditure may affect people's perceptions of the economy and decisions and actions. It can affect liquidity in the economy.

Titmuss (2001: 63) differentiated between three categories of welfare, one of which was fiscal welfare, the others being social welfare and occupational welfare. They are differentiated by their method of organization. Titmuss remarks that 'since the introduction of progressive taxation in 1907 there has been a remarkable development of social policy operating through the medium of the fiscal system' (Titmuss, 2001: 65).

Fiscal crisis refers to when government expenditure is greater than revenue and becomes a problem. It becomes a crisis when the government cannot reduce the deficit. O'Connor (1973) referred to the 'fiscal crisis of the welfare state': a deep-rooted problem associated with capitalism. It is to do with accumulation and legitimization.

Further reading

Titmuss, R. (2001) 'The Social Division of Welfare: Some Reflections on the Search for Equity, Lecture at the University of Birmingham in honour of Eleanor Rathbone (1955), in Alcock, P., Glennester, H., Oakley, A. and Sinfield, A. (eds.), *Welfare and Wellbeing: Richard Titmuss's Contribution to Social Policy*. Bristol: Policy Press, pp. 59–70.

FLEXICURITY

> Related entries: Labour; Welfare/well-being

The word 'flexicurity' is a combination of flexibility and security, meaning flexibility of workers and security for workers. Viebrock and Clasen (2009: 305) suggest flexicurity 'has recently become a buzzword in European labour market reform. It promises to deliver a magic formula to overcome the tensions between labour market flexibility on the one hand and social security on the other hand by offering "the best of both worlds"'.

In 2007, the European Commission committed to flexicurity (European Commission, 2007). It is concerned with

> **flexibility** of employees, who must be able to adapt to labour market developments and achieve their professional transitions. Similarly, this approach must

improve the flexibility of enterprises and work organisation in order to meet the needs of employers and to improve the balance between work and family life; **security** for employees, who must be able to progress in their professional careers, develop their skills and be supported by social security systems when they are not working.

(http://europa.eu/legislation_summaries/employment_and_social_policy/
community_employment_policies/c10159_en.htm)

Through flexicurity strategies the European Union (EU) aims to reduce unemployment and poverty rates and to help to facilitate the integration of the most underprivileged groups into the labour market, including young people, women, older workers and the long-term unemployed. It outlines the following mutually reinforcing principles which must underlie flexicurity strategies. These include: flexible and reliable work contracts, the introduction of lifelong learning strategies, effective active labour market policies (ALMP) and the modernization of social security systems, to provide financial support which encourages employment and facilitates labour market mobility.

To achieve this it calls for common principles at a European level: broadening the introduction of the Lisbon Strategy to improve employment and social cohesion within the EU; striking a balance between the rights and responsibilities of employers, employees, persons seeking employment and public authorities; adapting the principle of flexicurity to the circumstances of each Member State; supporting and protecting employees when they are not in work or during a period of transition, to integrate them into the labour market or to coach them towards stable work contracts; developing flexicurity within the enterprise as well as external flexicurity between enterprises, in order to support career development; promoting gender equality and equal opportunities for all; encouraging cooperation between the social partners, the authorities and other stakeholders; and a fair distribution of the budgetary costs and the benefits of flexicurity policies, especially between businesses, individuals and public budgets, with particular attention to small and medium-sized enterprises.

The European Foundation for the Improvement of Living and Working Conditions (2010) published an information pack on flexicurity in which it indicates that the EU has renewed interest in flexicurity as a means of dealing with the economic recession. Eurofound suggests:

> However, individual initiatives which are combining flexibility and security elements are hardly ever labelled 'flexicurity', even if they explicitly address various of the flexicurity dimensions and have been designed and are run by applying a multi-stakeholder approach. Interestingly, the majority of instruments analysed follow a multifaceted approach by combining various flexibility dimensions (external numerical, internal numerical, functional, labour cost) and security dimensions (job, employment, income, combination) and targeting several objectives.
>
> (European Foundation for the Improvement of Living and Working Conditions, 2010: 1)

Viebrock and Clasen (2009) conclude that, despite attempts at clarification and definition, the concept of flexicurity has remained ambiguous. This, they suggest, is

owing to its multidimensional character and the emphasis on particular policy components in some countries, but not in others. They suggest it is a buzzword, and state that
if 'Adopting a critical if not cynical approach, it could be argued that to some extent,
flexicurity has replaced the previous EU discourse on activation and is likely to be
replaced by the next fashionable and politically useful concept before long' (Viebrock
and Clasen, 2009: 331).

> Flexicurity is a crucial element of the Employment Guidelines and the European
> Employment Strategy as a whole. Integrated flexicurity policies play a key role
> in modernising labour markets and contributing to the achievement of the 75%
> employment rate target set by the Europe 2020 Strategy.
> Measures taken or initiated in this context include:
> - Agenda for new skills and jobs: for reducing segmentation and supporting
>   transitions by strengthening the flexicurity components and implementation;
>   equipping people with the right skills for employment; improving job quality
>   and the working conditions; and supporting job creation
> - New skills for new jobs: for upgrading, anticipating and better matching skills
>   and jobs
> - Youth on the Move: to help young people acquire skills, qualifications and
>   experience
> - anticipating, preparing and managing company restructuring
> - strengthening public employment services such as job search support, career
>   analyses, validation of experience, etc.
>   (http://ec.europa.eu/social/main.jsp?catId=102&langId=en)

Further reading

European Foundation for the Improvement of Living and Working Conditions (2010) *Flexicurity
Perspectives and Practice*. Dublin: Eurofound.
European Commission (2007) *Towards Common Principles of Flexicurity: More and Better Jobs
through Flexibility and Security*, COM(2007) 359 final. Brussels: European Commission.
Available at http://europa.eu/legislation_summaries/employment_and_social_policy/
community_employment_policies/c10159_en.htm
Viebrock, E. and Clasen, J. (2009) 'Flexicurity and Welfare Reform: A Review', *Socio-economic
Review*, 7: 305–331.

FUNCTIONINGS

> **Related entries: Capabilities; Equality; Needs**

Functionings is a concept introduced by Amartya Sen (1999). Whereas capabilities
refers to what a person can be, functionings refers to what a person manages to be.
Sen introduced the term and it has been taken up by other writers and organizations.
Sen suggests that well-being is to do with what people can do (capabilities) and what
people can be (functionings). Capabilities are to do with potential and functionings

are to do with realizing that potential and having achieved status, being part of something and being able to do something. This is a substantive approach, where outcomes are measurable, and is closely linked to social justice.

Sen stresses that

> the concept of functioning reflects the various things a person may value doing or being. The valued functionings may vary from elementary ones, such as being adequately nourished and being free from avoidable disease, to very complex activities or personal states, such as being able to take part in the life of the community and having self-respect.

(Sen, 1999: 75)

Functionings is very closely related to needs. The ideology underlying a particular welfare system will dictate to what extent it perceives its role in meeting needs and facilitating functioning.

In 2008, French President Sarkozy established *The Commission on the Measurement of Economic Performance and Social Progress* to explore the adequacy of current measures of economic performance, in particular those based on Gross Domestic Product figures, and to address broader concerns about the measurement of societal well-being, economic, environmental and social sustainability. The Commission was chaired by Professor Joseph E. Stiglitz, Columbia University. Professor Amartya Sen, Harvard University, was Chair Adviser. Professor Jean-Paul Fitoussi, Institut d'Etudes Politiques de Paris, President of the Observatoire Français des Conjonctures Economiques (OFCE), was Coordinator of the Commission. Its final report was published in September 2009. Stiglitz and colleagues argue that the capabilities approach

> conceives a person's life as a combination of various 'doings and beings' (functionings) and of his or her freedom to choose among these functionings (capabilities). Some of these capabilities may be quite elementary, such as being adequately nourished and escaping premature mortality, whereas others may be more complex, such as having the literacy required to participate actively in political life.

(Stiglitz *et al.*, 2009: 42)

Sen states: 'Individual advantage is judged in the capability approach by a person's capability to do things he or she has reasons to value . . . The focus here is on the freedom that a person actually has to do this or be that thing that he or she may value doing or being ' (Sen, 2009: 231–232).

Further reading

Sen, A. (1999) *Development as Freedom*. Oxford: Oxford University Press.
Sen, A. (2009) *The Idea of Justice*. London: Allen Lane.

GENDER

> Related entries: Discrimination; Equality; Feminism; Masculinities; Social
> divisions

Gender is concerned with social roles which are usually male and female. Sex describes biological differences between men and women. There is a distinction between sex and gender and it is commonly held that biological explanations are not adequate to explain gender inequalities. Assumptions about gender are now seen as embedded in society's institutions: the family, education, legal and political systems. We must look to social, cultural and structural reasons for differential access to resources. Gender identity is ascribed at birth and governs how we are treated and what is expected of us, with associated perceptions of femininity and masculinity. We live in a world which assumes men and women have different bodies, capabilities, needs and desires. Gender refers to the social process of dividing up people and social practices along the lines of sexed identities. This involves creating hierarchies, with one category privileged or devalued. Social policy is not gender neutral; policies reflect gender divisions inherent in society.

Beasley (2005) argues that a binary division of human beings and social practices can be oppositional, for example the opposite sex. Gender is concerned with socially constructed differences between being masculine and feminine. Gender differences are a feature of patriarchy: 'a social system in which men have come to be dominant in relation to women' (Holmes, 2007: 2). Understanding the life of a man or woman means understanding the society and time in which they live.

Orloff (2010: 254) defines gender as 'not an attribute of individuals but a social relationship, historically varying, and encompassing elements of labour, power, emotion, and language; it crosses individual subjectivities, institutions, culture, and language'. This is embedded in language, ideas, beliefs and norms, for example 'head of household', male-breadwinner and dependant. Power is institutionalized and hierarchical. Orloff is concerned with whether welfare states can promote gender equality. She refers to the two intellectual 'big bangs' of gender studies and regime analysis since the 1990s (Orloff, 2010: 252). Lewis (1992) introduced a male breadwinner model to understand welfare regimes. This, Pascall argues, is central to understanding gender equalities and inequalities in a comparative context (Pascall, 2012: 20). Pascall is concerned with the roots of gender difference in welfare institutions, and with gender equalities and inequalities. She asks if 'making room for care in everyone's lives – a universal caregiver approach – would take gender differences and gender inequalities apart at the roots' (Pascall, 2012: 4).

Esping-Andersen (2002: 69) states that 'gender equality is one of the key ingredients that must go into our blueprints for a workable new welfare architecture'. He explores what this equality might involve and suggests that 'if we want more gender equality our policies may have to concentrate on men's behaviour' (Esping-Andersen, 2002: 70). For Esping-Andersen (2002: 71) 'the issue is not so much that women are prohibited from embracing goals of lifetime careers. The issue is that if they do so they pay a high price if, that is, they also prioritize motherhood'. Depressingly, Esping-Andersen recognizes that

> the final and least insurmountable barrier to gender equality probably lies more on the 'constraint' side than on the 'choice' side. Even if women are as skilled, clever, or talented as men, competitively placed employers will rationally prefer male to female workers if they expect that women, not men, will experience a productivity decline owing to births. And if the cost of interruptions is wholly or even partly allocated to employers, then the gender bias will obviously strengthen. We face the age-old question of statistical discrimination. Employers are rational when they expect that their investment in women workers will yield comparatively less as long as women do, indeed, take time off for family reasons.
>
> (Esping-Andersen, 2002: 89)

Daly and Rake (2003) review literature on the welfare state and gender and suggest that there 'has been quite a polarized literature' (Daly and Rake, 2003: 10). They trace the beginning of discourse on gender and welfare to feminist scholarship. Feminist scholarship has deconstructed social policy to show how it is ideologically based, embracing assumptions about gender roles and responsibilities, for example the male breadwinner model. Feminist writers have drawn attention to the importance of the welfare state for women, as providers of welfare and as recipients. 'They elaborate the nature of women's closeness to the state in terms of three sets of relations; as citizens, employees and clients' (Daly and Rake, 2003: 13).

The *Gender Inequality Index* is a composite measure developed by the United Nations Development Programme to reflect inequality in achievements between women and men in three dimensions: reproductive health, empowerment and the labour market. The health dimension is measured by two indicators: the maternal mortality ratio and the adolescent fertility rate. The empowerment dimension is also measured by two indicators: the share of parliamentary seats held by each sex and by secondary and higher education attainment levels. The labour dimension is measured by women's participation in the workforce. The figure given is a country's ranking on the Index in relation to all other countries in the world.

Further reading

Beasley, C. (2005) *Gender and Sexuality*. London: Sage.

Daly, M. and Rake, K. (2003) *Gender and the Welfare State in Europe and the USA*. Cambridge, UK: Polity Press.

Esping-Andersen, G. (2002) 'A New Gender Contract', in Esping-Andersen, G., Gallie, D., Hemerijck, A. and Myles, J. (eds.), *Why We Need a New Welfare State*. Oxford: Oxford University Press, pp. 68–95.

Hearn, J. (2010) 'Reflecting on Men and Social Policy: Contemporary Critical Debates and Implications for Social Policy', *Critical Social Policy*, 30(2): 165–188.

Holmes, M. (2007) *What Is Gender? Sociological Approaches*. London: Sage.

Kjeldstad, R. (2001) 'Gender Policies and Gender Equality', in Kautto, M., Fritzell, J., Hvinden, B., Kvist, J. and Uusitalo, H. (eds.), *Nordic Welfare States in the European Context*. London: Routledge, pp. 55–78.

Lewis, J. (1992) 'Gender and the Development of Welfare Regimes', *Journal of European Social Policy*, 2(3): 159–173.

Orloff, A.S. (2010) 'Gender', in Castles, F. Leibfried, S., Lewis, J., Obinger, H. and Pierson, C. (eds.), *The Oxford Handbook of the Welfare State*. Oxford: Oxford University Press, pp. 252–264.

Pascall, G. (2012) *Gender Equality in the Welfare State?* Bristol: Policy Press.

Pilcher, J. and Whelehan, I. (2004) *50 Key Concepts in Gender Studies*. London: Sage.

Williams, F. (1989) *Social Policy: A Critical Introduction, Issues of Race, Gender and Class*. Cambridge, UK: Polity Press.

GLOBALIZATION

> **Related entries: Flexicurity; Global social policy; Migration**

Globalization, like many other social policy concepts, is highly contested. It is not a new phenomenon, as Kirby reminds us: 'though the term globalisation may be recent, it is widely accepted that flows of trade, information and migration linking distant parts of the world have existed for thousands of years, with ever growing intensity' (Kirby, 2004: 24). He traces the history of globalization, distinguishing different phases: the third phase 'gathered pace gradually from the mid-1970s' (*ibid.*) and has been fuelled by greater mobility of capital, the homogeneity of development models, the triumph of neo-liberalism, the increased dominance of global transnational corporations and restrictions on labour mobility.

In 1999, Ramesh Mishra recognized that 'globalization has spawned a vast literature, very little of which is about its impact on the welfare state' (Mishra, 1999: ix). Two years later Nicola Yeates remarked:

> academic social policy for its part has been traditionally oriented to the national sphere and, with the exception of the field of European social policy, has only relatively recently – since the mid 1990s – examined the global context of social policy. Even so, an intellectual project around globalization and social policy in the 'core' countries has already spawned a great deal of work.
>
> (Yeates, 2001: 1)

Since then, scholarship on globalization and social policy has mushroomed.

Mishra (1999: 15) suggests 'globalization, which must be understood as an economic as well as political and ideological phenomenon, is without a doubt now the essential context of the welfare state'. He defines globalization as 'a process through which national economies are becoming more open and thus more subject to supranational economic influences and less amenable to social control' (Mishra, 1999: 3–4). He warns, however, that 'the precise nature and extent of globalisation remain a matter of debate and contention' (Mishra, 1999: 4). Mishra differentiates between globalization and the internationalization of economics. These are ideal types which are not necessarily mutually exclusive. In the internationalization of economics, the principle economic units remain national although international aspects of the economy, for example trade, foreign direct investment and multinational enterprises, assume increasing importance.

In a similar vein, Yeates (2001: 4) contends that globalization is a contested term. She presents an overview of competing views of globalization and concludes: 'notwithstanding the reservations and limitations of globalization that have just been outlined, used carefully, a globalization perspective offers fruitful avenues for social policy analysis as it does for the social sciences generally'(Yeates, 2001: 17). Since then, Yeates has written extensively on globalization and global social policy (Yeates, 2008; Yeates and Holden, 2009).

Yeates, on globalization, states:

> at its core is an emphasis on the ways in which the conditions of human existence are characterized by dense, extensive networks of interconnections and interdependencies that routinely transcend national borders. These networks and links take a range of forms: flows of capital, goods, services and people; the global integration of business activities; flows of images, ideas, information and values through media and communications; the worldwide spread of ideologies such as consumerism and individualism; international movements of people (for leisure and work). They also take the form of 'new' collective responses, expressed in political cooperation and action across borders, as in the emergence of global, political movements directing their action at multilateral organisations in an attempt to shape how populations and territories are governed.
>
> (Yeates, 2008: 3)

She states that this process is more extensive and is happening at a quicker speed than has historically occurred.

Sykes (2010) presents four perspectives on the relationship between social policy and globalization and explores their effectiveness in explaining evidence on changes in social policy and welfare. He begins by looking at Mishra's (1999) argument that globalization has led to the decline in importance of nation states in terms of their autonomy in policy making, in pursuing full employment and economic growth. These conditions lead to a spiralling downwards in terms of welfare and employment conditions. In this context neo-liberalism becomes more widespread.

Sykes next presents Pierson's (2001) approach: the argument that globalization has little effect upon welfare states and that the welfare state will endure. The third approach, associated with Esping-Andersen (1996), is that globalization's effects on welfare states are mediated by national politics. Finally, welfare states generate globalization and limit its future development. This he associates with the writing of Rieger and Leibfried (2003).

There has always been an element of globalization, in that there has long been international trade and maritime exploration. After the Second World War, when Keynesian economics was in its ascendency and welfare states began to emerge, western economies were relatively closed and self-contained. There was an emphasis on the nation and closed economies. Until the 1970s, all western countries had strict control over capital movement and exchange rates were fixed. This changed during the 1970s when neo-liberalism was in the ascendant.

For Stiglitz (2002), globalization is neither good nor bad and has the power to do both. Stiglitz argues that the way globalization is managed has to change radically and he claims that decisions are often made because of ideology and politics, rather than evidence. The opening up of international trade has helped many countries develop quicker than they would have previously. There have also been improvements in standards of living and life expectancy, a reduced sense of isolation and greater access to knowledge. Stiglitz takes as examples the international landmines treaty and the dropping of national debt. He suggests that new foreign firms may hurt state-protected enterprises and lead to the introduction of new technologies, access to new markets and the creation of new industries. However, he argues that foreign aid has brought aid to millions and AIDS projects have been successfully developed.

Swank (2010) presents an overview of the theoretical arguments which link globalization with welfare state change. He suggests that literature in the 1990s was characterized by a 'race to the bottom' thesis. This was replaced by an emphasis on new demands for insurance because of heightened risks and diswelfares. He identifies a race to market-conforming social policy, in which globalization will constrain governments in their ability to sustain generous systems of public social protection, and the compensation thesis: 'a new theory of embedded liberalism' (Swank, 2010: 320). He also identifies that welfare systems provide social insurance against international risk to employment and compensation to those who lose out. Globalization could influence in predictable ways the preferences and political economic capacities of sector and classes in capitalist democracies.

Further reading

Mishra, R. (1999) *Globalization and the Welfare State*. London: Edward Elgar.

Swank, D. (2010) 'Globalization', in Castles, F. and Leibfried, S., Lewis, J., Obinger, H. and Pierson, C. (eds.), *The Oxford Handbook of the Welfare State*. Oxford: Oxford University Press, pp. 318–330.

Sykes, B. (2010) 'Globalization and Social Policy', in Alcock, P., May, M. and Rowlingson, K. (eds.), *The Student's Companion to Social Policy*, 3rd edn. Oxford: Blackwell, pp. 430–437.

Yeates, N. (2001) *Globalization and Social Policy*. London: Sage.

GLOBAL SOCIAL POLICY

Related entries: Globalization

Global social policy is concerned with social policy beyond nation states, as was the original focus of social policy. As welfare systems developed from the end of the nineteenth century and more rapidly after the Second World War, the focus was on nation building. However, since the mid-1990s in particular there has been a shift towards what has been defined as 'global social policy'.

Yeates, who has written extensively on global social policy (Yeates, 2008: 11), traces the term to Deacon and colleagues (1997), who defined it as 'a practice of supranational actors which embodies global social redistribution, global social regulation, and global social provision and/or empowerment, and . . . the ways in which supranational organisations shape national social policy' (Deacon *et al.*, 1997: 195).

Yeates (2008: 11) suggests that global social policy

> examines how social policy issues are increasingly being perceived to be global in scope, cause and impact; examines how cross-border flows of people, goods, services, ideas and finance relate to social policy development; examines the emergence of transnational forms of collective action, including the development of multilateral and cross-border models of governance; examines how these modes of governance and policy making shape the development and impacts of social policy around the world.

George and Wilding (2009: 27) call for a global approach to deal with global problems. They identify some of these global problems as crime and drugs, AIDS and water supply, and they state: 'the emergence and acceptance of a range of social problems as genuinely global stimulates pressures for the development of global social policies' (George and Wilding, 2009: 28). They feel this is necessary in order to avoid a race to the neo-liberal bottom. They highlight the emerging interest in global citizenship and human rights and view the expansion in international non-governmental organizations and social movements as a reflection of the interest in global citizenship. Yeates and Holden (2009: 280–290) outline the characteristics of global social policy as a field of research and study focusing on ideas, discourse, actors, agendas and practices, and global social policy in relation to history and place.

Further reading

Deacon, B., Hulse, M. and Stubbs, P. (1997) *Global Social Policy: International Organisations and the Future of Welfare*. London: Sage.
George, V. and Wilding, P. (2009) 'Globalization and Human Welfare: Why Is There a Need for a Global Social Policy?', in Yeates, N. and Holden, C. (eds.), *The Global Social Policy Reader*. Bristol: Policy Press, pp. 27–34.
Yeates, N. (ed.) (2008) *Understanding Global Social Policy*. Bristol: Policy Press.
Yeates, N. and Holden, C. (eds.) (2009) *The Global Social Policy Reader*. Bristol: Policy Press.

HEALTH

> Related entries: Welfare regimes; Welfare/well-being

Health is defined by the World Health Organization (WHO, 1946: 100) as: 'a state of complete physical, mental and social well-being and not merely the absence of disease or infirmity'. The WHO defines health policy as: 'decisions, plans, and actions that are undertaken to achieve specific health care goals within a society' (World Health Organization, *Health Policy*, http://www.who.int/topics/health_policy/en/). Health has long been one of the central concerns of social policy makers and scholars. Health status is often used as an indicator of poverty, for example in the Black Report (DHSS, 1980). Healthcare systems are a central part of welfare systems and in most industrialized countries health spending is a major concern of governments. Statistics on health expenditure for the Organisation for Economic Co-operation and Development (OECD) countries are available online at www.oecd.org.

Health insurance is insurance against meeting the costs associated with possible future ill health. Its introduction was associated with Bismarck in 1883. However, earlier forms of health insurance were associated with friendly societies. Different welfare regimes have different systems of health insurance across a spectrum from voluntary to compulsory contributions, and there is also a mix of public, private and voluntary provision. One of the most publicized developments in health care is Barack Obama's 2010 Patient Protection and Affordable Care Health Care Plan in the United States.

Esping-Andersen (1990) has been criticized for neglecting welfare services in his *Three Worlds of Welfare Capitalism* (Alber, 1995; Bambra, 2005b).

Reibling (2010) reviews three of the most influential health typologies as presented by the OECD (1987), Moran (1999, 2000) and Bambra (2005b). She outlines how the OECD (1987) developed one of the earliest categorizations of healthcare systems, distinguishing systems along three dimensions: (1) access to care measured by the degree of coverage; (2) the funding principle, for example taxation, public and private insurance; (3) the public–private mix of care provision. Based on these criteria, three system types were developed.

In countries with a national health service (NHS), as for example in the UK and Sweden, coverage is universal (based on residency requirements), funding is based on taxation, and the provision of care is almost exclusively public. At the other extreme is the private insurance system as it exists in the USA, in which both funding and care provision is organized through private actors and institutions. In most cases, private health insurance is purchased by the employer, who can offer an occupational healthcare plan to the employees. As a result of its voluntary nature, this system leaves a considerable number of people without health insurance and it therefore has a low degree of universality.

A middle way position is taken by the social insurance countries such as Germany and Austria. In this system type, we find a quasi-universal access to care through employer-based but compulsory health insurance. Funding is organized by non-profit insurance funds and with regard to service provision we find a mix of public and private providers. The theoretical dimension highlighted as being central to the development of these types is whether funding is based on taxation, public or private health insurance.

Reibling (2010) indicates that the next milestone in healthcare system classifications was Moran's (1999, 2000) typology of healthcare states. Moran stressed the role of the state and used three indicators for the development of his classification:

the governance of consumption, provision and technology. His analysis results in four families of healthcare states, which resemble the OECD system types. The entrenched command and control states include the NHS countries. They are characterized by universal access and a high degree of state control over costs and providers (hospitals and doctors), as well as a moderate level of control of health technology. The USA is the only real example of a supply state, which has non-universal access and a low degree of state control in all three arenas. The corporatist states conform to the social insurance countries. Access is quasi-universal, the degree of control of costs and providers is moderate, and control of health technology is rather low. The fourth type contains the southern European countries, which also have an NHS but a low regulative capacity in all three realms. As a result, these insecure command and control states can de facto not guarantee the formally existing rights. Even though Moran (2000) mainly reproduces the OECD types, he shifts the focus from organizational principles to government regulation and includes the regulation of health technology as an additional dimension.

The last typology reviewed was developed by Bambra (2005), who adapts Esping-Andersen's (1990) concept of decommodification and applies it to healthcare services. Her definition of health decommodification encompasses 'the extent to which an individual's access to health care is dependent upon their market position and the extent to which a country's provision of health is independent from the market' (Bambra, 2005: 33). The first part of this definition refers to the principle of decommodification, whereas the form of care provision reflects the principle of welfare mix. This borrowing of Esping-Andersen's (1990) principles is also present in the empirical indicators she uses for the 'health de-commodification index': (1) private health expenditure (% Gross Domestic Product); (2) private hospital beds (% total bed stock); (3) the percentage of the population covered by the healthcare system. Although the precise definitions differ, all three typologies use the public–private mix in the realms of funding and service provision as classification criteria.

Reibling (2010) suggests that healthcare systems are concerned with the provision of services to persons in need. She develops an analogy to decommodification for health care by proposing access as a central dimension for the comparative analysis of health systems. Putting access at the centre of a health typology strengthens a patients' perspective and thereby the impact of health services on individual health. A measure of access has been included in all previous typologies (OECD, 1987; Moran, 1999, 2000; Bambra, 2005). The definition of access used was restricted to a very narrow concept: the degree of coverage or universality of health systems.

Reibling extends the concept of access by looking at regulative aspects and financial incentives that shape entry and reception of care. As a result, three different modes of influencing healthcare access are proposed: legal regulations (e.g. gatekeeping), financial incentives (e.g. co-payments) and supply (e.g. availability of services). Based on empirical measurements for these dimensions, a cluster analysis is performed in order to develop a typology of healthcare access. Reibling reviews the most influential healthcare typologies and proposes a classification that takes access to healthcare services as its basis, thereby strengthening the position of the patients' perspective. She aims to highlight 'access to care' as one dimension that has been widely neglected in earlier studies

Further reading

Reibling, N. (2010) 'Healthcare Systems in Europe: Towards an Incorporation of Patient Access', *Journal of European Social Policy*, 20: 5–18.

WHO (1946) Preamble to the Constitution of the World Health Organization as adopted by the International Health Conference, New York, 19–22 June 1946; signed on 22 July 1946 by the representatives of 61 States (Official Records of the World Health Organization, no. 2) and entered into force on 7 April 1948.

HOUSEHOLD

Related entries: Dependency; Family; Male breadwinner

Household is a term that is widely used in social policy. It refers to a group of people who live together and share resources and responsibilities. It has been described as a 'black box' by Jan Pahl (1990), arguing that there is little knowledge of what occurs within it.

The term 'head of household' has been criticized by feminist scholars for its aggregation. The Organisation for Economic Co-operation and Development (OECD) suggests that household, in most countries, refers to a group of people living in the same dwelling, but, in some others, having a common provision for essential items is an additional requirement (OECD, 2008).

A household is defined as a collection of individuals who are sharing the same housing unit. In EU-SILC (European Union Statistics on Income and Living Conditions, http://epp.eurostat.ec.europa.eu/portal/page/portal/income_social_inclusion_living_conditions/methodology/main_concepts_and_definitions#) the following persons are regarded as household members: persons usually resident, related to other members; persons usually resident, not related to other members; resident boarders, lodgers, tenants (for at least six months); visitors (for at least six months); live-in domestic servants, au-pairs (for at least six months); persons usually resident, but temporarily absent from the dwelling; children of the household being educated away from home; persons absent for long periods, but having household ties; and persons temporarily absent (for less than six months) but having household ties.

Falkingham and Baschieri (2009: 123) discuss the usefulness of a unitary model of household expenses:

> this unitary model envisages the household as a single unit, implying the existence of a single household welfare function reflecting the preferences of all its members, and assumes that all members of the household pool their resources. As a result of this all members of the household are assumed to enjoy the same level of welfare.

They recognize that the unitary model of household expenses can mask gendered and generational inequalities, and as a result policies may be poorly targeted.

Sutherland (2005) explores the implications of examining the effect of policy changes on individual incomes, rather than household incomes, and argues that these are conceptual and associated with the treatment of collective resources and responsibilities, particularly children. Sutherland attempts to make this transparent by establishing a method of analysing policy at the individual (and gender-specific) level. She focuses on two policy-related issues: the impact of a minimum wage and the effect of introducing a minimum pension guarantee. She explores the implications of choosing the individual as the income unit and presents an analysis of the issue by gender. She concludes:

> the possibility that some individuals may benefit at the expense of other household members is an aspect of policy design that should be monitored, but is entirely absent from a household analysis. Policy analysis by gender illuminates the quite striking differences that continue to exist between the sexes. We find that the bottom of the individual distribution is dominated by women.
>
> (Sutherland, 2005: 22)

Further reading

European Foundation for the Improvement of Living and Working Conditions (2009) *Second European Quality of Life Survey*. Dublin: EFILWC.
Falkingham, J. and Baschieri, A. (2009) 'Gender and Poverty: How Misleading Is the Unitary Model of Household Resources?', in Yeates, N. and Holden, C. (eds.), *The Global Social Policy Reader*. Bristol: Policy Press, pp. 123–128.
OECD (2008) *The Distribution of Household Income in OECD Countries: What Are Its Main Features? Growing Up Unequal?* Available at http://www.oecd.org/els/social/inequality
Sutherland, H. (2005) 'Women, Men and the Redistribution of Income', *Fiscal Studies*, 18(1): 1–22.

HUMAN CAPITAL

> Related entries: Active welfare; Capabilities; Capitalism; Discrimination; Equality; Functionings

Human capital has been defined as 'knowledge, attitudes, and skills that are developed and valued primarily for their economically productive potential' (Baptiste, 2001: 185). The term is associated with the work of Jacob Mincer (1958), Theodore Schultz (1963) and Gary Becker (1975). They argue that human capital is similar to any other type of capital and that education is an investment in that it adds to human capital just as other investments add to physical capital. Investment in education, training and enhanced benefits can lead to an improvement in the quality and level of production. Human capital is relevant to debates on active labour market polices in which the emphasis is on enhancing people's skills so that they are more employable. It is closely associated with education and training and so it is directly relevant to social policy.

Baptiste (2001) provides a robust overview of the origins and development of Human Capital Theory, tracing it back to three diverse schools of thought. The first, he says,

> (represented by John Stuart Mill and Alfred Marshall) distinguished between the acquired capacities (skills and knowledge) of human beings, which are classed as capital, and human beings themselves. Having a deep-seated moral and philosophical commitment to human freedom and dignity, this group found the mere thought of humans as capital rather offensive.
>
> (Baptiste, 2001: 185)

The second school, Baptiste continues,

> (represented by Adam Smith, Irving Fisher, and the Chicago School) argued that human beings are themselves capital, that the notion of humans as capital is not incompatible with freedom and dignity, and that to the contrary, by investing in themselves, people enlarge the range of choices available to them and so enhance rather than limit their freedom.
>
> (Baptiste, 2001: 186)

Finally, he identifies that:

> Karl Marx represents the third camp. Like Adam Smith (1776/1937), he agreed that greater productivity alone does not account for the higher earnings of educated workers but that the cost of education (investment) also enters into the equation (Marx, 1867/1976). And, like Mill (1859/1956), Marx concurred that workers sell their capacities to labor (their 'labor power') rather than themselves. However, Marx argued that the capacity to labor itself is not a form of capital but that a worker's labor power becomes capital only when it is used in the process of production (Marx, 1867/1976, 1894/1981).
>
> (*ibid.*)

The World Bank has been concerned with human capital for half a century. In 2011, it launched its ten-year Education Strategy, which emphasizes learning *for all*. Its slogan is *Invest early, invest smartly, and invest for all.* It is based on consultation with governments, development partners, students, teachers, researchers, civil society and business representatives from more than 100 countries. It states: 'investments in quality education lead to more rapid and sustainable economic growth and development. Educated individuals are more employable, able to earn higher wages, cope better with economic shocks, and raise healthier children' (World Bank, 2011: v).

The World Bank recognizes that, although there has been progress in developing countries towards the Millennium Development Goals of universal primary education and gender equity, an abundance of evidence shows that 'many children and youth in developing countries leave school without having learned much at all' (*ibid.*).

The belief in education held by the World Bank can be summed up as:

Education is now the key to eliminating gender inequality, to reducing poverty, to creating a sustainable planet, to preventing needless deaths and illness, and to fostering peace. And in a knowledge economy, education is the new currency by which nations maintain economic competitiveness and global prosperity. Education today is inseparable from the development of human capital.

(*ibid.*)

The World Bank recognizes that access to education, a basic human right enshrined in the Universal Declaration of Human Rights and the United Nations Convention on the Rights of the Child, is also a strategic development investment:

The human mind makes possible all other development achievements, from health advances and agricultural innovation to infrastructure construction and private sector growth. For developing countries to reap these benefits fully – both by learning from the stock of global ideas and through innovation – they need to unleash the potential of the human mind. And there is no better tool for doing so than education.

(World Bank, 2011: 1)

The Education Strategy focuses on three areas: knowledge generation and exchange, technical and financial support, and strategic partnerships.

This commitment to education could be understood using Sen's (2009) capabilities approach. However, it could also be critiqued by Marxist theorists as serving the interests of capital; although by more liberal thinkers it could be viewed as empowering individuals to participate.

Further reading

Baptiste, I. (2001) 'Educating Lone Wolves: Pedagogical Implications of Human Capital Theory', *Adult Education Quarterly*, 51: 184–201.
Becker, G.S. (1975) *Human Capital: A Theoretical and Empirical Analysis, with Special Reference to Education*, 2nd edn. New York: Columbia University Press.
World Bank (2011) *Learning for All: Investing in People's Knowledge and Skills to Promote Development*. World Bank Group Education Strategy 2020. Washington: The International Bank for Reconstruction and Development/The World Bank.

HUMAN TRAFFICKING

> **Related entries: Asylum seeker; Citizenship; Globalization; Labour; Migration**

Human trafficking in people, or modern-day slavery, has received much media attention in recent years. In 2000, the United Nations reached an agreement on a definition that identifies three critical components to human trafficking. These are the act, the means and the purpose. The Palermo Protocol defines it as:

Trafficking in persons shall mean the recruitment, transportation, transfer, harboring, or receipt of persons, by means of the threat or use of force or other forms of coercion, of abduction, of fraud, of deception, of the abuse of power or of a position of vulnerability or of the giving or receiving of payments or benefits of exploitation. Exploitation shall include, as a minimum, the exploitation of the prostitution of others or other forms of sexual exploitation, forced labour or services, slavery or practice similar to slavery, servitude or the removal of organs. The consent of a victim of trafficking in persons to the intended exploitation set forth [above] shall be irrelevant where any of the means set forth [above] have been used.

(United Nations, 2000: Article 3)

The Palermo Protocol (http://www.palermoprotocol.com) is a useful source of information on human trafficking or trafficking in people.

Trafficking is complicated, as the victim can sometimes seem to be implicit in the act, for example when a woman agrees to migrate to another country to take up employment and then finds that she has been sold into slavery. It can include men and women of all ages and can take many different forms, including forced sex, begging, child soldiers, sex tourism, domestic labour and agricultural work.

The ILO (2012: 13) study, which covers the period from 2002 to 2011, estimates that 20.9 million people, or around three in every 1000 persons worldwide, were in forced labour at any given point in time over this ten-year period. It cautions that this is a conservative estimate, given the fact that human trafficking is a hidden crime. It indicates that human trafiicking affects

victims of forced labour globally, trapped in jobs into which they were coerced or deceived and which they cannot leave. Human trafficking can also be regarded as forced labour, and so this estimate captures the full realm of human trafficking for labour and sexual exploitation, or what some call 'modern-day slavery'.

(ILO, 2012: 13)

It classifies forced labour into three categories: that imposed by the state, by the private economy, and for either sexual or for labour exploitation. It states:

Of the total number of 20.9 million forced labourers, 18.7 million (90%) are exploited in the private economy, by individuals or enterprises. Out of these, 4.5 million (22% total) are victims of forced sexual exploitation, and 14.2 million (68%) are victims of forced labour exploitation, in economic activities such as agriculture, construction, domestic work and manufacturing. The remaining 2.2 million (10%) are in state-imposed forms of forced labour, for example in prison under conditions which contravene ILO standards on the subject, or in work imposed by the state military or by rebel armed forces.

(*ibid.*)

In June 2012, the European Commission adopted the *European Union Strategy towards the Eradication of Trafficking in Human Beings* (2012–2016) (European

Commission, 2012). This is a set of concrete and practical measures to be implemented over the next five years. These include the establishment of national law enforcement units specialized in human trafficking and the creation of joint European investigation teams to prosecute cross-border trafficking cases. The strategy includes prevention, protection and support of the victims, as well as prosecution of the traffickers. It identifies five priorities and outlines a series of initiatives for each of them, such as supporting the establishment of national law enforcement units specialized in human trafficking; creating joint investigation teams and involving Europol and Eurojust in all cross-border trafficking cases; providing clear information to victims on their rights under European Union (EU) law and national legislation, in particular their right to assistance and health care, their right to a residence permit and their labour rights; creating an EU mechanism to better identify, refer, protect and assist trafficked victims; establishing a European Business Coalition against trafficking in human beings to improve cooperation between companies and stakeholders; establishing an EU platform of civil society organizations and service providers working on victim protection and assisting Member States and third countries; and supporting research projects examining the Internet and social networks as increasingly popular recruitment tools for traffickers.

Rafferty (2008) presents a very comprehensive study on the impact of trafficking on children in which she focuses on the psychological and social policy perspectives. The effects include educational deprivation, physical health problems and reduced emotional well-being. She suggests that the solutions must be found in building a protective environment for children, which will require governments to acknowledge that trafficking is a violation of human rights and that such abuses are grounded in the marginalization of women and gender-based discrimination, and require the development of patriarchal structures that do not condone the commercialization of women and girls.

Rambaldini-Gooding (2012) has undertaken some very interesting research in which she explores best practice regarding policies and practice in relation to victims of sex trafficking. The comparative study looks at Ireland, Italy and the United Kingdom. Sex trafficking is an important issue for social policy. It involves exploitation and raises important issues about poverty and destitution in countries of origin and services and polices in destination countries in which victims can be aided or penalised according to regime type.

Further reading

European Commission (2012) *The European Union Strategy towards the Eradication of Trafficking in Human Beings (2012–2016)*. Brussels: European Commission.

ILO (2012) *Global Estimate of Forced Labour*, International Labour Organization Special Action Programme to Combat Forced Labour (SAP–FL). Geneva: ILO.

Rafferty, Y. (2008) 'The Impact of Trafficking on Children: Psychological and Social Policy Perspectives', *Journal of Society for Research in Child Development*, 2(1): 13–18.

Rambaldini-Gooding, D. (2012) *The Trafficking of Women into Ireland: A Model of Best Practice in Service Provision*. Unpublished PhD thesis, School of Applied Social Science, University College Dublin.

IDEOLOGY

Related entries: Citizenship; Democracy; Environmentalism; Equality; Feminism; Liberal; Needs

Wilson (1977: 7) reminds us that social policies are not neutral. They are not value free and come wrapped in ideology. George and Wilding (1994: 6) suggest that ideology is a view of the world and offers a critique of the existing socio-economic system, a vision of the future and some guidelines on how to achieve this ideal society. Welfare systems and social policies have to be understood in terms of ideologies, of which there is a wide spectrum.

Spicker (2008: 93) suggests that ideologies are 'commonly identified in terms of a spectrum running from "left" to "right"'. Generally, the left is assumed to support welfare, is in favour of public provision and institutional welfare and is collectivist in nature. The right is concerned with curtailing the state provision of welfare, against public provision, in favour of residual welfare and individualist in nature.

Right-wing or liberal ideologies are guided by three central concepts: 'freedom from coercion', justice and individualism. Left-wing ideologies are more concerned with 'freedom to', with achieving substantive equality and universal rights-based services. George and Wilding (1994) suggest there is a middle way which views the possibility of having a welfare state within a capitalist society. The middle way views the free market as the best way of organizing an economy, but consider that it needs managing and its effects need to be controlled and compensated for.

Spicker (2008: 93–98) explores seven strands of ideology: Marxism, socialism, social democracy, liberalism, conservativism, Christian democracy and the extreme right. George and Wilding explore the relationship between ideology and welfare and focus on Green and feminist ideologies as well as the right–left spectrum. Alcock and colleagues (2008b: 61–120) introduce a range of ideological approaches to welfare, which include neo-liberalism, conservativism, social democracy, socialism, the third way, feminism, Greenism and postmodernism.

George and Wilding indicate that welfare ideologies are value laden. Such ideologies provide guidance on how much the state intervenes, the positive and negative functions of state welfare provision for the political, economic and social life of the country and what organizational forms state intervention should take. They explore the ideal form of society for the future and how it differs from existing welfare states. They explore which methods/processes are necessary to maintain this. Esping-Andersen's (1990) *Three Worlds of Welfare Capitalism* and subsequent scholarship on welfare regimes explores the ideological foundations of welfare systems.

Further reading

George, V. and Wilding, P. (1994) *Welfare and Ideology*. London: Harvester Wheatsheaf.
Spicker, P. (2008) *Social Policy Themes and Approaches*, 2nd edn. Bristol: Policy Press.

INDIVIDUALISM

Related entries: Collectivism; Ideology; Liberal

Individualism can be seen to have two different but inter-related meanings: individualism as understood in free-market ideologies and individualism as an expression of individual freedoms. Individualism, as opposed to socialist collectivism, is central to the free-market philosophy, as is maximum individual choice in the economy. Individual rights are seen as central to the notion of social citizenship.

Individualist/anti-collectivist theorists embrace a number of perspectives associated with writers including Hayek (1949, 1972, 1976, 1979) and Friedman (1962, 1976; Friedman and Friedman, 1980) and institutions including the Institute of Economic Affairs (http://www.iea.org.uk) and the Adam Smith Institute (http://www.adamsmith.org). They agree on the broad principle of individualism: that the freedom of the individual is paramount, as is freedom of the market.

Kennedy (2002) classifies individualist theorists as asociological, astructural, consensual and gender blind. They are asociological in that they do not allow for individual differences associated with health, ability and intelligence; astructural in that they accept the status quo and do not challenge structural inequalities; consensual in that they assume social relations are based on consensus; and gender blind in that they do not, for the most part, allow for the social construction of gender differences. In relation to welfare, these theorists advocate a minimal role for the state: a residual model of welfare. Statutory intervention is viewed as a disincentive to work, wasteful and inefficient, authoritarian, limiting choice and destroying initiative and self-reliance. They tend to have a more economic dimension, as Williams concludes: 'the principles of economic life are to be reflected in social life, initiative, responsibility, discipline, authority and ultimately through these, freedom' (Williams, 1989: 27).

The main principles of individualist theorists are outlined by Bosanquet (1983), who presents the idea of a thesis and an anti-thesis model, the former associated with the Austrian school and the latter with the Chicago school. By thesis he means that the main source of order is the result of human action but not human design: 'government and conscious design are not the main source of order and institutions in society; in fact they are more likely to inflict damage than to confer benefit' (Bosanquet, 1983: 6). Left alone, society has a natural tendency to grow.

The main features of the thesis school are: society has inherent tendencies towards justice and order; men are driven by self-interest and self-love; and man naturally wants to please himself and others, which leads to a natural justice. This will shape the distribution of income; inequality is inevitable. Capitalism as a system has ensured growth and improved living standards, and the entrepreneur is a key figure in the success of capitalism. Economic growth will first reduce and then eliminate poverty in absolute poverty.

Bosanquet's anti-thesis model emphasizes state intervention as being associated with the beginnings of politicization, which is viewed as negative. It is associated with increased public spending and a tendency towards centralization, which in turn weakens government. 'Politicization leads to a more intense class conflict between groups which will shake the social fabric' (*ibid.*). This will lead to increased public expenditure and industrial subsidies. It challenges the belief that economic interventions will often have social costs or impacts on third parties which justify state intervention. He sums the anti-thesis model up:

> The atmosphere of class conflict will grow more sullen. The power of producer groups will increase. Politics will be concerned with vote-buying rather than with general rules to help along the process of creative destruction.

> (*ibid.*)

Further reading

Bosanquet, N. (1983) *After the New Right*. London: Heinemann.

INDIVIDUALIZATION

Related entries: Dependency; Equality; Gender; Household

Individualization is the term used when referring to a system of social security based on individual entitlement and a system of taxation based on individual assessment of personal income. This is in contrast to systems which are based on aggregation of the means and incomes of more than one person, for example when a couple is jointly assessed or where dependants, such as children, are included in the assessment. The policy shift in the direction of the individualization of the welfare and taxation systems is generally seen as a reflection of a move away from the traditional breadwinner model to one based on the value of equality. The main argument put forward in favour of the individualization of the social security and taxation systems is that the traditional approach based on the male breadwinner model is not suited either to the current labour market composition or to the evolution of new family forms of life. Individualization, by treating men and women equally, would change the status of many women from that of dependency to that of economic independence.

Further reading

Villota, P. and Ferrari, I. (2001) *The Impact of the Tax/Benefit System on Women's Work* (El impacto de los impuestos y transferencias sociales en el empleo remunerado de las mujeres). Comisión Europea, DGV. Available at http://europa.eu.int/comm/employment_social/equ_opp/women_work.pdf

KEYNESIAN

Related entries: Beveridgian welfare; Employment

Keynesian economics (Keynesianism and Keynesian theory) is a school of macroeconomic thought based on the ideas of the economist John Maynard Keynes (1883–1946). He first presented his theory in *The General Theory of Employment, Interest and Money* (Keynes, 1936). Keynesian economics challenged the classical political economy based on Say's law of supply and demand, which argued that every supply creates its own demand and thus government intervention is unnecessary.

Keynes argued for government intervention in macroeconomic policy, especially in times of economic recession, in particular through public sector job creation and monetary policy actions by the central bank, and fiscal policy actions by the government. Keynesian economics advocates a mixed economy, with a role for the private sector, government and public sector. Roosevelt's New Deal in America in the 1930s was influenced by Keynesian economics. It was also influential during the Second World War, and during the post-war economic expansion (1945–73). It lost some influence following the stagflation of the 1970s. There has been a renewed interest in Keynesian economics since the beginning of the global financial crisis in 2008.

In relation to the British welfare state, Alcock and colleagues (2008b: 35–36) state that 'the range of policies which made up the post-war consensus are those stemming from the economic philosophy of John Maynard Keynes and the social philosophy of Sir William Beveridge in what has come to be called the Keynesian Welfare State'. They explain such policies as

> ones which assumed, or were consistent with, the intervention of government through fiscal and monetary techniques to regulate demand and encourage full employment. Beveridgian social polices were intended to contribute to the development of comprehensive welfare services, access to which would confer a sort of social citizenship. Accordingly, Keynes plus Beveridge were seen to equal Keynesian social democracy, or welfare capitalism or consensus.
>
> (Alcock *et al.*, 2008b: 36)

Further reading

Keynes, J.M. (1936) *The General Theory of Employment, Interest and Money*. London: Macmillan.

LABOUR

Related entries: Active welfare; Commodification and decommodification; Earnings; Models of welfare; Occupational welfare

Labour is generally understood as meaning work that is paid or unpaid. Labour is central to social policy, as individuals often access welfare entitlements through their status as members of the labour force. Labour is the most certain route out of poverty. In his three models of welfare – residual, industrial-achievement and institutional-redistribution – Titmuss identified the importance of welfare accessed through labour market participation. Bismarck had introduced such occupational welfare in the nineteenth century.

The International Labour Organization (ILO) is a useful source of information on labour internationally. The ILO was created in 1919, as part of the Treaty of Versailles following the First World War. It was established with the aim of achieving a more secure, humanitarian world. The ILO Constitution's Preamble states that the High Contracting Parties were 'moved by sentiments of justice and humanity as well as by the desire to secure the permanent peace of the world' (ILO, 2010: 5). It was concerned with the exploitation of workers in industrializing nations. There was also increasing understanding of the world's economic interdependence and the need for cooperation to obtain similarity of working conditions in countries competing for markets. Reflecting these ideas, the Preamble states:

> Whereas universal and lasting peace can be established only if it is based upon social justice; and whereas conditions of labour exist involving such injustice hardship and privation to large numbers of people as to produce unrest so great that the peace and harmony of the world are imperilled; and an improvement of those conditions is urgently required.
>
> (*ibid.*)

The areas of improvement listed in the Preamble remain relevant today: the regulation of the hours of work including the establishment of a maximum working day and week; the regulation of labour supply, prevention of unemployment and provision of an adequate living wage; the protection of the worker against sickness, disease and injury arising out of his or her employment; the protection of children, young persons and women; the provision for old age and injury; the protection of the interests of workers when employed in countries other than their own; the recognition of the principle of equal remuneration for work of equal value; the recognition of the principle of freedom of association; the organization of vocational and technical education; and other measures (http://www.ilo.org/ilolex/english/iloconst.htm).

Labour markets are central to writing on welfare regimes (Esping-Andersen, 1990) where one's ability to survive outside the market, decommodification, is strongly related to social rights. Subsequent writers have focused on gender (Lewis, 1993) and migration (Morrisens and Sainsbury, 2005).

Further reading
International Labour Organization: www.ilo.org

LIBERAL

> Related entries: Ideology; Individualism

Liberal ideology is committed to the individual enjoying maximum freedom. O'Brien and Penna (1998) refer to confusion regarding liberalism. They say it is more accurate to refer to 'liberalisms' as a series of related philosophies regarding the roles and functions of individuals, groups and institutions in managing, directing and controlling the character and progress of human social life. Some see personal autonomy and freedom as the only goal of social organizations whereas others are more open to collective strategies while still emphasizing individual freedom. Some see state interference as evil or dangerous, others see it as justifiable in order to bring about reform.

Heywood (2007) suggests that liberalism is committed to a distinct set of values and beliefs: the individual, freedom, reason, justice and toleration. There are different strands of liberalism. Classical liberalism is characterized by a commitment to a 'minimal state'. This state would intervene only in relation to maintaining domestic order and personal security. Modern liberalism proposes that the state should help people to become self-sufficient. Heywood describes how liberal ideas were radical ideas that emerged with industrialization. The English revolutions of the seventeenth century and the American and French revolutions of the eighteenth centuries embraced notions of liberalism. They advocated constitutional and representative government in place of divine power, associated with monarchies.

Heywood (2007: 25) suggests that the nineteenth century was the liberal century. It shaped industrial capitalism, a belief in the free market and free trade, which spread worldwide. He suggests it is the most powerful political ideology to shape western politics. However, liberalism became increasingly conservative. He defines classical liberalism as 'a tradition within liberalism that seeks to maximize the realm of unconstrained individual action, typically by establishing a minimal state and a reliance on market economies' and 'modern liberalism' as 'a tradition within liberalism that provides (in contrast to classical liberalism) a qualified endorsement for social and economic intervention as a means of promoting personal development' (*ibid.*). He suggests that 'the twentieth century appeared to culminate in the worldwide triumph of liberalism'. The liberal model of representative government and market-based economics 'spread remorselessly throughout the globe' (*ibid.*).

Heywood defines neo-liberalism as a revival of economic liberalism which has occurred since the 1970s. He suggests that 'neoliberalism amounts to a form of market fundamentalism. The market is seen to be morally and practically superior to government any form of political control' (2007: 52). Liberalism is sometimes known as neo-liberalism or market liberalism. It combines political ideology with a specific economic approach. Freedom of the individual is paramount. Liberals believe in the free market as the best way to determine levels of production in society and they accept market failure.

George and Wilding (1994) suggest that right-wing ideologies are concerned with the three central concepts of freedom, justice and individualism. They see freedom as the absence of coercion. Freedom is being free to do something, and processes and procedures can be defined in terms of justice. There is no such thing as society, only individuals and families. Faith in the free market is paramount, competition is essential and it is impossible to create a comprehensive welfare state. They are suspicious of welfare states.

Fiona Williams (1989) differentiates between liberal and libertarian feminist approaches to social policy. Libertarian views women's oppression as caused by state intervention and views liberty as achievable through the freedom of the market. Libertians maintain the division between the public and the private and tend to be blind to class and racial differences. Liberal feminists view oppression as resulting from sex discrimination and sex-biased laws and look to the state to implement equality legislation as a means of achieving greater equality. In a similar vein, writing on social policy and the environment, Tony Fitzpatrick (2011a) differentiates between libertarians, conservatives and liberals.

Further reading

George, V. and Wilding, P. (1994) *Welfare and Ideology*. London: Harvester Wheatsheaf.
Heywood, A. (2007) *Political Ideologies: An Introduction*, 4th edn. London: Palgrave Macmillan.

LIBERTY

Related entries: Autonomy; Capabilities; Citizenship; Equality; Functionings; Ideology; Individualism

Liberty is a concept central to social policy. It is associated with political philosophy. It is often used in relation to equality and social justice. Negative freedom means freedom from coercion, property rights and freedom of choice. Spicker (2008: 86) suggests that negative freedom is characterized by non-interference from other people, freedom from coercion by other people and freedom from coercion by government. The welfare state is perceived as potentially imposing on individual freedom through regulation and taxation.

Positive freedom refers to freedom as autonomous: to have control over one's own life choices. This is freedom to participate and can be viewed in relation to Sen's (2009) capabilities approach. It involves taking cognisance of resources. Sen states:

'since the idea of capability is linked with substantive freedom, it gives a central role to a person's actual ability to do the different things that she values doing' (Sen, 2009: 253).

Further reading

Spicker, P. (2008) *Social Policy Themes and Approaches*, 2nd edn. Bristol: Policy Press.

LONE PARENTS

> Related entries: Discrimination; Family; Household; Poverty

Lone (single) parents have received much attention in social policy. They are often demonised. Lone-parent families are defined by the Canadian census as:

> a mother or a father, with no spouse or common law partner present, living in a dwelling with one or more children. This includes children living with one parent following a parental breakup, single parents of adopted children, a grandparent or other family member who is responsible for the day-to-day care of the children, and widows or widowers.
>
> (http://www.statcan.gc.ca/pub/85–002-x/2009001/definitions-eng.htm)

Lone parenthood refers to one adult parenting alone, and welfare entitlements are often tied to the dependency of a child/children within the household. More women parent alone and live in poverty as a result. Millar (1989) researched lone parents in the 1980s and scholarship in the area has developed ever since. Pascall reminds us that from the point of the male breadwinner model 'lone mothers are an anomaly', and she goes on to explain: 'The Beveridge system designed them out, as they were neither full-time workers nor dependent wives doing full-time work' (Pascall, 2012: 110). She asks the perennial question: should lone mothers be perceived as workers or carers?

Millar and Ridge (2001) provide a critical summary of research on families, focusing on lone parents and low-income couples, in order to review evidence about what works in respect of policies intended to promote employment among these families and to identify gaps in our knowledge about the needs and circumstances of such families. They focus on family patterns and dynamics, poverty and living standards, and employment patterns, barriers to work and the impact of welfare to work programmes.

The European Commission (2007) published a study on poverty and social exclusion among lone parents in Europe (http://ec.europa.eu/employment_social/social_inclusion/docs/2007/study_lone_parents_en.pdf). They acknowledge that there are variations across countries and within families and that there are multiple routes into lone parenthood: 'widows, unmarried single mothers, divorced mothers and lone fathers have usually followed quite different routes to lone parenthood, and also, they experience lone parenthood in different periods of their life course' (European Commission, 2007: 12). They suggest that if we want to understand the reasons why lone parent households experience higher poverty and social exclusion we need to take into account both the specific cultural, economic and welfare context of lone parenthood, and the specific path to lone parenthood (*ibid.*).

Haux (2011: 8) presents seven characteristics of lone parents not in employment based on a review of the literature. These are: having a child under the age of five, having three or more children, a health problem, not having qualifications, not having any recent work experience, being a social housing tenant and not looking to move into work. Haux (2011) identifies the international trend over the last twenty years towards activation measures for lone parents. She explores the perception of lone parents as mothers and as workers. She focuses on three groups of lone parents: those with children between the ages of seven and fifteen, between five and seven and between three and four. 'Ability to work' is frequently discussed in terms of the age of the child. Haux challenges this: 'the level of disadvantages among lone parents with older children exposes the assumption that the age of the youngest child can be equated with ability to work in the case of lone parents as incorrect and one-dimensional' (Haux, 2011: 12).

Burstrum and colleagues (2010) examine the welfare arrangements, living conditions and health among lone and couple mothers in Italy, Sweden and Britain: three different welfare regimes. They find that lone mothers had significantly worse health, were more likely to suffer from material disadvantage and were more likely to smoke than couple mothers. 'They could be considered a disadvantaged group in particular need in all three countries, irrespective of policy regime' (Burstrum *et al.*, 2010: 912). However, they argue that, in relation to lone motherhood, regime type does matter: 'there were telling differences in the prevalence of lone motherhood, their composition, rates of joblessness, poverty and health status of lone mothers in relation to couple mothers in each country' (*ibid.*). It is also linked to culture and tradition. Both lone mothers and couple mothers fare better in Sweden in the usual earner family model, which 'Has clearly protected Swedish mothers in general and lone mothers in particular from the degree of poverty experienced among British lone mothers and helps them achieve higher rates of employment than in both Italy and Britain' (Burstrum *et al.*, 2010: 919).

Further reading

Burstrum, B., Whitehead, M., Clayton, S. and Fritzell, S. (2010) 'Health Inequalities between Lone and Couple Mothers and Policy under Different Welfare Regimes: The Example of Italy, Sweden and Britain', *Social Science and Medicine*, 70(6): 912–920.

Haux, T. (2011) 'Activating Lone Parents: An Evidence-Based Policy Appraisal of Welfare-to-Work Reform in Britain', *Social Policy and Society*, 11(1): 1–14.

Millar, J. and Ridge, T. (2001) *Families, Poverty, Work and Care: A Review of Literature on Lone Parents and Low Income Couple Families with Children*. Department for Work and Pensions Research Report No. 153. Leeds: Centre for Disability Studies.

Millar, J. and Rowlingson, K. (eds.) (2001) *Lone Parents, Employment and Social Policy: Cross-national Comparisons*. Bristol: Policy Press.

MALE BREADWINNER

Related entries: Dependency; Gender; Household; Welfare regimes

Male breadwinner is the term used to describe the situation in which men are providers, working in the paid labour market and supporting women and children. This idea is the backbone of many welfare systems. Beveridge's model emphasized the importance of insuring the male head of the household: 'Housewives as mothers have vital work to do in ensuring the adequate continuance of the British race and of British ideas in the world' (Beveridge, 1942: 53). This was the institutionalization of the male breadwinner model which insured that women had a separate social insurance. Their work, unlike the male breadwinner, was viewed as dispensable and despite their crucial role they were deemed dependent.

A social security system based on the male breadwinner model was essentially discriminatory against women, as women were marginalized in the paid labour market and their labour in the home was generally unseen or undervalued. The importance of a contributory record in such a system discriminated against women. Women, because of their prescribed role as carers in the home, were generally unable to develop a contributions record and were, thus, denied access to benefits. Colwill highlights Beveridge's demarcation of different types of contributors, for example self-employed as against employed. This concept of differential status had particular significance for women and with reference to married women's distinct status: 'Patriarchal relations within a capitalist society could thus be faithfully reproduced within the social security system; upon marriage women were quite literally to undergo an economic and social transformation in which the world of work gave way to the world of dependent motherhood' (Colwill, 1994: 56).

Lewis (2001: 153) states that 'The male breadwinner model built into the post-war settlement assumed regular and full male employment *and* stable families in which women would be provided for largely via their husbands' earnings and social contributions'. She reminds us that a pure male breadwinner model never existed, that women always engaged in the labour market during historical periods in some countries and that there was also a class dimension. Interestingly, Lewis remarks that the male breadwinner model was a prescription in many countries in which policy makers

> treated it as an 'ought' in terms of relationships between men and women, and in many countries it served to underpin both social policies that assumed female dependence on a male wage and family law, which made the same assumptions about the marriage contract in terms of stability and the nature of the contribution made by men and women in families, seeking to enforce them through fault-based divorce.
>
> (*ibid.*)

Lewis (1992) presented a theoretical model to incorporate the gendered dimension of welfare systems. It is a three-tiered model of strong, modified and weak male breadwinner welfare states. Since then dual-worker models and one-and-a-half worker models have been identified. An 'adult-worker model' assumes that all adults are in the labour market. This is explored by Daly (2011) in a comparative study of social policy reform in Europe. She concludes: 'the empirical analysis reveals a strong move towards individualization as social policy promotes and valorizes individual agency and self-sufficiency and shifts some childcare from the family. Yet evidence is also found of continued (albeit changed) familism' (Daly, 2011: 1).

Further reading

Daly, M. (2011) 'What Adult Worker Model? A Critical Look at Recent Social Policy Reform in Europe from a Gender and Family Perspective', *Social Politics*, 18(1): 1–23.

Lewis, J. (1992) 'Gender and the Development of Welfare Regimes', *Journal of European Social Policy*, 2(3): 159–173.

Lewis, J. (2001) 'The Decline of the Male Breadwinner Model: Implications for Work and Care', *Social Politics*, 8(2): 152–169.

MATERNITY

> Related entries: Care; Citizenship; Family; Gender; Labour

Maternity is central to welfare systems, as women are increasingly being compensated through legislation for maternity leave and benefits. When does maternity begin? Does it end? Kennedy (2002) presents the concept of the maternity period to describe the period in a woman's life from conception through pregnancy, childbirth and the first year of the child's life, arguing that in terms of understanding social policies this is a specific period in a woman's life. It involves a change of identity. Kennedy also introduces a three-dimensional model of motherhood to explore social policies which affect a woman during the maternity period. These include health, welfare and labour market policies. Leira (1992) in her study of mothers in Scandinavia writes of mother as citizen and as carer.

The feminist scholar Adrienne Rich (1977) distinguishes between biological motherhood and the institution of motherhood. She comments on the 'strange lack of material to help us understand' motherhood despite its importance, as she states:

> All human life on the planet is born of woman. The one unifying, uncontrollable experience shared by all women and men is that months-long period we spent unfolding inside a woman's body. Because young humans remain dependent upon nurture for a much longer period than other mammals, and because of the division of labour long established in human groups, in which women not only bear and suckle but are assigned almost total responsibility for children, most of us know both love and disappointment, power and tenderness in the person of a woman. We carry the imprint of this experience for life, even into dying. Yet there has been a strange lack of material to help us understand and use it.
>
> (Rich, 1977: 11)

There has been a huge lacuna in the analysis of social policies which directly affect women during this period of their lives. Leira states that:

> Even though not all women personally experience motherhood, hardly any woman in present day welfare states is unaffected by its potentiality, and most women actually do become mothers. Considering, too, that the gender-differentiated family is a central character of welfare state design, an investigation of welfare state motherhood also sheds light on the welfare state approach to women more generally.
>
> (Leira, 1992: 3)

Budig and colleagues (2012) suggest that mothers' employment and earnings partly depend on social policies and cultural norms supporting women's paid and unpaid work. They examine country variation in the association between motherhood and earnings, in cultural attitudes surrounding women's employment and in childcare and parental leave policies. They model how cultural attitudes moderate the impact of policies on women's earnings across countries. Parental leave and public childcare are associated with higher earnings for mothers when cultural support for maternal employment is high, but have less positive or even negative relationships with earnings in which cultural attitudes support the male breadwinner/female caregiver model. They refer to the motherhood penalty and suggest: 'While factors such as education and experience explain some of the motherhood penalty, a significant portion remains unexplained by individual-level factors' (Budig *et al.*, 2012: 167).

Further reading

Budig, M.J., Misra, J. and Böckmann, I. (2012) 'The Motherhood Penalty in Cross-National Perspective: The Importance of Work–Family Policies and Cultural Attitudes', *Social Politics*, 19(2): 163–193.
Kennedy, P. (2002) *Maternity in Ireland: A Woman-Centred Perspective*. Dublin: Liffey Press.

MARXISM

> Related entries: Capitalism; Class; Ideology; Labour

Marxism is a political ideology based on the writing of Karl Marx (1818–83). It gathered momentum in social policy studies from the 1970s. Pascall (1986) indicates how theorists concerned with the lack of explanatory power in the social administration school, and with the emerging crisis in the welfare state, turned to Marxist theory in an attempt to understand the welfare state. These theorists adhered closely to Marxist theory. Klein (1993: 7), in an interesting article, classes three of the leading neo-Marxists together: O'Connor (1973), Gough (1979) and Offe (1984). He refers to them collectively as 'O'Goffe', as 'the leading exponents of neo-Marxist theories', and outlines the main features of their theories. He refers to 'O'Goffe's tale', that what distinguished O'Goffe from the myriad of other scholars wringing their hands about the plight of the welfare state at a time of economic turmoil was that they sought to explain these troubles by involving the nature of capitalist states (Klein, 1993: 7).

The problems of welfare states are an inherent feature of capitalist societies because of the inevitable conflict between needs of legitimization and consumption and the demands of capital accumulation. Furthermore, 'the conflict could be resolved and the welfare state saved, O'Goffe concluded, only in a new kind of socialist society' (Klein, 1993: 8). This debate was useful as it articulated the existence of conflict within capitalist societies and illuminated the relationship between welfare policies and economic policies. It exposed issues around class and power: 'the welfare state could be understood only as the product of economic and political forces; as part of the total social environment' (ibid.). Mishra acknowledges that Marxists offer structural explanations of the limits of state welfare, seeing the state as 'a creature of the mode of production' that is concerned with both maintaining and reproducing the capitalist system. At the same time, state welfare meets the needs of the economic system, thus constraining the possibilities for social reform; 'in short, the policy structure of the capitalist system itself explained the limits of social policy' (Mishra, 1984: 68).

Pascall (1986: 13) states that 'it could be argued that Marxism gives fruitful openings both for analysing women's position and explaining their oppression'. These two useful 'openings' are, first of all, the analysis of women's place in the reserve army of labour and, second, women's role in the reproduction of the labour force. Ginsburg (1979: 26) states that 'the social security system not only reflects but strengthens the subordinate position of women as domestic workers inside the family and wage workers outside the family'. He sees the welfare state as using its power to modify the reproduction of labour power and in maintaining the non-working population in capitalist societies. One of the major criticisms of Marxist theory is that it concentrates on the relationship of woman to the state to the neglect of the relationship of woman to man, that is, it tends to ignore gender relations.

Socialist feminists (Wilson, 1977; Barrett, 1980; Barrett and McIntosh, 1991) introduced the concept of social reproduction to the debate. Williams (1989: 60), in an evaluation of socialist feminism, suggests that from a theoretical viewpoint there are different approaches within socialist feminism. She summarizes the broad areas of agreement as the importance of understanding men and women's behaviour as socially constructed, a recognition of the differential as well as shared experiences of oppression of different classes, races, ages and cultures, and a belief that the personal is political. The broad areas of disagreement are the extent to which women's liberation can be achieved without a massive reorganization of the economic and social structures or without the mobilization of women and the working class; the relationship between patriarchy and capitalism in the creation of oppression; and 'central to these early analyses was an analysis of the family as the site of oppression, with the ideology of familism permeating all areas of state provision and restricting women's role to that of wife and mother' (Williams, 1997: 261).

George and Wilding (1994) provide a comprehensive account of Marxist theory as it relates to welfare.

Further reading

George, V. and Wilding, P. (1994) *Welfare and Ideology*. London: Harvester Wheatsheaf, pp. 102–129.

Ransome, P. (2010) 'Karl Marx, Capitalism and Revolution', in Ransome, P., *Social Theory for Beginners*. Bristol: Policy Press, pp. 65–98.

MASCULINITIES

> Related entries: Equality; Gender; Ideology; Sexuality; Social divisions; Theory

Masculinity is derived from the Latin *masculinus*, meaning male or of masculine gender. Like sexuality, masculinity can be understood in terms of biological essentialism and social constructionism. The former implies that masculinity is based on physiological differences and associated with hormones and chromosomes (Goldberg, 1979); the latter perceives masculinity in terms of social and cultural beliefs and context (Connell, 1995). There is a wide spectrum and overlap between the two explanations. Increasingly, scholarship on masculinity stresses masculinities, recognizing the social divisions in society and that men are a heterogeneous group. Multiple masculinities is a term used to explain the relationship between masculinity and other social divisions, including age, race, ethnicity and disability (Shuttleworth *et al.*, 2012). Writing in 2000, Phoenix (2000: 94) noted: 'the topic of men and the associated concept of "masculinity" are now, just about, on political and policy agendas'. A plethora of scholarship in social policy has emerged since then.

Hegemonic masculinity refers to the accepted status quo in society. Connell (1995) has developed this area. It acknowledges a gender hierarchy which places a certain perception of men at the top. Connell refers to *complicit masculinities*, which is a lower level, and lower again is *subordinated masculinities*, which incorporates homosexual masculinity. Keenan (2010: 120) explains: 'the problem is that hegemonic masculinities can produce an array of models of admired masculine conduct that do not correspond closely to the lives of actual men, therefore creating contradictions'. Interestingly, she notes: 'the theory also suggests the gender order is not fixed and struggles for hegemony can occur, as older forms of masculinity are displaced by new ones, and a more humane, less oppressive means of being a man could become hegemonic. It also suggests that the gender order differs from country to country, culture to culture, and time to time' (Keenan, 2010: 121).

Hearn and colleagues (2012) discuss the status of the concept of hegemonic masculinity in relation to their research on men and boys in Sweden, and examine how the concept has been used and developed. They suggest that since the late 1990s there has been a move beyond the theory of hegemonic masculinity and 'Some contemporary work on men and masculinities stresses insights from queer theory, discourse theory, science and technology studies, postcolonialism, intersectionality, and "third-wave feminism"' (Hearn *et al.*, 2010: 37).

Hearn (2010: 167) describes his own approach as supporting 'profeminist Critical studies on Men that are interdisciplinary, historical, transnational, cultural, relational, materialist, deconstructive, anti-essentialist'.

Hearn explores the relationship between social policy and masculinities, recognizing that, although social policy has always been concerned with men, 'what is newer is the explicit *naming* of men in social policy' (*ibid.*). He outlines the range of approaches to studying men. These are an explicit focus on men and masculinities; a more general critical gender scholarship; understanding men and masculinities as socially constructed, produced and reproduced; seeing men and masculinities across time, space and culture; men's relationships to gendered power; the emphasis on the material and discursive; and finally intersections of men and gender with other social divisions.

Hearn (2010) gives an interesting account of men's health as an important focus of social policy, indicating that, even though men fare better in terms of health determinants, their outcomes are worse. This may be related to lifestyles and risk taking.

Further reading

Hearn, J. (2010) 'Reflecting on Men and Social Policy: Contemporary Critical Debates and Implications for Social Policy', *Critical Social Policy*, 30(2): 165–188.

Hearn, J., Nordberg, M., Andersson, K., Balkmar, D., Gottzén, L., Klinth, R., Pringle, K. and Sandberg, L. (2012) 'Hegemonic Masculinity and Beyond: 40 Years of Research in Sweden', *Men and Masculinities*, 15: 31–55.

Shuttleworth, R., Wedgwood, N. and Wilson, N.J. (2012) 'The Dilemma of Disabled Masculinity', *Men and Masculinities*, 15(2): 174–194.

MEANS TESTING

> Related entries: Redistribution; Selectivity; Stigma

This is a tool used to decide whether an individual/family is entitled to a payment/service/benefit in kind. One's means are assessed and the decision is based on this. Means tested payments are selectivist payments. They are not guaranteed as a right but are allocated based on means. These payments are generally perceived as inferior to entitlement/rights-based payments.

Further reading

Bahle, T., Pfeifer, M. and Wendt, C. (2010) 'Social Assistance', in Castles, F., Leibfried, S., Lewis, J., Obinger, H. and Pierson, C. (eds.), *The Oxford Handbook of the Welfare State*. Oxford: Oxford University Press, pp. 448–461.

MIGRATION

> Related entries: Citizenship; Equality; Social divisions

Migration, from the word *migrare* (to move), is a feature of human living. The International Organization for Migration (IOM) is an intergovernmental organization established in 1951, committed to the principle that humane and orderly migration benefits migrants and society, and the IOM provides a useful source of information on the topic (www.iom.org). IOM defines migration as:

> The movement of a person or a group of persons, either across an international border or within a State. It is a population movement, encompassing any kind of movement of people, whatever its length, composition and causes; it includes migration of refugees, displaced persons, economic migrants, and persons moving for other purposes, including family reunification.
> (http://www.iom.int/jahia/Jahia/about-migration/key-migration-terms/lang/en)

Migration was identified as a basic human right by the United Nations in 1948. It is a global phenomenon and it is increasing. The IOM indicate that the number of international migrants has increased from an estimated 150 million in 2000 to 214 million persons in 2008. Thus, one of out of every thirty-three persons in the world today is a migrant, as compared with one out of every thirty-five persons in 2000. Approximately 49 per cent of migrants worldwide are women (http://www.iom.int/jahia/Jahia/about-migration/facts-and-figures/lang/en).

The IOM acknowledges the importance of remittances sent by migrants, which have increased from an estimated US $132 billion in 2000 to an estimated US $440 billion in 2010, even with a slight decline owing to the current economic crisis. The IOM indicates that the actual amount, including unrecorded flows through formal and informal channels, is believed to be significantly larger (http://www.iom.int/jahia/Jahia/about-migration/facts-and-figures/lang/en).

Migration is a challenge for welfare systems, particularly when we consider that often resources are redistributed based on entitlement criteria linked to citizenship status. Migration raises issues around inclusion and exclusion, racism, multicultural-ism and integration. Castles and Schierup (2010) suggest that immigration and ethnic diversity have been neglected in scholarship on the development of welfare systems in Europe and the North America. They define immigrants as:

> foreign-born persons who have immigrated to Europe or North American countries; and ethnic minorities, which includes the previous category but also embraces their descendants, who may or may not have been born in their county of residence, but who are categorized as different from the majority population through appearance, religious practices, language use and customs.
> (Castles and Schierup, 2010: 279)

As Law (2010: 106) indicates, 'Migrants are now subject to increasingly high levels of control and regulation. Growing national concerns with the economic, political and social consequences of immigration have increasingly led to attempts to lower and restrict inflow of migrants'. This has major consequences for social policy.

The IOM indicates that there is no universally accepted definition of a migrant, yet the United Nations (UN) defines a migrant as 'an individual who has resided in a foreign country for more than one year irrespective of the causes, voluntary or involuntary, and the means, regular or irregular, used to migrate' (http://www.iom.int/cms/en/sites/iom/home/about-migration/key-migration-terms-1.html).

Bloch (2008: 411) argues that migrant can be used as a generic term 'but for social policy analysis, it is important to understand who migrants are and the differing categories they fall into'. Migrants are often classed as *documented* and *undocumented*. The former is a migrant who enters a country legally and remains there in line with the entry requirement. The latter refers to a migrant who has entered the country illegally, or who entered legally but no longer meets the specified criteria to remain there. An *economic migrant* is one who has migrated for economic reasons rather than to flee persecution.

Asylum seeker is a term which has appeared more noticeably in policy documents since the end of the 1990s, and many national and international debates have evolved in relation to rights and needs of asylum seekers and appropriate policy responses. The IOM defines an asylum seeker as:

> A person who seeks safety from persecution or serious harm in a country other than his or her own and awaits a decision on the application for refugee status under relevant international and national instruments. In case of a negative decision, the person must leave the country and may be expelled, as may any non-national in an irregular or unlawful situation, unless permission to stay is provided on humanitarian or other related grounds.
> (http://www.iom.int/jahia/Jahia/about-migration/key-migration-terms/lang/en#Asylum-Seeker)

A *refugee* is defined as a person who, 'owing to a well-founded fear of persecution for reasons of race, religion, nationality, membership of a particular social group or political opinions, is outside the country of his nationality and is unable or, owing to such fear, is unwilling to avail himself of the protection of that country' (Art. 1(A)(2), Convention relating to the Status of Refugees, Art. 1A(2), 1951 as modified by the 1967 Protocol). In addition to the refugee definition in the 1951 Refugee Convention, Article 1(2), the Organization of African Unity (OAU) Convention defines a refugee as any person compelled to leave his or her country 'owing to external aggression, occupation, foreign domination or events seriously disturbing public order in either part or the whole of his country or origin or nationality' (OAU, 1969: 3). Similarly, the 1984 Cartagena Declaration states that refugees also include persons who flee their country 'because their lives, security or freedom have been threatened by generalised violence, foreign aggression, internal conflicts, massive violations of human rights or other circumstances which have seriously disturbed public order' (UNHCR, 1984).

Based on data from the UN High Commissioner for Refugees, the number of refugees stood at 15.4 million in 2010 compared with 15.9 million in 2000 – a decline of around 500,000. However, because of a change in classification and estimation methodology in a number of countries, figures since 2007 are not fully comparable with pre-2007 figures.

Castles and Schierup (2010) identify three current research perspectives on ethnic diversity and the welfare state. These they identify as (1) endeavouring to link an understanding of racism and discrimination to the analysis of citizenship and social exclusion/inclusion; (2) a growing body of specialized research focused on the analysis of international migration, gender and changing institutional contingencies of care work; and (3) a comprehensive scholarly research and debate on multiculturalism, citizenship and the welfare state (Castles and Schierup, 2010: 280).

Morrisens and Sainsbury (2005) recognize that comparative welfare research has devoted little attention to the social rights of migrants or the ethnic, racial dimension. They attempt to redress this by comparing the social rights of migrants and citizens across welfare regimes. They focus on participation in social transfer programmes and the impact of transfers on migrants' ability to sustain a socially acceptable standard of living compared with the rest of the population.

Morrisens and Sainsbury's research unearths major discrepancies between migrants and non-migrants and that discrepancies are wider for members of visible minorities. They show that intra-regime variations exist in the case of liberal and social democratic countries. They also argue that country analysis seems to be the only analysis of race/ethnicity in relation to welfare regimes and suggest that the growing disparities between the social rights of refugees, asylum seekers and other migrants are not usually addressed (Morrisens and Sainsbury, 2005: 638). Morrisens and Sainsbury suggest that the main criterion for evaluating social rights is decommodification: 'the degree to which they provide a decent standard of living independently of market forces' (*ibid.*). They are concerned with the accessibility of benefits, their generosity and duration, and the range of entitlements, and they define an acceptable standard as above the poverty line. They look at the extent to which welfare states provide migrants, and particularly those outside the labour market, with the possibility of a socially acceptable life (*ibid.*).

Morrisens and Sainsbury refer to conditions of eligibility and benefit levels stratifying people. They distinguish between formal rights and substantive rights. They try to determine the incidence of households having a socially acceptable standard of living, that is, the proportion of households above the poverty line; this income is a combination of the result of market income and social benefits.

Further reading

Bloch, A. (2008) 'Migrants and Asylum-Seekers', in Alcock, P., May M. and Rowlingson, K. (eds.), *The Student's Companion to Social Policy*. Oxford: Blackwell, pp. 410–417.

Castles, S. and Schierup, C. (2010) 'Migration and Ethnic Minorities', in Castles, F., Leibfried, S., Lewis J., Obinger, H. and Pierson, C. (eds.), *The Oxford Handbook of the Welfare State*. Oxford: Oxford University Press, pp. 278–291.

IOM (International Organization for Migration) (2004) *IOM Glossary on Migration*, International Migration Law Series No. 25. Available at http://www.iom.int/jahia/Jahia/about-migration/key-migration-terms/lang/en#Immigration

Law, I. (2010) *Racism and Ethnicity: Global Debates, Dilemmas, Directions*. Harlow: Pearson.
Morrisens, A. and Sainsbury, D. (2005) 'Migrants, Social Rights, Ethnicity, and Welfare Regimes', *Journal of Social Policy*, 34(4): 637–660.
UN DESA (United Nations Department of Economic and Social Affairs) (2008) *Trends in International Migrant Stock: The 2008 Revision*. Available at http://esa.un.org/migration/index.asp?panel=1
United Nations (2002) *International Migration*. New York: United Nations.

MIXED ECONOMY OF WELFARE

> Related entries: Comparative social policy; Models of welfare; Welfare

The 'mixed economy of welfare' and 'welfare pluralism' are used interchangeably to describe the combination of the four sectors involved in welfare formulation, delivery, financing and regulation. These are the state, the private (commercial) sector, the voluntary (non-governmental organization/not-for-profit/third) sector and the informal (family, friends and neighbours) sector. The combination varies in different welfare regimes and across time. Johnson (1999: 30) looks to Dunleavey and O'Leary to define the characteristics of the state as a 'recognizably separate . . . set of institutions, so differentiated from the rest of its society as to create identifiable public and private spheres' (Dunleavy and O'Leary, 1987: 2).

Private/commercial welfare involves the sale and purchase of welfare services and products in markets of one kind or another. The sellers of these services are usually aiming to make a profit. Welfare services can be sold in the same way as any other product or service. Holden (2008: 197) suggests that there are two reasons why welfare services should be distinguished from other goods and services: first, because they are so important for the meeting of basic human needs that governments should take action to ensure that citizens have some access to them; second, because the market often does not provide welfare services efficiently, partly because when making choices in these areas people are more dependent on professionals. The type of welfare system in a country will influence the extent of commercial welfare.

Holden explains the types of commercial welfare as those that directly provide welfare services to the public; for example healthcare and education services; firms that produce essential goods such as medicines and educational material; firms that supply services to organizations, such as cleaning, catering or delivery services; firms that provide insurance or financial services such as pensions or mortgages; firms involved in the design and building and maintenance of premises; and finally firms that provide occupational welfare to their own employees. Holden (2008: 201) points out that with private provision the state has to be conscious of two factors if it is to direct services effectively. They need to be cognizant of the type of behaviour associated with those who are trying to maximize profit and, second, the regulation of providers. Holden (2008: 202) suggests that the biggest concerns are equity, quality and regulation. He states: 'the principle of equity is at the heart of the welfare state, and markets may have profound implications for both equitable access to services and for equitable outcomes'. Johnson (1999) identifies some of the arguments associated with the role of commercial welfare as including efficiency, choice, freedom and rights, equity and equality.

Kendall defines the non-profit sector as: 'formally organised entities which are constitutionally/legally separate from the state, bound not to distribute surpluses (profits) to owners, and demonstrably benefiting from some degree of voluntarism (uncoerced giving) of money ("donations") or time ("volunteering")' (Kendall, 2008: 214). Furthermore, he suggests that types of non-profit sector organizations can be identified by social functions such as service provision, advocacy, innovation, community building, and community development. He suggests that other taxonomies focus on values, norms and the motivations of actors, while others focus on resource base, financial or human resource size and others focus on governance/control rights distribution (*ibid.*).

The voluntary sector (non-governmental organization/the third sector/not-for-profit sector) is 'the contribution of organizations between the market and the state to social well-being – embraces an extraordinarily diverse range of activities' (Kendall, 2008: 212). These allow needs to be met which may otherwise go unrecognised. They can be seen as more cost-effective, responsive and sensitive to the needs of service users. Kendall indicates that since the 1980s the voluntary sector has become a field of study in its own right (Kendall, 2008: 213). Johnson claims that there are links between the commercial and voluntary sector in that voluntary organizations have become increasingly involved in quasi-markets; there is a blur between large voluntary organizations and commercial operators and their increasing role reflects their deduction of state provision. Johnson (1999: 143) refers to the social significance of the voluntary sector in terms of democracy, solidarity and civil society.

The informal sector is usually concerned with the provision of care. Glendinning and Arksey (2008) define informal care as 'the extra help given to ill, disabled and older people by friends and relatives, as distinct from that given as part of a formal paid job such as nursing, care assistant, home help, or support worker' (Glendinning and Arksey, 2008: 219). Informal care refers to 'care provided in addition to the normal support that family members give each other as a matter of course'. They elaborate that informal care can involve personal or physical care, or other practical help such as shopping and cooking, or keeping someone company or out of danger (Glendinning and Arksey, 2008: 224).

Glendinning and Arksey explain that carers are more likely to be women, or to be close relatives or live in the same household as those that they care for, and to have sole responsibility for the provision of care. They are cognizant that doing such work can have a negative impact on the carer. For example, it can impact on the carer's mental health and well-being, the risk of which increases with the intensity and duration of care (Glendinning and Arksey, 2008: 220). Although they report that emotional rewards act as motivation for care work, they recognize that many carers are denied income and career opportunities because of caring (Glendinning and Arksey, 2008: 221). They argue that carers experience many of the factors that contribute to social exclusion, including isolation, difficulty in obtaining help for their own health problems, and difficulties in obtaining other services to help in the provision of care (*ibid.*). They recognize that government support of carers is an issue and they ask if carers or those in receipt of care should be the target of policies. They look at models of informal care in policy and practice and indicate that social and health profession-als respond to carers in four ways: (1) they perceive the carer as resource; (2) as a co-worker; (3) as co-clients; (4) they refer to the 'superseded' carer. Glendinning and Arksey identify emerging issues in the informal sector to be the future demand for informal care, competing priorities, and caregiving versus employment.

Further reading

Bartlett, W. (1991) *Quasi-markets and Contracts: A Market and Hierarchies Perspective on NHS Reform*. Bristol: School for Advanced Urban Studies.

Glendinning, C. and Arksey, H. (2008) 'Informal Care', in Alcock, P., May, M. and Rowlingson, K. (eds.), *The Student's Companion to Social Policy*. Oxford: Blackwell, pp. 219–225.

Holden, C. (2008) 'Commercial Welfare', in Alcock, P., May, M. and Rowlingson, K. (eds.), *The Student's Companion to Social Policy*. Oxford: Blackwell, pp.196–202.

Johnson, N. (1999) *Mixed Economies of Welfare, a Comparative Perspective*. London: Prentice Hall.

Kendall, J. (2008) 'Voluntary Welfare', in Alcock, P., May, M. and Rowlingson, K. (eds.), *The Student's Companion to Social Policy*. Oxford: Blackwell, pp. 212–218.

MODELS OF WELFARE

Related entries: Comparative social policy; Families of nations; Mixed economy of welfare; Welfare regimes

A model is a typology, a way of classifying welfare systems to make sense of them. Titmuss (1974) introduced models of welfare. He classified welfare systems as three types: the residual, the industrial achievement and the institutional-redistributive model. He argued that models are concerned with principles which are intended to guide welfare states: 'The purpose of model building is not to admire the architecture of the building but to help us see some order in all the disorder and confusion of facts, sys-tems and choices concerning certain areas of our economic and social life' (1974: 30).

Ramesh Mishra (1977) built on Titmuss's work, suggesting that residual was conservative and institutional was liberal/social democratic, and he identified a third model: structural. For Mishra, 'models are prescriptions regarding social policy and incorporate both normative and explanatory propositions derived from wider social theories and philosophies' (Mishra, 1977: 23) which 'must engage in the task of identifying the principle models of welfare, analysing their normative bases and assumptions and evaluating the underling explanatory theories and concepts' (Mishra, 1977: 24). Mishra argued that 'at the very least models offer a terrain, a relevant base, from which both normative and explanatory theories relevant to welfare can be explored systematically' (Mishra, 1977: 8).

Mishra's work was prophetic when he identified that models would help to develop a large body of concepts related to welfare and work which would be cumulative, provide meaning and relevance and which would provide an excellent vantage point; a point of departure as well as return – from which to examine normative and explanatory theories and a point of departure in that they provide meaning for wider explorations, e.g. the nature of social justice, the locus of power in modern society, which otherwise remain somewhat abstract and remote from the concerns of social administration (this seems to be the case at present); a point of return in that wider normative and positive explorations, in turn, help evaluate the policy models themselves and in this way inform social choice and policy decisions.

(Mishra, 1977: 24)

Scholarship on models of welfare gathered momentum in the 1970s. Parker (1975) used models to analyse governments' responses to problems of poverty and inequality and distinguished three models: laissez faire, liberal and socialist. The last of these models stresses equality, that is the right to take part in political, social and economic activities; an emphasis on 'freedom to' rather than 'freedom from'; distribution that is according to need; and state responsibility for facilitating similar standards and opportunities. The laissez faire model is based on a simple form of individualism; it stresses economic growth, maximizing wealth, individual free choice and minimal state intervention; and poverty and inequality are taken for granted and linked to an absolute definition of poverty. The liberal model lies between the first two. It stresses liberty and individual freedom, attaches importance to the market as a means of redistribution, admits government responsibility for guaranteeing minimum standards of living and opportunities and is related to the living standards of the rest of the community.

There emerged a significant commitment to developing models, which continued to gather momentum, and one of the most seminal works focusing on welfare regimes was published in 1990. In *The Three Worlds of Welfare Capitalism*, Esping-Andersen (1990) describes welfare regimes as belonging to three clusters: social democratic, liberal and conservative corporatist. As Goodin and Rein (2001: 771) conclude:

The story begins with the seminal inaugural lecture of Richard Titmuss on the 'Social Division of Welfare', in Britain in the mid-1950s, and it culminates 35 years later in Esping-Andersen's influential *Three Worlds of Capitalism*, based on Titmuss's early work. It is the continuity of thought, and the stable structure of argument on which welfare state types are based, that we want to stress here.

Arts and Gelissen (2010: 581) also point out that:

in evaluating models of the welfare state, one has to realize that each model, however complex, is always simplification of reality. Moreover, it is important to keep in mind that models have a dual function of explanation and description. Regarding explanation one should prefer highly simplified (and therefore often very unrealistic) models that have the advantage of great analytical power; concerning description one should prefer highly complex models that often have the advantage of realistic descriptiveness, but which are analytically less powerful. So there is a trade-off between analytical power and empirical accuracy.

Further reading

Arts, W.A. and Gelissen, J. (2010) 'Models of the Welfare State', in Castles, F., Leibfried, S., Lewis, J., Obinger, H. and Pierson, C. (eds.), *The Oxford Handbook of the Welfare State*. Oxford: Oxford University Press, pp. 569–584.

Castles, F., Leibfried, S., Lewis, J., Obinger, H. and Pierson, C. (eds.) (2010) *The Oxford Handbook of the Welfare State*. Oxford: Oxford University Press.

Mishra, R. (1977) *Society and Social Policy: Theories and Practice of Welfare*. London: Macmillan.

Parker, J. (1975) *Social Policy and Citizenship*. London: Macmillan.

Titmuss, R. (1974) *Social Policy: An Introduction*. London: Allen & Unwin.

NEEDS

Related entries: Capabilities; Citizenship; Functionings; Poverty; Social justice

Need is usually understood in terms of requiring something essential and is viewed in terms of lack or absence. Wants and needs are closely linked, yet, although there may be consensus that social policy meets needs, there is equal consensus that social policy is not concerned with 'wants'. Thus, although we need food to survive, the cuisine we want is irrelevant. Although we need clothes for warmth and modesty, the brand we want is not at issue. Lister (2010: 169) recognizes that sometimes we identify a need only when it is not met: 'a need implies that, unless it is met, a person will be harmed in some way'. Need is central to welfare provision. Resources are limited in all societies so the question arises of how such resources should be redistributed. Should decisions in relation to allocation be made on the basis of need or rights? Policy makers often claim to target resources at 'those in need'.

Theorists have tried to define need, as a concept, for decades, while they have also discussed who is best placed to define need: service users or professionals. Dean (2010: 2) suggests that need is 'arguably the single most important organizing principle in social policy'. He suggests that how we measure need depends on the values we hold. There are difficulties in measuring common human needs. Definitions of need can be subjective or can attempt to be objective. Some of the prominent theorists who have tried to define need include Abraham Maslow (1943), Jonathon Bradshaw (1972), Antony Forder (1974), Len Doyal and Ian Gough (Doyal and Gough, 1991).

One of the most enduring theories of human need is that presented by the psychologist Maslow (1943). His hierarchy of human needs suggests that one need is dependent on the fulfilment of a previous need. Furthermore, needs are inter-related. Maslow's hierarchy of needs, organized in a pyramid, begins with physiological needs, which he suggests are 'the most pre-potent of all needs' (Maslow, 1943: 373). These include food, water and shelter. The next level of needs he refers to as safety needs. These include a preference for stability and order and a preference for the familiar over the unfamiliar. Next are love needs: the need for love, affection and belongingness. These are followed by the need for self-esteem, a need for a highly based self-evaluation and finally self-actualization needs, when one can realize one's full potential. Looking at this classification in the context of social policy it is clear that policies can influence the degree to which each of these needs is met.

A taxonomy of need was developed by Jonathan Bradshaw (1972) in which he distinguished four ways in which people define need. The first of these are felt needs, when individuals are conscious of their needs. This is a subjective definition of need. The next stage is expressed needs, when people vocalize their needs. Next he refers to normative needs, when needs are classified according to professional norms and standards. Finally, Bradshaw distinguishes comparative needs, which are based on relative judgement, in a social context. Anthony Forder (1974) suggests that values determine which needs are prioritized by service providers. He refers to a subjective identification of need as defined by the recipients of services. This is felt need. He refers to needs identified by experts as normative as they draw on established norms and procedures. He draws on ideal norms, which are the goals of social services to define need. He uses the concept of minimum standards. Then he focuses on comparative need, which is related to the standards of the community. He then discusses felt need, drawing on the individuals' own assessment.

In their classic study *A Theory of Human Need*, Doyal and Gough (1991) developed a theory of need which has subsequently been drawn on by many social policy analysts. They argue that humans have common universal needs which we can take for granted. 'It is possible to identify objective and universal human goals which individuals must achieve if they are able to optimize their life chances' (Doyal and Gough, 1991: 3). They conclude that human needs 'are universal and knowable, but our knowledge of them and of the satisfiers necessary to meet them, is dynamic and open-ended' (Doyal and Gough, 1991: 4). They ask which needs are universal and ascertain that autonomy and health are the basic needs that people must have met in order to participate in society. They recognize the importance of good physical health: 'to complete a range of tasks in daily life requires manual, mental and emotional abilities with which poor physical health usually interferes' (Doyal and Gough, 1991: 56). To be autonomous they describe as 'to have the ability to make informed choices about what should be done and how to go about doing it' (Doyal and Gough, 1991: 53). Based on this criterion they present the following list of basic universal needs: nutritional food and clean water, protective housing, a non-hazardous physical environment, appropriate health care, security in childhood, significant primary relationships, physical security, economic security, appropriate education and safe birth control and childbearing (Doyal and Gough, 1991: 157–168). Many of these basic needs mirror Sen's (2009) capabilities approach, which links capabilities to well-being and argues for this approach as a constitutional guarantee. It is concerned with those things people need in order to thrive.

Fraser (1989) distinguishes between 'thin needs', which refer to universal needs, and 'thick needs', which are more specific. She focuses on homeless people to explain that, whereas thin needs relate to the need for shelter, thick needs relate to the specific type of provision required (Fraser, 1989: 163). Thus, thick needs will be socially specific. Dean (2010) builds on this distinction, linking it with well-being. Thin needs prevent harm but thick needs facilitate flourishing and social quality, and a recognition of the importance of social relationships. Fraser (1989) writes of the politics of needs interpretation. She identifies three stages: the establishment of the political status of needs, the practical interpretation and the satisfaction of needs.

Dean (2010), in *Understanding Human Need*, presents thirty different concepts of need. He suggests that need has been an elusive and contested concept in social policy (Dean, 2010: 1). He suggests that there are four discourses on need: moralistic, related to what people ought to be able to do in order to be able to survive; economistic, to do with preferences expressed in the free market; paternalistic, related to what people ought to have; and humanistic, an ideal vision of human fulfilment. He explores the distinction between absolute and relative need, focusing on inherent and interpretive definitions and thin and thick definitions. Like Bradshaw, Dean presents a taxonomy of need; in it he applies the inherent and interpreted conceptualisations of need and thin and thick conceptualisations to relate to the four discourses which are part of social policy development. These are circumstantial, particular, common and universal. He is concerned with how needs can be translated into social rights and argues that rights to welfare can be framed as conditional, selective, protective or citizenship-based, depending on the understanding of need adapted.

Further reading

Bradshaw, J. (1972) 'The Concept of Social Need', *New Society*, 30: 640–643.
Dean, H. (2010) *Understanding Human Need*. Bristol: Policy Press.
Doyal, L. and Gough, I. (1991) *A Theory of Human Need*. London: Macmillan.
Forder, A. (1974) *Concepts in Social Administration: A Framework for Analysis*. London: Routledge & Kegan Paul.
Fraser, N. (1989) *Unruly Practices*. Cambridge, UK: Polity Press.
Lister, R. (2010) 'Needs', in Lister, R., *Understanding Theories and Concepts in Social Policy*. Bristol: Policy Press, pp. 167–194.
Maslow, A.H. (1943) 'A Theory of Human Motivation', *Psychological Review*, 50: 370–396.
Sen, A. (1985) *Commodities and Capabilities*. Amsterdam: Elsevier Science Publishers.

NEW SOCIAL MOVEMENTS

> Related entries: Globalization; Power; Social divisions

Organizations of people campaigning for social change form movements. Traditional social movements include the labour movement. Since the 1970s a wide range of organizations agitating for change have emerged, linked to gender, identity and the environment. Crossley (2002: 1) suggests that there is no neat way of defining new social movements and he criticizes some definitions in the literature as being too broad. He suggests they are collective, but questions what that means in relation to size, obligations for attendance and so on. He refers toWittgenstein's (1953) understanding of movements as involving 'family resemblance', sharing common features.

Croft and Beresford (1996) explain the emergence of new social movements. In the 1970s new movements emerged including those organized around women, gay, black and environmental issues. They were concerned with a genuine struggle for participatory democracy, social justice and equality. They involved alternative models of organization at local, national and international levels. They had alternative ideologies and a focus on alternative service provision. They emphasized the positive aspects of their identities and there was a recognition of the overlap of ideologies. Croft and Beresford (1996: 177) draw on Oliver's typology of new social movements, which characterizes them as being located on the periphery of the traditional political system and sometimes deliberately marginalized. They offer a critical evaluation of society as straddling older forms of domination and newer emerging forms of opposition concerned with quality of life, rather than just material need; they are internationalist.

Williams refers to campaigns by new social movements and by welfare users since the 1970s, having exposed first the limitations of a 'false' universalism, a limited egalitarianism and an exclusive rather than inclusive citizenship inherent in the post-war welfare state.

> In doing this they also highlighted new social risks – for example, domestic violence, racial violence, forms of discrimination, child sexual abuse, lack of autonomy, rights circumscribed according to sexual preference, environmental risks from pollution. The identification of these risks emerged from claims against cultural and social injustices caught up in unequal relations of power in society. These relations were refracted in welfare through the hierarchical relations between providers and users, through the constitution of moral categories of desert and medical categories of physical, mental and sexual invalidity, and through forms of restricted access to resources by marginalised social groups. Thus, central to many of their demands has been the reconstitution of the welfare subject as an active citizen participating in the democratic organisation of welfare services.
>
> (Williams, 1999: 673)

The identification of these risks emerged from claims against cultural and social injustices caught up in unequal relations of power in society.

Further reading

Croft, S. and Beresford, P. (1996) 'The Politics of Participation', in Taylor, D. (ed.), *Critical Social Policy*. London: Sage, pp. 175–198.

Crossley, N. (2002) *Making Sense of Social Movements*. Buckingham: Open University Press.

Williams, F. (1999) 'Good Enough Principles for Welfare', *Journal of Social Policy*, 28(4): 667–687.

OCCUPATIONAL WELFARE

Related entries: Citizenship; Commodification/decommodification; Models of welfare

Occupational welfare is associated with paid employment. This may involve money, goods or services, for example a pension, sick pay, meals or health service. Titmuss first referred to occupational welfare, in his classification of welfare systems as models, when he referred to the industrial-achievement model (Alcock *et al.*, 2001: 181). Goodin and Rein describe occupational welfare as 'market-driven social benefits provided by private employers and the state in its role as employer' (Goodin and Rein, 2001: 772). Occupation-based welfare has long been a feature of people's lives. The traditional guild structure guaranteed that members of traditional trades looked after their own. Similarly, in the nineteenth century industries such as Guinness and Rowntree were very much involved in welfare provision in relation to housing and social services. The Bismarckian model was associated with access to welfare through employment. Esping-Andersen (1990) describes how Germany pioneered social insurance, but benefits there have depended almost entirely on contributions and thus on work and employment.

Greve (2007: 33) develops a typology to classify occupational welfare based on two of its elements. These are, first, the extent to which it is supplementary, a substitute for or outside the scope of public welfare and, second, the degree to which the various elements of occupational welfare have a direct or indirect impact on companies.

May (2008: 203) defines occupational welfare as 'the non-wage elements of the reward packages provided by employers that enhance employee well-being'. May suggests that there are two views of occupational welfare, one which focuses on arrangements voluntarily provided by employers, and the other, broader definition, which embraces mandatory schemes too (May, 2008: 204). She says it can be categorized along nine dimensions based on the type of support offered and there are cross-cutting variables, depending on whether spouses and children are included (May, 2008: 205). The nine forms of voluntary and mandatory occupational welfare presented by May are: social security, social care, healthcare, education and training, housing, transport, leisure, concierge services and community participation. Looking at Britain, May (2008: 207–208) concludes that there is variation in relation to organizational size, sector, and industry and employment status. There is a gender dimension owing to women's concentration in smaller forms and lower tiers of employment. The same applies to ethnic groups. May explores modes of service delivery range, mix and service type and how these change over time (May, 2008: 206).

Further reading

Goodin, R.E. and Rein, M. (2001) 'Regimes or Pillars: Alternative Welfare State Logics and Dynamics', *Public Administration*, 79(4): 769–801.

Greve, B. (2007) *Occupational Welfare: Winners and Losers*. Cheltenham: Edward Elgar.

May, M. (2007) 'Occupational Welfare', in Powell, M. (ed.), *Understanding the Mixed Economy of Welfare*. Bristol: Policy Press, pp. 149–176

May, M. (2008) 'Occupational Welfare', in Alcock, P. May, M. and Rowlingson, K. (eds.), *The Student's Companion to Social Policy*. Oxford: Blackwell, pp. 203–211.

Titmuss, R., Abel-Smith, B. and Titmuss, K. (1987) *The Philosophy of Richard Titmuss: Selected Writings of Richard M. Titmuss*. London: Allen & Unwin.

PATH DEPENDENCY

Related entries: Critical junctures

Changes and continuities in social policy have been discussed widely by path dependency theorists, emphasizing the historicity of policy making (Room, 2008). Path dependency is associated with the scholarship of Paul Pierson (2004), who suggests that policies develop along a trajectory or path which is closely related to history. Once these are in place, path dependency and 'institutional lock-in' can occur. It limits, but does not prevent, the scope for future change, and organizations, institutions and nations can be constrained to move.

Pierson (2004) holds that critical junctures occur in policy development. Studying these helps us to understand welfare settlements in a nation's history. Once a policy develops along a certain path, 'institutional lock-in' will limit the scope for future change. Such lock-in insures that path trajectories – organizations, institutions and nations – are limited in terms of development. Decisions, once made, will shape and influence policy and politics for the future (Greer, 2008). Present policies have emerged from a historical context whose structures influence present resources and prospects for shaping viable political strategies. The start of a path, taking place in a specific type of situation, often called a 'critical juncture' or 'breakage point', is often crucially important for subsequent policies. In these critical junctures the development curve transforms into a new trajectory.

Lessenich (2005: 345) suggests that the combination 'of historical legacies, policy feed-back and lock-ins, increasing returns and self-reinforcing processes became part of the conceptual tool kit of mainstream social policy research'. Policy, as Hinrichs (2001) suggests, can be slow to move.

Room (2008) argues that, as we live in times of rapid global change with global restructuring, technological change, economic and environmental change, new, more vigorous and coordinated responses are demanded. He suggests that we need more appropriate indicators so that policy makers can see 'tipping points'. Path dependency can help us to understand critical junctures in the development of welfare systems. Pierson (2004) refers to the creative 'first mover' and the well trodden trail. Ebbinghaus (2005) argues that path dependency involves road junctures, in which an actor must choose at a fateful juncture. Ebbinghaus suggests that the first mover is locked in by investment costs, and the well-trodden path is locked in as it is a low-cost option. The two paths are closely interdependent.

Further reading

Ebbinghaus, B. (2005) *Can Path Dependence Explain Institutional Change?* Cologne: Max-Planck-Institut fuer Gesellschaftsforschung.

Lessenich, S. (2005) '"Frozen Landscapes" Revisited: Path Creation in the European Social Mode', *Social Policy & Society* 4(4): 345–356.

Room, G. (2008) 'Social Policy in Europe: Paradigms of Change', *Journal of European Social Policy*, 18: 345–352.

Pierson, P. (2004) *Politics in Time, History, Institutions and Social Analysis.* Princeton, NJ: Princeton University Press.

PATRIARCHY

> Related entries: Citizenship; Discrimination; Equality; Feminism; Household; Male breadwinner; Social justice

Patriarchy means male rule or rule by the father. Since the 1970s feminist writers in social policy have placed patriarchy at the centre of social policy debates. Walby (1990: 20) defines patriarchy as 'A system of social structures and practices in which men dominate, oppress and exploit women'. Holmes (2007: 2) defines it as: 'a social system in which men have come to be dominant in relation to women'. Some of the pioneers in this work include Elizabeth Wilson (1977), Hilary Land (1980), Barrett and McIntosh (1991), Mary McIntosh (1996), Gillian Pascall (1986) and Fiona Williams (1989).

Further reading

Holmes, M. (2007) *What Is Gender? Sociological Approaches.* London: Sage.

McIntosh, M. (1996) 'Feminism and Social Policy', in Taylor, D. (ed.), *Critical Social Policy, A Reader.* London: Sage, pp. 13–26.

Pilcher, J. and Whelehan, I. (2004) *50 Key Concepts in Gender Studies.* London: Sage.

Walby, S. (1990) *Theorizing Patriarchy.* London: Blackwell.

Williams, F. (1989) *Social Policy: A Critical Introduction, Issues of Race, Gender and Class.* Cambridge, UK: Polity Press.

POVERTY

> Related entries: Capabilities; Functionings; Household; Need; Social exclusion

Poverty is generally understood to mean lacking resources. The complexity of trying to define and measure poverty is clear from Spicker and colleagues (2007), who present in excess of 200 terms in their glossary on poverty. There are two broad conceptions of poverty – absolute and relative – but many other closely related concepts, such as primary poverty, secondary poverty, measurement of poverty, dynamic poverty, risk of poverty, consistent poverty and the feminization of poverty, are found in the literature. Pinker (1999: 1) observes that explanations on the causes of poverty tend to be structural, focusing on the institutionalization of inequality and macro-economic issues and, on the other hand, on the behaviour of people, which can extend beyond generations. Poverty has held a central place in social policy literature for generations of scholars. Harris (1977: 3) refers to the discovery of poverty in the 1880s to 1890s, referring undoubtedly to the pioneering work of Charles Booth (1840–1916) and Seebohm Rowntree (1871–1957). Booth, a philanthropist whose work can be accessed online through the London School of Economics (http://booth.lse.ac.uk/), conducted major studies of poverty in London. *Life and Labour of the People* stretched to seventeen volumes published between 1889 and 1903. He was committed to the idea of a poverty line, defined in terms of minimal requirements for survival. He defined the very poor as those whose means were insufficient 'according to the normal standards of life in this country' (Booth, 1892: 33). Thus, he understood poverty in relative terms.

Rowntree carried out a comprehensive survey of 11,560 families or 46,754 individuals in York, during which investigators visited every 'working class' home. It was published as *Poverty, a Study of Town Life* (1901). Many of the terms associated with poverty studies in social policy literature can be traced back to this work. Like Booth, he was committed to the notion that it is possible to draw a poverty line which indicates an absolute minimum standard of living. He drew on nutritional studies to determine the number of calories necessary for people to function and then he costed these. This is also known as the *subsistence* or *budget standard approach*. By this method one defines and costs a set of goods and services which are considered to be the minimum necessary for physical survival. The income needed to cover this minimum is then the poverty line. According to Rowntree, those living below the poverty line were those with 'an income insufficient to obtain the minimum necessaries for the maintenance of merely physical efficiency' (Rowntree, 1901: 134). Rowntree did not allow for any spending on 'The maintenance of mental, moral or social sides of human nature' (Rowntree, 1901: 86). He differentiated between primary and secondary poverty. The former includes those who did not have enough income to meet the costs of their basic needs. Secondary poverty includes those who have sufficient income to meet their basic needs but spend it on other items. In 1936 Rowntree conducted a second study, *Poverty and Progress*, in which he took a more relative approach. He allowed for the inclusion of such items as postage stamps, radios, books, tobacco, beer, presents, holidays and, interestingly, trade union membership. He recognized that needs are specific to time and place. People's standards of living must be viewed in relative terms. In 1951 Rowntree published *Poverty and the Welfare State*. In the interim the welfare state had developed in Britain and its blueprint proposed in the Beveridge Report (1942) incorporated Rowntree's concepts of poverty.

In the US the Department of Agriculture used a variation of Rowntree's method in its Social Security Administration Poverty Index in 1959 and in 1964 when the Council of Economic Advisors set the official poverty line for the US (Ahmed, 2007:

56). The US adopted an official poverty line in 1969, known as the Orshansky Scale, after Molly Orshansky (MacPherson and Silburn, 1998: 9). It is a combination of nutritional-based and income-based methods.

Poverty studies in the UK from the 1960s onwards were associated with Peter Townsend (1928–2009), who argued that poverty could be understood only in terms of relative deprivation. In his seminal work *Poverty in the UK* (1979), Townsend argued that poverty can only be understood as a relative concept. He suggested that 'Individuals, families, and groups in the population can be said to be in poverty when they lack the resources to obtain the types of diet, participate in the activities, and have the living conditions and amenities which are customary, or are at least widely encouraged, or approved in societies to which they belong' (Townsend, 1979: 31). Townsend developed a methodology to measure poverty objectively and scientifically. He wanted to establish who was living in poverty by examining real socio-economic conditions, the distribution of resources between individuals and differences in their styles of living, and concluded: 'Their resources are so scarcely below those commanded by the average individual or family that they are in effect excluded from ordinary living patterns, customs and activities' (ibid.). In 1968/1969 he conducted major surveys in the UK, questioning a sample of 2000 households, collecting data on each individual's resources in an attempt to build a more comprehensive picture of resources. These included cash incomes; capital assets; benefits in kind; public social services (housing); and private income in kind. Second, it collected data on styles of living and replaced consumption with a more comprehensive concept, a *deprivation index* which was based on sixty indicators from all the common activities in society related to diet, clothing, fuel, light, home amenities, housing, immediate environment, recreation, education and health. Townsend then compiled a deprivation index based on twelve of the items. He suggests that 'conditions of deprivation' cannot be independent of 'feelings of deprivation' (Gordon, 2010: 199). He suggests that material objects cannot be evaluated without reference to how people view them. Townsend and other writers including Mack and Lansley (1985) are associated with the *consensual approach*. The latter based their work on a general survey of households in which individuals were asked to identify the necessities of life.

Another milestone in poverty studies was the publication of the Black Report (DHSS, 1980). It used *relative health standards* to define poverty. It linked poverty to health status. It examined the mortality rates of different social classes and at all stages of the life cycle. It found that those in homes where the head of household is unskilled were disadvantaged compared with others. Poverty can cause ill health and ill health can lead to poverty. Housing, diet and heating are linked to health status. As there is a link between living standards and health, it has been suggested that health could provide a basis for a relative poverty line.

Nolan and Whelan (1996) focus on the overlap between income and deprivation. They are concerned with identifying the poor and explore the income–deprivation relationship. They advocate the use of *relative income poverty lines* and outline the advantages of the method: it incorporate the relative nature of the concept directly and transparently; it can be used for individual countries or for international comparison; and one can assess the sensitivity of results by varying the poverty line. They acknowledge that the challenges are where to place the threshold and that it may not appeal to everyone (Nolan and Whelan, 1996: 44). The relative income poverty line defines poverty line incomes as fixed proportions of average incomes, adjusted for family size and composition using equivalence scales. The cut-off can be at 40 per cent, 50 per cent or 60 per cent of average income. In Ireland, poverty data is collected by the Central Statistics Office using the annual EU Survey on Income and Living Conditions (EU-SILC). The CSO calculates the number of people in poverty using *Relative Income Poverty* and *Consistent Poverty*. This is also known as *relative poverty*, *income poverty* or *risk of poverty*. It is measured by setting a *relative income poverty line*, which shows how an individual's or household's income compares with the average (http://www.cpa.ie/povertyinireland/measuringpoverty.htm). The European Community Household Panel (ECHP) conducted by EUROSTAT includes data that can be used for comparative analysis.

Another measurement of poverty is the Food Ratio Method, whereby the proportion of income spent on food is used as a measurement of poverty. The Social Security Poverty Line is another measurement when the lowest level of social welfare payment is used as a poverty line. This approach was used by Brian Abel-Smith and Peter Townsend in 1965 in *Poor Britain*.

The UN Millennium Declaration adopted by world leaders in 2000 at the Millennium Summit committed nations to a new global partnership to reduce extreme poverty by 2015. It set out a series of time-bound targets: the Millennium Development Goals (MDGs). These are the world's targets for addressing extreme poverty including income poverty, hunger, disease, lack of adequate shelter, and exclusion. At the same time it is committed to promoting gender equality, education, environmental sustainability and basic human rights, those of each person on the planet to health, education, shelter, and security. The United Nations Development Programme (UNDP, 2005) links poverty with human development, and uses three composite indexes to define and measure poverty: the Human Development Index (HDI), Human Poverty Index (HPI) and Gender-Related Development Index (GDI). The HPI concentrates on the deprivation in the three essential elements of human life: longevity, knowledge and a decent standard of living. The HPI is derived separately for developing countries (HPI-1) and a group of select high-income OECD countries (HPI-2) to better reflect socio-economic differences and also the widely different measures of deprivation in the two groups. The first deprivation relates to survival – the likeliness of death at a relatively early age – and is represented by the probability of not surviving to the ages of 40 and 60 respectively for the HPI-1 and HPI-2. The second dimension relates to knowledge – being excluded from the world of reading and communication – and is measured by the percentage of adults who are illiterate. The third aspect relates to a decent standard of living; in particular, overall economic provisioning. For the HPI-1, it is measured by the unweighted average of the percentage of the population without access to safe water and the percentage of underweight children for their age. For the HPI-2, the third dimension is measured by the percentage of the population below the income poverty line (50 per cent of median household disposable income). In addition to the three indicators mentioned above, the HPI-2 also includes social exclusion, which is the fourth dimension of the HPI-2. It is represented by the rate of long-term unemployment. These are based on Sen's capabilities approach, which argues that income is a means to an end. For Sen, well-being is to do with what people can do and be. He focuses on *functionings*, being part of something, being able to do something and achieved status, and *capabilities*, which are to do with potential.

Social exclusion is a term used in relation to poverty. Lister (2004) points out the difficulties of this in that not all who are excluded lack money. Household are generally the focus of poverty studies. Pahl (1990) wrote about the 'black box' of the household and how it is necessary to look within this to view how income is distributed within households. Diana Pearce (1990) introduced the term *the feminization of poverty* to refer to the reality that women are more likely to experience poverty at some times of their life than men and to experience recurrent and longer periods of poverty. *Time poverty* has been introduced by feminist writers to refer to the pressures women can experience in their dual role as worker and carer and also in managing poverty (Glendinning and Millar, 1992). *Dynamic poverty* is a term used to recognize that risk of poverty can change during one's life cycle.

Further reading

Álvarez Leguizamón, S. and Gordon, D. (eds.) (2006) *Poverty: An International Glossary*, 2nd edn. London: Zed Books.
Gordon, D. (eds.) (1999) *Poverty: An International Glossary*. London: Zed Books.
Lister, R. (2004) *Poverty*. Cambridge, UK: Policy Press.
Nolan, B. and Whelan, C. (1996) *Resources, Deprivation and Poverty*. Oxford: Clarendon Press.
Saunders, P. (2010) 'Inequality and Poverty', in Castles, F., Leibfried, S., Lewis, J., Obinger, H. and Pierson, C. (eds.), *The Oxford Handbook of the Welfare State*. Oxford: Oxford University Press, pp. 526–538.
Spicker, P. (2007) *The Idea of Poverty*. Bristol: Policy Press.

POWER

> Related entries: Capitalism; Class; Gender; Patriarchy; Social divisions

Power is understood in terms of strength and capacity to exercise one's intentions. Giddens (2006: 1029) defines power as

> the ability of individuals, or the members of a group, to achieve aims or further the interests they hold. Power is a pervasive aspect of all human relationships. Many conflicts in society are struggles over power, because how much power an individual or group is able to achieve governs how far they are able to realize their own wishes as the expense of the wishes of others.

Spicker (2008: 33) argues that there are three questions to answer when discussing power. These are what kind of power is being considered, where power is concentrated and who benefits. In relation to types of power, Spicker differentiates between economic, social and political, which are distinctly different yet connected. Looking at how power is concentrated he differentiates between different theoretical approaches which view power as exercised by elites or pluralists. Elitism refers to the theory that power is held in society by a certain group. The power of the state is viewed as important and as possessed by those with economic and political resources. Pluralism sees power as widely distributed within societies. In relation to the final question, who benefits, he states: 'this question represents an important challenge to many of the assumptions behind welfare policy; welfare policy is not necessarily intended to benefit the recipients' (Spicker, 2008: 33).

The sociologist Max Weber presented a theory of power in which he distinguished between forms of power that are coercive and those that have authority (Ransome, 2010). He discussed ideal types of authority suggesting that there are three sources of authority. These are traditional authority, charismatic authority and rational-legal authority. Traditional authority is associated with tradition and established patterns. Charismatic authority is associated with the personality attributes of an individual. Rational-legal authority is associated with power which is legitimized through rules and regulations.

Many writers have drawn on Stephen Luke's three-dimensional theory of power as presented in *Power: A Radical View* (Lukes, 1974). The first dimension relates to the ability to make one's own decisions in a conflict situation; the second refers to the ability to control what issues are decided on; the third relates to 'the manipulation of desires', which involves exercising power over people so that they go against the desires of others. Lukes illustrates that a full critique of power should include the interests of those excluded by the political process. This is an important argument in relation to social policy, as it draws attention to participation, inclusion and exclusion.

Watson (2000: 67), writing on Foucault's theory of power and the study of social policy, indicates that, whereas power is often viewed as negative and repressive, for Foucault, power is exercised rather than possessed. It is a fluid, complex entity which involves a dynamic relationship. Power is exchanged and present in all social relationships. Foucault's work is very pertinent to social policy, as he was concerned with such institutions as prisons, hospitals and schools. He was concerned with discourse and how power shapes attitudes, and that expert discourses can be met by resistance.

Watson suggests that one of the important elements of Foucault's theory of power is that power and knowledge are very closely interlinked: power 'produces reality, it produces a domain of objects and rituals of truth' (Watson, 2000: 194). Watson identifies other key elements which relate to power in Foucault's work. These include Foucault's work on discipline in *Discipline and Punish* (Foucault, 1977), and bio-power, which is concerned with the social, medical and psychiatric professions. Foucault also wrote on the power dimensions of confession, and Watson writes that

> confession in this sense plays a key part in social policy, social administration and social research. Surveys, questionnaires and interviews all investigate and intrude upon the most intimate aspects of personal and social life. In order to qualify for assistance or benefits the notion of privacy is stripped away. The homeless person, the criminal, the social security claimant are constantly monitored and surveyed and called upon to give information which may be prejudicial to them.
>
> (Watson, 2000: 69)

Watson very succinctly summarizes Foucault's importance for social policy in his exploration of 'new forms of power'. Referring to the normalization of classification, data collection in the form of censuses, commissions, surveys and other things 'was an increasing appeal to decisions based on statistical measures of what is normal as opposed to decisions based on notions of right and wrong or justice' (*ibid.*). This is very important, as it raises key questions for the ideological basis of social policy and its guiding principles of justice, equality and others.

Power is central to feminist critiques of social policy. Walby (1990: 20) defines patriarchy as 'A system of social structures and practices in which men dominate, oppress and exploit women'. Such structures are central to welfare provision.

Further reading

Lukes, S. (1974) *Power: A Radical View*. London: Macmillan.
Watson, S. (2000) 'Foucault and Social Policy', in Lewis, G., Gewirtz, S. and Clarke, J. (eds.), *Rethinking Social Policy*. London: Sage, pp. 66–77.

POWER RESOURCES

Related entries: Welfare regimes

Power resources is a term employed by Walter Korpi (1983) in attempting to shed light on theories of structure, change, power and conflict in societies. He focuses on class and the distribution of power between collectivities and classes. He explores the role of interest groups' involvement in public policy and reviews the pluralist industrial tradition, the *logic of industrialism*, which explains the development of industrial technology as the chief driver of societal change. This societal change leads to a multiplicity of interest groups, and 'through multiple and overlapping associational memberships, criss-crossing lines of interest conflicts emerge' (Korpi, 1983: 8). This in turn leads to the development of institutional structures for the resolution of conflict.

Korpi looks also at the corporatist tradition, a term he claims 'has been used inter alia, to refer to possible changes not only in modes of interest mediation (from pluralism to corporatism), but also in the form of the state (from parliamentarism to corporatism), but also in the mode of production' (Korpi, 1983: 349). Korpi asserts that both theories are inadequate. He offers an alternative:

> an analytical approach which takes class and the distribution of power resources in society as the point of departure. In contrast to the pluralist views, my guiding hypothesis is that in a capitalist society the working class is a subordinated class in relation to capital. However, in contrast to the Leninist interpretation of Marx, my hypothesis is that, through its political and union organisations, the working class can decrease its disadvantage in power resources in relation to capital.
>
> (Korpi, 1983: 354)

115

He argues that 'the degree of disadvantage of the power resources of the wage-earners can vary significantly over time and as well as between countries' (*ibid.*). Korpi explains power resources as

> characteristics which provide actors – individuals or collectivism – with the ability to punish or reward other actors. These resources can be described in terms of a variety of dimensions. Power resources can thus vary with regard to domain, which refers to the number of people who are receptive to the particular types of rewards and penalties. They can also differ in terms of scope – the various kinds of situation in which they can be used. A third important dimension is the degree of scarcity of a power resource of a particular type. Furthermore, power resources can vary in terms of centrality, i.e., they can be more or less essential to people in their daily lives. They also differ with regard to how easily they are convertible into other resources. The extent to which a power resource can be concentrated is a crucial dimension. Of relevance also are the costs involved in using a power resource and in its mobilization in making it ready for use. Power resources can furthermore differ in the extent to which they can be used to initiate action or are limited to responses to actions by others.
>
> (Korpi, 1983: 355)

He explains that these power resources need not be activated to have consequences for others. It is necessary to consider how such resources are deployed in terms of efficiency.

Korpi describes different types of power resources, some basic in that they have the capacity to reward or punish other actors. He identifies violence as one basic type of power resource. Another is capital and control over the means of production. A third is human capital, that is labour power, education and occupational skills (Korpi, 1983: 356).

In relation to social policy, Korpi claims 'the distribution of power resources between the main collectivisms or classes in a country affects the form and direction of public interventions in the direction of public interventions in the distributive processes and thereby the extent of inequality in a country' (Korpi, 1983: 377). He tests this hypothesis using OECD data for eighteen countries and indicates that 'one way of elucidating the distribution of power is to analyse what instruments and resources of power different groups and collectivisms society have at their disposal in the interaction which takes place between them over long periods of time' (Korpi, 1983: 14).

Further reading

Korpi, W. (1983) *The Democratic Class Struggle*. London: Routledge & Kegan Paul.

PUBLIC POLICY

Related entries: Mixed economy of welfare

Colebatch (2002: 84) writes that in searching for definitions of public policy 'what governments do' is the common denominator. He elaborates: 'to a large degree, this means translating the process of government into a pattern of goal-oriented direct action' (Colebatch, 2002: 85).

Spicker (2008: 76) indicates that public policy incorporates broad areas such as economic policy, foreign policy and 'domestic' policy. He suggests that social policy can be viewed as a 'subcategory of domestic policy, along with law, and other issues like culture, environmental policy or the public services' (*ibid.*). However, he recognizes that social policy is complex and straddles a diverse spectrum. This was recognized by Titmuss (1974), who was concerned with a wealth of areas from blood transfusion to air pollution. He defined policy as 'action about means as well as ends and it therefore implies change: changing situations, systems, practices, behaviour' (Titmuss, 1974: 23).

Hill (2009: 19) suggests that 'special claims are made about the legitimacy of state policy and its primacy over other policies'. This, he argues, takes us into a debate about the nature of the state and the special justifications used for the role of the state as a provider of policies. He defines the state as 'a set of institutions with super ordinate power over a specific territory' (*ibid.*) which can be defined both in terms of its component institutions and their functions. These institutions take different forms and are located at national, regional and local levels. He also acknowledges the role of supra-state institutions, for example the European Union, the United Nations and the World Trade Organization.

Further reading

Hill, M. (2009) *The Policy Process in the Modern State*, 5th edn. Harlow: Pearson.
Colebatch, H.K. (2002) *Policy*, 2nd edn. Buckingham: Open University Press.

QUALITY OF LIFE

Related entries: Capabilities; Functionings; Well-being/welfare

Quality of life has increasingly received attention from social policy scholars. A study commissioned by the European Foundation for Living and Working Conditions (Eurofound) indicates that quality of life refers 'to the overall level of well-being of individuals in a society' (Fahey *et al.*, 2003: 1). Enabling people to achieve their goals

117

is thus an important aspect of quality of life. Fahey and colleagues (2003: 1) remind us that

> this has to be achieved, of course, within the constraints imposed by economic sustainability and respect for the rights and needs of others. It also takes place in a particular institutional and policy setting, and in the context of a community and a society. The nature of an individual's relationships with others in their household, their community and beyond, as well with institutions and policies, are fundamental influences on quality of life.

Fahey and colleagues (2003) are concerned with developing sound measurements of quality of life, suggesting it is necessary to employ a multidimensional approach and employ a wide range of indicators. These must include both 'objective indicators' (living conditions) and 'subjective indicators' (how people feel about their lives). They argue: 'Monitoring quality of life entails focusing on "outcomes" (the choices people make), subjective assessments (reflecting adaptation) and resources (the factors that condition, facilitate and constrain their choices)' (Fahey et al., 2003: 1). They acknowledge the key role of public provision in affecting quality of life in that access to, and the quality of, education, health care, housing and social services influence the quality of life experienced by citizens of any country. Such measurements should capture the 'interconnectedness of people with others in the community and the broader society' (Fahey et al., 2003: 16) by focusing on social cohesion, social integration and social capital. Fahey and colleagues (2003: 2) state:

> The conclusion reached is that quality of life can serve as an overarching frame encompassing many of these other concepts that apply at the level of the individual, family, community and society. Combating social exclusion and promoting an inclusive society, for example, involves enhancement of the capacity of people to participate in the life of their society, which is central to quality of life. Similarly, discussions of the concept of social quality emphasise elements such as socio-economic security and empowerment, which play a central role in quality of life

Stiglitz and colleagues (2009) similarly argue that

> quality of life depends on people's objective conditions and capabilities and that steps should be taken to improve measures of people's health, education, personal activities and environmental conditions. In particular, substantial effort should be devoted to developing and implementing robust, reliable measures of social connections, political voice, and insecurity that can be shown to predict life satisfaction.
>
> (Stiglitz et al., 2009: 15)

Stiglitz and colleagues suggest there are three useful conceptualisations of quality of life. These are subjective well-being, capabilities and fair allocations. Fahey and colleagues (2008) completed a major study of quality of life in Ireland. It explores the social impact of the economic boom and has important lessons for social policy analysts.

Further reading

Fahey, T., Nolan, B. and Whelan, C.T. (2003) *Monitoring Quality of Life in Europe*. Dublin: European Foundation for the Improvement of Living and Working Conditions.

Fahey, T., Russell, H. and Whelan, C.T. (eds.) (2008) *Quality of Life in Ireland: Social Impact of Economic Boom*. New York: Springer.

Stiglitz, J., Sen, A. and Fitoussi, J. (2009) *Report by the Commission on the Measurement of Economic Performance and Social Progress*. Available at http://www.stiglitz-sen-fitoussi.fr, www.communities.gov.uk/publications/communities/childwellbeing2009

RACE

> Related entries: Citizenship; Discrimination; Equality; Ethnicity; Social divisions

Race, racism and racist are terms used every day, yet they are seldom defined. Fanning (2012: 12) reminds us:

> it is important not to conflate all forms of prejudice under the label of racism. It is possible, even useful to distinguish between racisms, xenophobias, sectarianisms and other forms of prejudice while at the same time acknowledging the impact and consequences of race thinking on beliefs about distinctive groups within dominant ideologies, beliefs and stereotypes.

He recognizes that race has more than one meaning and is socially constructed.

Platt (2008) writes of the emotive and contested nature of the language of race and discusses how the term is a part of popular discourse and policy. She defines racism as

> behaviour that uses physical markers of difference such as skin colour as the basis of assumed inferiority and as a justification for less favourable treatment, whether through verbal or physical abuse (racial harassment), through denying employment or by obstructing access to opportunities or services.
>
> (Platt, 2008: 370)

Law (2010) looks at the complexity of defining race and suggests that it has a wealth of meanings 'from which emerged the central understanding that it refers to a "rhetoric of descent"' (Law, 2010: 2). He defines race as

> the social and cultural significance assigned to a group of people who are recognized as sharing common physical or physiognomic characteristics and/or a common lineage of descent, hence for Goldberg (1993) race refers to a 'rhetoric of descent' resulting from cultural choices in naming a set of markers of difference between human beings.
>
> (*ibid.*)

Law (2010: 3) defines racism as comprising:

two core elements in all historical and geographical situations, it presupposes that some concept of race is being mobilized and involves negative attribution of a specified racial group. Identifying how race is being utilized and presented and how negative attribution is being articulated in particular situations are the two central problems that social scientists face in establishing the existence of racism across the globe.

Williams (1989) focuses on the neglect of both gender and race in social policy scholarship:

particularly in terms of a failure to, first, acknowledge the experiences and struggles of women and of Black people over welfare provision; secondly, to account for racism and sexism in the provision of state welfare; thirdly, to give recognition to work which does attempt to analyse the relationship between welfare state and the oppression of women and of Black people (and, historically, other racialized groups such as the Irish and Jews); and fourthly to work out a progressive welfare strategy which incorporates the needs and demands which emerge from such strategies and analyses.

(Williams, 1989: xi)

Williams (1989) outlines the basis for an anti-racist critique of the welfare state. She examines approaches which have the greatest relevance to welfare theory and policy. These she distinguishes as, first, those associated with the sociology of race relations, which incorporates assimilation theory and cultural pluralism, and, second, those from studies of race and class, which include the 'relative autonomy' and 'autonomy' approach and the 'racialized class fraction' approach (Williams, 1989: 89).

Lieberman (2002) explores the politics of race in the development of modern welfare systems. Looking at the United States, Great Britain and France he argues that racial rule in each country led to the development of different welfare systems. He identifies: 'a comparative exploration of the links between racial politics and the welfare-state is important not only for the study of race as a political phenomenon that is increasingly central to national and international politics but also for the study of the welfare-state' (Lieberman, 2002: 105). He suggests that the welfare state is 'a particularly useful focus for the comparative study of race relations. It is among other things a mechanism of social solidarity, a means of linking citizens to the state through a set of social rights and to each other by ties of inter-dependence' (Lieberman, 2002: 386).

Further reading

Law, I. (2010) *Racism and Ethnicity: Global Debates, Dilemmas, Directions*. Harlow: Pearson.
Lieberman, R. (2002) 'Political Institutions and the Politics of Race in the Development of the Modern Welfare State', in Rothstein, B. and Steinmo, S. (eds.), *Restructuring the Welfare State: Political Institutions and Policy Change*. New York: Palgrave, pp. 102–128.
Platt, L. (2008) '"Race" and Social Welfare', in Alcock, P., May, M. and Rowlingson, K. (eds.), *The Student's Companion to Social Policy*, 3rd edn. Oxford: Blackwell, pp. 369–377.

RATIONING

Related entries: Citizenship; Eligibility; Means testing; Needs; Redistribution; Selectivity; Universality

Rationing means allocating scarce resources. It occurs when demand exceeds supply, which is the norm in relation to welfare resources. Rationing can be based on meeting one's needs or meeting one's entitlements. How it is done is linked to the ideological view one holds. Spicker (2008) presents a very clear overview of the intricacies of rationing. He explains: 'rationing means that supply is balanced with demand at the point where services are delivered' (Spicker, 2008: 169). He draws on a model of rationing put forward by Scrivens (1980), who presents two options for limiting supply: restriction and dilution. Restriction can be done by denial, restricting access and eligibility criteria, filtering through deflection and referral, and delay (Spicker, 2008: 169–173). On the other hand, dilution means some form of reduction of the service. In relation to demand Spicker suggests that demand can be managed in several ways: through charging for services, limiting access or through deterrence (Spicker, 2008: 177–178).

Examples of rationing can be seen in all areas of social policy. For example, in relation to health care, there can be charges, waiting lists and eligibility criteria. In relation to social housing, there are also usually criteria which have to be satisfied. These can include age, marital status and family size, and often waiting lists are established. In relation to education, age limits can be introduced, for example in relation to pre-school places.

Further reading

Scrivens, E. (1980) 'Towards a Theory of Rationing', in Leaper, R. (ed.), *Health, Wealth and Housing*. Oxford: Blackwell, pp. 223–239
Spicker, P. (2008) *Social Policy Themes and Approaches*, 2nd edn. Bristol: Policy Press.

REDISTRIBUTION

Related entries: Citizenship; Equality; Means testing; Models of welfare; Needs; Rationing; Selectivity; Social justice; Universal

Redistribution involves transferring resources from one individual or group to another individual or group. Redistribution can be vertical or horizontal. Vertical redistribution involves taking resources from one socio-economic group and giving them to another; this usually means from the wealthy to the poor, but not necessarily. Horizontal redistribution involves redistribution across groups, in which needs rather than income are considered. Fraser (1995) insists on the importance of redistribution, arguing that it is linked to recognition and an egalitarian society cannot have one without the other. Korpi (1993: 374) asserts that 'the issue of redistribution in social policy is a complicated one'.

Lowi (1972: 298) identifies four types of policy. These are distributive policy, which involves the distribution of new resources; redistributive policy, which involves changing the distribution of existing resources; regulatory policy, which involves regulating activities; and constituent policy, which involves establishing or reorganizing institutions. Redistribution policy involves government interference, which can be perceived as positive or negative depending on one's ideological stance. Redistribution is a feature of all welfare systems but how it is done differs. Models of welfare help us to explore the nature of redistribution.

Hills (2008) presents a taxonomy to understand the complexity of assessing distributional effects. These are: vertical redistribution, from rich to poor; horizontal redistribution, on the basis of need, between people with similar incomes but different needs; redistribution between different groups, by dimensions such as class, gender, ethnicity or age; insurance against adversity; efficiency justifications – universal, compulsory and possibly state-provided systems can be cheaper than if the market is left to itself; life cycle distribution – most welfare services are unevenly spaced over the life cycle; compensating for 'family failure' – distribution between and within families; and external benefits – some services may have a spill over, benefiting those beyond the intended group, for example promoting education for the affluent (Hills, 2008: 140–141).

Measuring how welfare is distributed is complex. Hills (2008: 141–147) presents a conceptual framework to work towards this. He writes of the counterfactual: 'to answer the question, "how are welfare services distributed?", you have to add, "compared to what?"'. Next, he refers to incidence – 'who really benefits from a service?' – and valuation: 'to look at the combined effects of different services, their values have to be added up in some way, most conveniently by putting a money value on them'. He highlights the importance of assessing distribution between which groups, distribution of what, and time and data collection problems.

Korpi differentiates between marginal and institutional social policy, arguing that:

> in the long run, an institutional social policy will decrease inequality more than a marginal type of policy because it tends to have redistributive and political consequences which differ from the marginal type. In areas where universal programmes exist, an institutional social policy decreases inequality by making it possible for the lower socio-economic strata to enjoy roughly the same services as other groups.
>
> (Korpi, 1993: 374)

Further reading

Fraser, N. (1995) 'From Redistribution to Recognition? Dilemmas of Justice in a "Post-socialist" Age', *New Left Review*, 212: 68–92.

Hills, J. (2008) 'The Distribution of Welfare', in Alcock, P., May, M. and Rowlingson, K. (eds.), *The Student's Companion to Social Policy*, 3rd edn. Oxford: Blackwell, pp. 139–148.

Lowi, T.A. (1972) 'Four Systems of Policy, Politics and Choice', *Public Administration Review*, 32: 298–310.

RESILIENCE

Related entries: Capabilities; Environmentalism; Functionings; Sustainable development

---

Resilience means bouncing back, having the ability to cope, recover and move on. It is a skill, talent or attribute that people carry in varying quantities. It is associated with overcoming adversity, surviving and, for some people, coming out of a crisis situation stronger and more resourceful.

Walsh (2003: 1) defines resilience as 'The ability to withstand and rebound from disruptive life challenges'. She refers to Luthar, Cicchetti and Becker's observation that 'It involves dynamic processes, fostering positive adaptation within the context of specific adversity' (*ibid.*). Walsh contrasts those who get stuck in a victim position with those who bounce back, as resilient. She suggests that 'Resilience involves key processes over time that foster the ability to "struggle well" surmount obstacles and go on to live and love fully' (*ibid.*). Referring to the work of Luthar and Zigler (1991) who emphasized personal traits possessed by the 'rugged individual', Walsh suggests that this view has changed over time to incorporate family and wider socio-economic influences.

Dyer and McGuinness (1996) suggest that, historically, resilience was used to describe a pliant or elastic quality of a substance or organ. Reviewing several sources, they highlight the importance of bouncing back, rebounding, adaptability and buoyancy. They define resilience as 'a global term describing a process whereby people bounce back from adversity and go on with their lives' (Dyer and McGuinness, 1996: 226). 'It is a dynamic process highly influenced by protective factors', which they describe as specific competencies 'that are necessary for the process of resilience to occur' (Dyer and McGuinness, 1996: 277). They indicate that 'competencies are simply the healthy skills and abilities that the individual can access'. They exist in three domains: individual competencies, interpersonal competencies and familial competencies. Dyer and McGuinness note that there 'is a shifting balance between vulnerability and resilience' (*ibid.*) and they identify adversity as an antecedent to resilience. They write of the importance of the presence of at least one other caring person in the person's life at some point, even briefly: 'The example of this caring individual and the mirroring of the person's inherent worth are crucial to the development of resilience' (*ibid.*).

Effective coping, Dyer and McGuinness argue, is the primary consequence of resilience and the sense that, having overcome one adversity, the person has mastered the skill to overcome more. The critical attributes they identify are, first of all, 'malleability and pliancy' – rebounding towards a direction in life. Second is 'a sense of self' – not just high self-esteem but a sense of one's unique path in life. This involves acceptance and appreciation of what has happened in one's own life: 'the thread of enduring values weaves the foundational fabric for the sense of self' (*ibid.*). Third, they refer to determination, 'stick-to-it-iveness', 'a quality to persevere until the task is completed, or the goal is achieved': 'It is a value of fortitude with conviction, tenacity with resolve. An acknowledgement that the difficulties in life are to be expected and dealt with' (*ibid.*). They suggest that 'there is little black or white thinking, that the resilient person addresses the shades of gray and resourcefully problem solves'. Finally, they stress the importance of a pro-social attitude: the ability to draw people into one's life during times of adversity supports the process of resilience. Pro-social behaviours can also be learned through the support of others.

In relation to the relationship between welfare and resilience, the National Economic and Social Council's (2009) study of well-being draws on the idea of resilience:

> We know from the well-being literature that resilience is a component of our make-up which can be harnessed, given supportive conditions. This understanding derives from the notion of human flourishing which embodies autonomy, self determination, interest and engagement, aspiration and motivation, and whether people have a sense of meaning, direction or purpose in life.
>
> (NESC, 2009: 8)

Resilience can be advanced through the acknowledgement and development of people's capabilities. These capabilities can be enhanced by public policy, at the same time as public policy can be informed by participatory democracy. This two-way relationship is central (Sen, 1999: 18). People live and operate in a world of institutions (the market, the democratic system, the public distribution system, civil society, the media), so that people's opportunities and well-being depend not only on what institutions exist, but on how they function, which in turn is influenced by the prevailing values in society. As well as individuals showing resilience, institutions need to demonstrate resilience in changing and challenging circumstances, and to be able to adapt to be 'fit for purpose'.

Resilience is increasingly employed by writers on environmental policy to refer to the earth's capacity to bounce back and recover from environmental degradation (Anderies *et al.*, 2012).

Further reading

Anderies, J.M., Folke, C., Ostrom, E. and Walker, B. (2012) *Aligning Key Concepts for Global Change Policy: Robustness, Resilience, and Sustainability*. CSID Working Paper Series No. CSID–2012–002, Center for the Study of Institutional Diversity, Arizona State University, Tempe, AZ. Available at http://hdl.handle.net/10535/8063

NESC (National Economic and Social Council) (2009) *Well-Being Matters: A Social Report for Ireland*. Report Number: 119 volumes 1 and 2. Dublin: NESC.

Dyer, J.D. and McGuinness, T.M. (1996) 'Resilience: Analysis of the Concept', *Archives of Psychiatric Nursing*, 10(5): 276–282.

Luthar, S.S. and Zigler, E. (1991) 'Vulnerability and Competence: A Review of Research on Resilience in Childhood', *American Journal of Orthopsychiatry*, 61: 6–22.

Luthar, S.S., Cicchetti, D. and Becker, B. (2000) 'The Construct of Resilience: A Critical Evaluation and Guidelines for Future Work', *Child Development*, 71(3): 543–562.

Walsh, F. (2003) 'Family Resilience: A Framework for Clinical Practice', *Family Process*, 42(1): 1–18.

RISK

> Related entries: Agency; Autonomy; Collectivism; Globalization; Social insurance; Welfare/well-being

Risk is associated with potential harm, danger and adversity. It is a focus of much social policy scholarship (Taylor-Gooby, 2000; Edwards and Glover, 2001; Kemshall, 2002). Collective insurance is a key feature of welfare systems since first introduced by Bismarck in the nineteenth century. Taylor-Gooby holds that 'public policy is our collective response to risk' (Taylor-Gooby, 2000: 1). He says that 'in part uncertainty results from decay of the mechanisms that had previously dealt with risks. The retreat of the welfare state is part of this process' (Taylor-Gooby, 2000: 3).

Kemshall (2002) explores the relationship between social policy and risk and holds that risk is replacing need as the key principle of social policy formation and delivery. This is a response to the risk society (Beck, 1992). Beck proposes that we are living in a 'risk society' and he argues that late modernity produces risks. It begins where nature and tradition ends and the shift from natural risks are replaced by those caused by modernization and industrialization. This leads to uncertainty for individuals as well as increased choices. Social and economic conditions can cause risks too. Risk is concerned with the future. Beck views global risks as a feature of postmodernity, referring to the uncertainty over future outcomes and impacts. Giddens (1999) refers to 'the runaway world', characterized by internally produced or manufactured risks in contrast to external risks of the natural world. Technology expands the range of personal choice and also expands uncertainties and risk. This results in unintended side effects and consequences, expansion of choice and reduction of traditional norms and social bonds: 'as customary ways of doing things become problematic, people must choose in many areas which used to be governed by taken-for-granted norms' (Giddens, 1998a: 5). In this context personal anxiety stakes rise, traditional bonds such as those between family and community are eroded and individuals are increasingly exposed to risk. Both Beck and Giddens employ reflexivity, which means self-monitoring, where people have to look more closely at their own behaviours and circumstances and make decisions accordingly (Giddens, 1998a).

Beck (1992) suggests that the socially disadvantaged are most likely to experience risk and not have resources to deal with it. Furthermore, risks are under-regulated and the social control previously imposed upon technology is now absent. The end of traditional bonds exacerbate risk. Risks have their source in social change, economic forces, scientific development and technological change.

Social risks have been identified as a result of economic and social changes associated with the transition to what some social scientists call 'a post-industrial society'. According to Taylor-Gooby (2004), four processes demonstrate this transition. The first involves a move by large numbers of women into paid work, at the same time as a fall in the proportion of men who are economically active. Second, an increase in the absolute and relative numbers of older people has implications for welfare state pensions, social care and the health services. Third, labour market changes have strengthened the link between education and employment. Finally, there is an expansion of private services. These 'post-industrial social risks' tend to affect particular subgroups of the population. Vulnerable groups are likely to experience needs in three areas. These are, first of all, in relation to family and gender roles (balancing paid work and family responsibilities, especially childcare, and being called on to care for a frail elderly relative (or becoming frail themselves and lacking family support); second, in relation to labour market changes (lacking the skills necessary to gain access to an adequately paid and secure job, or having skills and training which have become obsolete and being unable to upgrade them through life-long learning), and third, in relation to welfare state changes (because of private provision that supplies an insecure or inadequate pension or unsatisfactory services).

It has been argued that post-industrial society brings with it 'discontinuities' in family and working lives, which can entail insecurities and vulnerabilities. These 'discontinuities' require a different type of engagement with the institutions of the state from previously: greater flexibility, differentiated routes and pathways, activation on the part of the state and of citizens, and a shift towards an 'enabling state', with agreed standards and greater regulation (Leisering, 2003).

Further reading

Beck, U. (1992) *Risk Society: Towards a New Modernity*. London: Sage.

Giddens, A. (1998a) 'Risk and Responsibility', *Modern Law Review*, 62(1): 1–10.

Giddens, A. (1998b) 'Risk Society: The Context of British Politics', in Franklin, J. (ed.), *The Politics of Risk Society*. Cambridge, UK: Polity Press, pp. 23–44.

Kemshall, H. (2002) *Risk, Social Policy and Welfare*. Buckingham: Open University Press.

Leisering, L. (2003) 'Government and the Life Course', in Mortimer, J.T. and Shanahan, M.J. (eds.), *Handbook of the Life Course*. New York: Academic Publishers.

Taylor-Gooby, P. (2004) 'New Risks and Social Change', in Taylor-Gooby, P. (ed.), *New Risks, New Welfare: The Transformation of the European Welfare State*. Oxford: Oxford University Press, pp. 1–28

SELECTIVITY

Related entries: Deserving/undeserving; Eligibility; Means testing; Redistribution; Social assistance; Universality

Selectivity is the strategy of targeting government transfer payments to meet the needs of individuals and groups. They are usually targeted at those in lower socioeconomic groups to supplement existing standards and to meet exceptional needs. There are two basic systems of social protection: social insurance and social assistance. Social insurance payments are based on entitlement and are earned through contributions and financed mainly from the social insurance fund. Social assistance payments are means-tested payments to persons in need. They are financed through tax revenue.

Social assistance payments are individual payments and can also include dependants payments. These are generally means tested and are selectivist payments.

Titmuss suggested that, in a selective service, both client and service suffer a loss of status, or stigma, despite the fact that the claimant is often being compensated for diswelfares. The challenge is how to target resources to those most in need and to avoid stigma. The administration of selectivist payments necessarily involves a system of rules and procedures. Consistency and accountability are important; however, discretionary powers allow for flexibility. Supplementary allowance schemes are designed to meet exceptional needs. Although inconsistency and bias can be a feature of discretionary payments, they also offer flexibility and can be responsive to need. Selectivity has received much attention in social policy literature.

Reddin (1978) completed a comprehensive study of universalist and selectivist payments on behalf of the National Economic and Social Council (NESC). It addressed the role of the citizen as taxpayer and the citizen as recipient. Reddin suggests the attractions of universality and selectivity can only be understood in the context of a specific time and context, and any discussion of universality and selectivity must involve a discussion of sources of finance, forms of finance, utilization (how much/ by whom), sense of time, how long financing will take, and how long benefit will be paid for or received. This involves evaluating the impact of policy, measuring the outcome of policy choices and avoiding presumptions that events subsequent to a policy act are necessarily its consequences. He argues that there is a need to acknowledge unintended consequences, for example underutilization, identification and the claiming process (by agencies and by self), income and the unit to be tested, and issues associated with dependants.

Reddin identifies risk associated with being refused, disclosing one's health status, inability to cope, poverty and other factors. He refers to investigating the incidence of revenue sources, to decipher whose taxes go to pay for what. For example, should those without children pay taxes towards paying child benefit? He refers to the incidence of benefit and how to accurately define the size of the potential population to benefit. He addresses cost and argues that where the financing comes from is relevant. If it comes from the poor, is it wasteful? If it comes from cigarettes or alcohol, is it counterproductive? Reddin suggests that a more detailed analysis might reveal a considerable selectivization around the visible universality. He draws our attention to visibility, being conspicuous or concealed. Political sympathy for the group is also an issue. Reddin refers to non-means-tested selectivities for example where the health service targets the sick rather than the healthy. He refers to negative discrimination, when there are constraints on one group to appropriate limited resources. He discusses tax allowances and regressive selectivity, private health care, private pensions, home ownership and area selectivity.

Reddin is concerned with teasing out the intricacies of the acceptance of strategies, social acceptability, generosity of benefits and claiming for others. He identifies the role of the citizen as taxpayer as unexplored territory, as are the opinions of taxpayers. He is concerned with the idea of the conspicuous taxpayer, which leads to polarization, when it is perceived that only the well-paid pay tax. He identifies the existence of the low-paid taxpayer.

Reddin also looks at the impact on beneficiaries and suggests that a longitudinal dimension blurs the lines of demarcation. He suggests that it may be worthwhile to extend it to cover many. It is necessary to evaluate efficiency and effectiveness in the context of specific schemes. Efficiency implies an overall optimal use of resources. He asks whether, if efficiency implies stigma, the strategy is optimal. He is concerned with alienation, stigma and social inefficiency. If the attitude of non-recipients is one of hostility, is this efficient, as it may make the long-term position of the non-poor more vulnerable? He asks if it is possible to assist the needy without disabling them. Reddin suggests that social justice, allocation of resources to where most needed, would appear to justify selectivity.

Reddin outlines four important dimensions. (1) What benefits are provided; to whom are they directed; to what extent are they used by those at whom they are directed; who pays; and how do they pay? (2) Is there a distributional incentive and what are the effects of the way in which costs are met and for how long? (3) What changes are likely to occur over time for those who pay and those who receive? (4) How do those who pay judge those who benefit, and how do those who benefit judge those who pay?

Further reading

Reddin, M. (1978) *Universality and Selectivity: Strategies in Social Policy*. Dublin: NESC.

SEXUALITY

Related entries: Equality; Feminism; Gender; Masculinities; Power; Social divisions

Sexuality is understood as something natural, intrinsic to our being and an important part of our identity. It is used to differentiate between male and female bodies. Sexuality is both identity, how we define ourselves as gay, straight, bisexual, and activity, what we do, for example whether we are celibate or sexually active. Despite the prevalence of sexuality in the media, in common discourse, in our daily lives it has received very little explicit attention in social policy literature, with some notable exceptions, particularly Jean Carabine (1996a,b, 2004), Jeffrey Weeks (1998, 2001) and Diane Richardson (1997, 2004). Sexuality, when examined closely, is central to welfare, education, housing, health and the personal social services, for example in relation to the 'co-habitation rule', same-sex marriage, gay and lesbian health services, sex education, gendered accommodation and hospital wards and personal care. Social policy may not focus particularly on sexuality, yet all of the areas with which it is concerned contain assumptions about sexuality.

Weeks (2001) refers to insecurity among policy makers in relation to sexuality. This insecurity poses considerable challenges for those concerned with developing policy. Weeks (2001: 49) argues that 'the formulation of policy towards the sexual sphere is fraught, hazardous and usually unrewarding'. Governments have often 'shuffled away from direct responsibility' (*ibid.*). He suggests that there are challenges for social policy in that sexuality raises very profound questions about the social order. Weeks views sexuality as socially constructed and writes of 'remaking sexuality', and that 'sexuality is a product of structure and agency. We make sexual history as much as sexuality makes us' (Weeks, 2001: 51). He suggests that we redraw boundaries between 'appropriate and inappropriate' and 'right' and 'wrong' behaviour (Weeks, 2001: 48). For Weeks, 'the revolution is clearly unfinished there are local battles, symbolic moments, moral panics, infinitesimal shifts, moves forwards and back' (Weeks, 2001: 49).

Carabine, writing on sexuality and social policy for more than two decades, indicates that, although it is generally understood that sexuality is a private issue, closer examination reveals that there is the 'focus of implicit and explicit social regulation and control' (Carabine, 1996c: 37). She draws attention to the relationship between sexuality and power and suggests there is an absence of analysis of the effects of normative ideas about sexuality on the formulation, implementation and practice of social policy. She looks at the issue of social control and includes institutions other than the state, for example the family, marriage and motherhood. When women and men define or identify their own sexuality as other than heterosexual, they are usually penalised. Class, gender, race and ethnicity are related to sexuality. Co-habitation rules, for example, assume that a sexual relationship means one person is a dependant whereas the other, usually the male, is expected to provide financially. Carabine (2004: 165) writes that the personal when viewed 'through the lens of sexuality' is 'simultaneously private and public'. Shildrick (2004: 125) suggests that

> sexuality is never simply a matter of what a person does but more importantly it is to do with who he or she is. That is not to say that identities are ever fixed: because sexual practices change and develop over a lifetime and divergent meanings are attached to a person's sexuality, identity is always in a process of construction.

Sexuality is often understood as essentialist/biologically determined (Carabine, 2004; Richardson, 1997; Weeks, 1986; Weeks *et al.*, 2003) but also as socially constructed. Thus, we discuss sexuality in terms of sex drives, instinct and hormones as being biologically determined: the essentialist view. Yet how these drives are acted out will differ according to social context: the social constructionist view. Social divisions such as gender, race, class, ability and ethnicity are often used in sexuality discourse in relation to perceptions of how different groups of individuals behave. Richardson (1997: 155) explores the literature on theories of sexuality, focusing on the extreme views of essentialism/biological determinism and social constructionism. The former views sexuality as 'doing what comes naturally' (*ibid.*), that is biologically determined. Sexuality is an instinct or a drive, which needs fulfilment through sexual activity. It is normal for it to be directed at the opposite sex, have a reproductive function and involve vaginal intercourse. It is 'a natural phenomenon, universal and unchanging' (*ibid.*). Men are usually assumed to have stronger sex drives than women. Those belonging to a certain race or class can also be perceived to have different sexual appetites. Some groups are perceived as less sexually responsible. This approach has been criticized by those who argue that sexuality is socially constructed. Shildrick, writing on sexuality and disability, concludes: 'the way in which the sexuality of people with

disabilities is shaped and given meaning by the combination of sociocultutral assumptions, the physicality of the body, the personal experience of desire, the operation
of social policy, and so on, indicates the highly constructed nature of all sexuality'
(Shildrick, 2004: 124).

Richardson, reviewing social constructionist approaches, suggests that sexuality
and sexual identities are a result of social and historical forces which are shaped by
'religion, law, medical definitions, social policies, psychiatry and popular culture'
(Richardson, 1997: 155). She draws on anthropological and historical studies which
show that what is normal differs cross-culturally and also historically. Sexuality is a
political issue. There is an essentialism/biological determinism continuum. She concludes that: 'the capacities of the body gain their power to shape human behaviour
through the meanings given them in particular historical, cultural and interpersonal
contexts' (Richardson, 1997: 156).

Carabine (2004: 3) suggests that 'personal lives and sexualities are constructed in
and through social policy and practice'. She views sexuality as institutionalized and
that it 'is about much more than individual practices and personal relationships. It is
legally sanctioned and informs and structures everyday life through the social institutions and social practices of marriage, reproduction and parenting' (Carabine, 2004:
10). She writes of the role of social policy in constituting sexual norms and suggests
that it 'implicitly and explicitly conveys messages about appropriate and acceptable
sexualities' (Carabine, 2004: 3). Carabine (1996b) asserts that the normative values of
sexuality are replicated, asserted and reasserted in social policies through the ideology
of heterosexuality.

Feminists argue that sexuality has been constructed in the interests of men. The
institution of heterosexuality is linked to the idea of *heteronormativity*. Feminist
writers have drawn attention to the relationship between sexual abuse and violence
and the relationship to normal ideas and practices regarding heterosexuality, arguing
that power and domination are central to the social construction of sexuality and
that male dominance in sexual relations gives licence to male dominance in all other
spheres (Richardson, 1997). Carabine (2004: 7) writes of the gendered nature of
sexuality, that male and female sexualities differ. In heteronormative societies there
are assumptions around women's childbearing and fertility. This has direct relevance
for social policy, particularly in relation to debates around dependency, breadwinners
and parental leave.

Heterosexism is the assumption that being heterosexual is the typical and 'normal'
sexual orientation, with an underlying assumption that it is the superior sexual orientation. This assumption often results in an insensitivity, exclusion or discrimination
towards other sexual orientations and identities, including those that have lesbian, gay,
bisexual or transexual orientations. *Heteronormativity* is the cultural bias in favour
of opposite-sex relationships of a sexual nature, and against same-sex relationships
of a sexual nature. Because the former are viewed as normal and the latter are not,
lesbian and gay relationships are subject to a heteronormative bias. *Heteronormative*,
or the 'heterosexual norm', refers to the assumption that heterosexuality is the only
sexual orientation. It is closely related to 'heterosexism' and can often cause other
sexual orientations to be ignored and excluded. Pilcher and Whelehan suggest that
heterosexism was first defined in the Oxford English Dictionary in 1979 as 'prejudice

and antagonism shown by heterosexual persons towards homosexuals; discrimination against homosexuals' (Pilcher and Whelehan, 2004: 68). This mirrored a distinction that was emerging in relation to sexism as discrimination against all women and heterosexism as discrimination against gay and lesbian people.

Homosexuality is a term used to describe someone who is sexually and romantically attracted to a person of the same sex. Michel Foucault (1979), in *The History of Sexuality*, suggests that homosexuality and heterosexuality emerged as terms only in 1869. He indicates that from then onwards: 'homosexual became a personage, a past, a case history, and a childhood, in addition to being type of life, a life form, and a morphology, with an indiscreet anatomy and possibly a mysterious physiology. Nothing that went into his total composition was unaffected by his sexuality' (Foucault, 1979: 43).

Weeks (1996: 100) suggests that there are three positions that can be taken in relation to the regulation and control of sexuality. One is the 'absolutist position', which views sex as 'dangerous, disruptive and fundamentally antisocial'; if we follow this position then we are likely to embrace a moral and political stance which proposes tight authoritarian regulation. Second, he identifies a libertarian stance: if 'we believe that the powers of desire are basically benign, life-enhancing and liberating we are liable to adopt a relaxed, even radical set of values, to support'. Between these two extremes he identifies a liberal-pluralist position which 'is perhaps rather less certain about whether sex itself is good or bad; it is convinced, however, of the evils both of moral authoritarianism and of excess'. This is a useful framework for analysing social policies in relation to sexuality, as social policies always reflect ideology.

Carabine (2004: 20) writes on empowerment in relation to sexuality. She suggests that, in relation to sexuality, individuals seek empowerment through self-definition and identity, sexual practice, demands for collective rights and through refusing to accept existing definitions and categorisations.

Intimate citizenship is a term used by Plummer (2003: 38–39):

> this speaks to an array of concerns too often neglected in past debates over citizenship, and which extended notions of rights and responsibilities. I call this 'Intimate Citizenship' because it is concerned with all those matters linked to our most intimate desires, pleasures and ways of being in the world. Some of this must feed back into traditional citizenship; but equally, much of it is concerned with new spheres, new debates, and new stories. For many people in the late modern world there are many decisions that can, and increasingly have to, be made about a life; making decisions around *the control (or not)* over one's body, feelings, relationships; *access (or not) to* representations, relationships, public spaces, etc.; and *socially grounded choices (or not) about* identities, gender experiences, erotic experiences.

Weeks (1998) refers to the 'sexual citizen', a term used also by Richardson (2000: 105) differentiating between conduct-based, identity-based and relationship-based rights claims.

Sexuality Research and Social Policy is a multidisciplinary journal which publishes original research on sexuality, theoretical and methodological discussions, and the implications of this evidence for policies across the globe regarding sexual health, sexuality education, and sexual rights in diverse communities (http://www.springer.com).

Further reading

Carabine, J. (1996a) 'Heterosexuality and Social Policy', in Richardson, D. (ed.), *Theorising Heterosexuality*. Milton Keynes: Open University Press, pp. 55–74.

Carabine, J. (1996b) 'Constructing Women: Women's Sexuality and Social Policy', in Taylor, D. (ed.), *Critical Social Policy*. London: Sage, pp. 113–126.

Carabine, J. (1996c) 'A Straight Playing Field or Queering the Pitch? Centering on Sexuality in Social Policy', *Feminist Review*, 54: 31–64.

Carabine, J. (2000) 'Constituting Welfare Subjects through Poverty and Sexuality', in Lewis, G. *et al.* (eds.), *Rethinking Social Policy*. London: Sage, pp. 78–93.

Carabine, J. (ed.) (2004) *Sexualities: Personal Lives and Social Policy*. Bristol: Policy Press.

Richardson, D. (ed.) (1996) *Theorising Heterosexuality*. Milton Keynes: Open University Press.

Richardson, D. (1997) 'Sexuality and Feminism', in Robinson, V. and Richardson, D. (eds.), *Introducing Women's Studies*, 2nd edn. London: Macmillan, pp. 152–174.

Richardson, D. (2000) 'Constructing Sexual Citizenship: Theorizing Sexual Rights', *Critical Social Policy*, 20: 105–135.

Weeks, J. (2001) 'Live and Let Love? Reflections on the Unfinished Sexual Revolution of Our Times', in Edwards, R. and Glover, J. (eds.), *Risk and Citizenship: Key Issues in Welfare*. London: Routledge, pp. 48–63.

Weeks, J., Holland, J. and Waites, M. (eds.) (2003) *Sexualities and Society: A Reader*. Cambridge, UK: Polity Press.

SOCIAL ADMINISTRATION

> **Related entries: Social policy; Fabianism**

Social administration is concerned with the planning and delivery of services. It is concerned with structures, decision making, management and finance. Social administration as a subject was first taught in the London School of Economics at the turn of the last century. Blakemore (1998: 8) suggests that 'three important strands of learning and training were fused together: social work, sociology and social administration, the last being the study of local and central government institutions, and of the framework in which services to the poor and needy were to be delivered'.

Richard Titmuss was appointed the first Professor of Social Administration in 1950 at the London School of Economics. Although recognizing Titmuss's important contribution to social policy as a subject in the 1950s and 1960s, Blakemore suggests that 'much of the subject of social administration seemed to have developed into a rather complacent and technical description of existing social services and how they were to be delivered' (Blakemore, 1998: 10). Social administration tends to be descriptive, for example describing the detail of health policies and how services are structured. It describes funding sources and bureaucratic structures. Social administration is concerned not with whether or not a service should exist but rather with the nature of that service or policy.

Donnison and colleagues (1970: 26) describe the subject of social administration as 'the development of collective action for the advancement of social welfare'. It may focus on the statutory or non-governmental organization sectors, the private and the informal. Donnison and colleagues (1970: 232) describe administration as 'consisting of all the processes that play a part in determining the volume, character and distribution of the service being studied. The service is the outcome of these processes – the product provided for the public – not the agency providing it'.

Spicker (2008: 298) defines social administration as the 'study of the development, structure and practices of the social services'. Social administration, therefore, is concerned with the mixed economy of welfare. Welfare originates from the state, the voluntary sector, the informal and the private spheres. Each of these organizes welfare provision and services differently. Administration involves administrators who can be professionals or bureaucrats, for example public and civil servants and service users. Looking at the structure of services, Spicker differentiates between different people working in the social services: bureaucrats, professionals and semi-professionals, management, radical alternatives and effective organizations (Spicker, 2008: 159). Spicker identifies different aspects of service delivery, production of welfare, priorities, resources, rationing, equity and procedural fairness, managing demand and delivery of services (Spicker, 2008: 165). Administration is concerned with looking at systems and how they operate, their objectives and rules. It is concerned with operational issues.

Spicker writes of the need to look at the administration of welfare, which is complex. There is no one system of administration. There is national government and regional government. He suggests that there are three main differences between different types of services. These are functional – what services do; client based – targeted at certain groups; and finally area based – based on geographical grounds, for example national, regional and community.

Further reading

Blakemore, K. (1998) *Social Policy an Introduction*. Buckingham: Open University Press.
Donnison, D., Chapman, V., Meacher, M., Sears, A. and Urwin, K. (1970) *Social Policy and Administration Studies in the Development of Social Services at the Local Level*, 3rd edn. London: Allen & Unwin.
Spicker, P. (2008) *Social Policy Themes and Approaches*, 2nd edn. Bristol: Policy Press.

SOCIAL ASSISTANCE

Related entries: Deserving/undeserving; Means testing; Needs; Social insurance; Stigma

Social assistance is sometimes described as welfare. The International Labour Organization (ILO) defines social assistance as: 'benefits to persons of small means as of right in amounts sufficient to meet minimum standards and financed from taxation' (ILO, 1942). Social assistance payments are usually selectivist or means-tested payments. Bahle and colleagues (2010: 448) equate social assistance with need. They explain how, in the USA, welfare is the preferred term. In the European Union, social protection is the term most commonly used to describe income maintenance payments. They suggest that social assistance has two meanings: a broad one, which means means-tested benefits, and a narrow one, a minimum income to all members of society (universal) or to selected groups (categorical). The last they perceive as an income of last resort: 'Historically, it was the first important public social policy that paved the way for welfare state development' (Bahle *et al.*, 2010: 448). They note that since the nineteenth century, as social insurance has become the norm, social assistance has become secondary.

Social assistance payments are generally perceived as inferior to social insurance payments as they are means tested and stigmatizing, and they are allocated according to means rather than entitlement.

Further reading

Bahle, T., Pfeifer, M. and Wendt, C. (2010) 'Social Assistance', in Castles, F., Leibfried, S., Lewis, J., Obinger, H. and Pierson, C. (eds.), *The Oxford Handbook of the Welfare State*. Oxford: Oxford University Press, pp. 448–461.

SOCIAL DIVISIONS

Related entries: Citizenship; Disability; Equality; Ethnicity; Gender; Race

Social policy is concerned with people and society. Societies are complex and heterogeneous. Diversity is a feature of human nature and society, and social policies have to respond to this challenge. Payne (2000) explores the dimensions of social divisions. He indicates that 'when we talk about social divisions we mean those substantial differences between people that run throughout our society' (Payne, 2000: 2). He presents two categories of social division, each with distinct material and cultural features. He suggests that

> one category is better positioned than the other, and has a better share of resources because it has great power over the way our society is organised. Membership of a category is closely associated with a social identity that arises from a sense of being similar to other members, and different from other categories. This affects how people conduct their social interaction. Movement from one category to another is not easy.
>
> (*ibid.*)

Payne outlines how social divisions are socially constructed. He identifies nine core characteristics of social divisions: gender, ethnicity, national identity, age, childhood, sexuality, disability, health and class. These are 'a principle of social organisation result-ing in a society-wide distinction between two or more logically interrelated categories of people, which are socially sanctioned as substantially different from one another in material and cultural ways' (Payne, 2000: 242). Each of these is explored in detail in Payne's edited collection. Payne suggests that a social division is 'long-lasting and sustained by dominant cultural beliefs, the organisation of social institutions, and the situational interaction of individuals' (*ibid*.). He asserts that a social division is socially constructed, that it 'confers unequal opportunities of access to desirable "resources" of all kinds – and therefore different life chances and life styles – from membership of other categories' (Payne, 2000: 243). Payne also suggests that the extent of this differ-entiation differs according to social division, but movement between divisions is rare. It produces shared identities for those within a category. He suggests that 'each social division encompasses all members of society in one or other of its categories, but individuals seldom have matching profiles of category membership across the range of social divisions' (*ibid*.). Payne also indicates that 'an examination of life chances and life styles is an empirical method of identifying social divisions and categories' (*ibid*.) and finally that 'however much specific social divisions are opposed by those disad-vantaged by them, the principle of social divisions is a universal systematic feature of human society' (*ibid*.).

Further reading

Payne, G. (2000) *Social Divisions*. Basingstoke, UK: Palgrave.

SOCIAL EXCLUSION

> **Related entries: Capabilities; Functionings; Needs; Poverty**

Exclusion generally means being left out or marginalized. In social policy literature, social exclusion is usually linked to poverty. However, individuals and groups can be excluded or marginalized for reasons other than poverty, for example gender, race, ethnicity, age, sexual orientation and disability. Burchardt and colleagues (2002: 2) suggest that in the USA 'ghettoization', 'marginalization' and 'underclass' are used as concepts in a similar way. Room (2008) suggests that an analysis of social exclusion raises three methodological questions. These are: how is it conceptualized? How is it measured? And 'to what theoretical and policy purposes is the investigation and analysis of social exclusion to be considered?' (Room, 2008: 341).

Adam Smith, writing over 200 years ago, was concerned with social exclusion:

> By necessaries I understand not only the commodities which are indispensably necessary for the support of life, but whatever the custom of the country renders it indecent for creditable people, even the lowest order, to be without . . . Custom

has rendered leather shoes a necessary of life in England. The poorest creditable person of either sex would be ashamed to appear in public without them.

(Smith, 1776/1976: 351–352)

This trend has developed throughout the years. Peter Townsend's relative approach to poverty emphasizes exclusion:

Individuals, families, and groups in the population can be said to be in poverty when they lack the resources to obtain the types of diet, participate in the activities, and have the living conditions and amenities which are customary, or are at least widely encouraged, or approved in societies to which they belong. Their resources are so scarcely below those commanded by the average individual or family that they are in effect excluded from ordinary living patterns, customs and activities.

(Townsend, 1979: 31)

The term 'exclusion' is accredited to René Lenoir (1974) in France, where the term was used to describe those who fell through the safety net of the social insurance system, and who were described as 'les exclus'. The term is associated with French social policy, where there is an emphasis on solidarity, and it can be traced back as far as to the sixteenth century (Spicker, 2007: 65). Lister (2005) traces the historical use of the concept to Weber's reference to social closure of groups as a way of securing and maintaining privilege; this was followed on in the work of Durkheim and Merton, and in relationship to citizenship in Marshall's work.

Writing on social exclusion, Levitas (2004) identifies three discourses: RED, redistributive, egalitarian discourse, linked to citizenship and social justice; MUD, a moralistic discourse linked to underclass and dependency; and SID, a social integrationist discourse. Sen (2000: 13) suggests we need to understand social exclusion in the context of the capability literature:

Being excluded can sometimes be in itself a deprivation and this can be of intrinsic importance on its own. For example, not being able to relate to others and to take part in the life of the community can directly impoverish a person's life. It is a loss on its own, in addition to whatever further deprivation it may indirectly generate. This is a case of constitutive relevance of social exclusion.

He identifies exclusions as having instrumental importance as 'they may not be impoverishing in themselves, but they can lead to impoverishment of human life through their causal consequences (such as the denial of social and economic opportunities that would be helpful for the persons involved)' (ibid.). He distinguishes between active and passive exclusion. An example is policy in relation to asylum seekers in which asylum seekers are actively excluded from the welfare system which is available to the indigenous population, as for example in Ireland, where asylum seekers receive direct provision, which guarantees the provision of accommodation and food, rather than cash payments as received by other welfare recipients. On the other hand passive exclusion is unintended.

The Department for International Development defines social exclusion as

> a process by which certain groups are systematically disadvantaged because they are discriminated against on the basis of their ethnicity, race, religion, sexual orientation, caste, descent, gender, age, disability, HIV status, migrant status or where they live. Discrimination occurs in public institutions, such as the legal system or education and health services, as well as social institutions like the household.
>
> (DFID, 2005)

Kahn (2012: 2) outlines three important aspects of social exclusion: it is multidimensional in that it encompasses social, political, cultural and economic dimensions, and operates at different social levels; it is dynamic, in that it impacts on 'people in various ways and to differing degrees over time'; and it is relational, in that 'it is the product of social interactions which are characterised by unequal power relations, and it can produce ruptures in relationships between people and society, which result in a lack of social participation, social protection, social integration and power'.

Internationally, social exclusion has received much attention. In 1997 the London School of Economics established the Economic and Social Research Council-funded Centre for Analysis of Social Exclusion (http://sticerd.lse.ac.uk/case/_new/publications/default.asp). In 1997 the UK government established a Social Exclusion Unit. It was abolished in 2006 and was replaced by the Social Exclusion Task Force, which was in turn abolished in 2010.

The Australian Government professes

> a vision of a socially inclusive society as one in which all Australians feel valued and have the opportunity to participate fully in the life of our society. This necessitates all Australians having the resources, opportunities and capability to: Learn by participating in education and training; Work by participating in employment, in voluntary work and in family and caring; Engage by connecting with people and using their local community's resources; and have a voice so that they can influence decisions that affect them.
>
> (http://www.socialinclusion.gov.au/)

In Canada, the Laidlaw Foundation has drawn attention to social exclusion and social inclusion, as it relates to children, through their Children's Agenda Program. Since 2001 its Working Paper Series has commissioned research on Perspectives on Social Inclusion (http://www.laidlawfdn.org/working-paper-series-social-inclusion).

The European Union has embraced the concept of social exclusion. The Amsterdam Treaty (http://europa.eu/legislation_summaries/institutional_affairs/treaties/amsterdam_treaty/index_en.htm) undertook to fight social exclusion. The European Commission's *Towards a Europe of Solidarity* (COM (92) 542) describes social exclusion as the result of

> mechanisms whereby individuals and groups are excluded from taking part in the social exchanges, from the component practices and rights of social integration and of identity. Social exclusion goes beyond participation in working life; it is

felt and shown in the fields of housing, education, health and access to services.

(European Commission, 1992: 8)

In 1993 the European Commission observed that 'social exclusion affects individuals, groups of people and geographical areas. Social exclusion can be seen, not just in levels of income, but also matters such as health, education, access to services, housing and debt. Phenomena which result from social exclusion therefore include: the resurgence of homelessness' (Tiemann, 1993: 48). It viewed the causes of social exclusion as related to structural factors: persistent long-term unemployment; industrial change; breakdown of family structures; changes to value systems, weakening of cohesion and traditional forms of solidarity; social fragmentation; and changes in migration. It views social exclusion as dynamic, affecting individuals, groups and areas, and multidimensional. It recognizes that 'the European Union cannot be developed without internal cohesion and support for European integration depends on development of the "social dimension"' (Tiemann, 1993: 49).

In 2000 the Lisbon European Council announced the Social Inclusion Strategy to focus on social exclusion and deprivation (http://www.europarl.europa.eu/summits/lis1_en.htm). It agreed to adopt the open method of coordination, with common objectives on poverty and social exclusion. This would include national action plans against poverty and social exclusion; joint reports on social inclusion and regular monitoring, evaluation and peer review; development of common indicators to provide a means of monitoring progress and comparing best practice; and a Community Action Programme to encourage cooperation between Member States to combat social exclusion.

Combating poverty and promoting social inclusion are key priorities of the Commission's Social Policy Agenda 2006–10, supporting two of the Commission's strategic goals for the next five years which are prosperity and solidarity. The Agenda launched a Community initiative to examine minimum income schemes and the integration of people excluded from the labour market, and designated 2010 as the European Year of Combating Exclusion and Poverty acknowledging:

> Poverty and exclusion do not only strike at the well-being of individuals, their ability to take an active part in the life of society; they also impair economic development. The Union wishes to reaffirm the importance of collective responsibility in combating poverty; this doubtless involves the decision-makers, but it also calls for a response from the actors in the public and private sectors. Among its aims, the European Year will seek to give a voice to those who daily experience poverty and social exclusion.
>
> (http://ec.europa.eu/employment_social/2010againstpoverty/extranet/
> About_the_Year/factsheet_EY2010_en.pdf)

It identified four cross-disciplinary issues: 'Recognition', recognizing the fundamental right of persons experiencing poverty and social exclusion to live in dignity and to take an active part in society; 'Shared responsibility and participation', promoting public support for social inclusion policies, emphasizing collective and individual responsibility in combating poverty and social exclusion, and fostering commitment by all public and private actors; 'Cohesion', promoting a more cohesive society, where no one doubts that society as a whole benefits from the eradication of poverty; and 'Commitment and practical action', renewing the pledge of the European Union and its Member States to combat poverty and social exclusion, and involving all levels of authority in the pursuit of that aim.

Further reading

Burchardt, T., Le Grand, J. and Piachaud, D. (2002) 'Introduction', in Hills, J., Le Grand, J. and Piachaud, D. (eds.), *Understanding Social Exclusion*. Oxford: Oxford University Press, pp. 1–12.

Kahn, R. (2012) *Topic Guide on Social Exclusion*. International Development Department, University of Birmingham.

Lister, R. (2004) 'Poverty and Social Exclusion', in Lister, R., *Poverty*. Cambridge, UK: Polity Press, pp. 74–98.

Sen, A. (2000) *Social Exclusion: Concept, Application and Scrutiny*. Social Development Papers No. 1, Office of Environment and Social Development. Manila: Asian Development Bank.

SOCIAL INSURANCE

> Related entries: Benefit; Beveridgian welfare; Bismarckian model; Citizenship; Means testing; Needs; Selectivity; Social assistance; Universalism

Social insurance is a strategy which is concerned with insulating individuals against contingencies. Esping-Andersen (1990: 24) suggests that the social-insurance model promoted by Bismarck and von Taffe was 'a form of class politics'. Insurance payments were central to the Beveridge welfare system, which was built on the premise that people face risks as they go through life which may lead to a loss of income, and social insurance payments compensate for this. McKay and Rowlingson (2008: 307) summarize the main issues which arise with social insurance as: 'why should the state provide this service, rather than private insurance?; what risks should be covered; on what basis should contributions be made, or be deemed to be made?'.

Insurance payments are perceived as superior to assistance payments because they are rights based rather than needs based. There is a gender dimension to insurance payments in that women generally have weaker links to the labour market than men and thus are more likely to have an interrupted contribution history and may have paid lower contributions.

The Bismarckian model of social policy is mostly associated with Germany; however, it was developed in other countries including Austria, France, Italy and the Netherlands. Hinrichs and Lynch (2010) note that the United States introduced a light version in the 1930s and southern European countries followed suit between the 1960s and 1970s. Otto von Bismarck (1815–98) became Prime Minister of Prussia in 1862 and was Chancellor of the German Empire from 1887 to 1890. He is credited with introducing social insurance legislation which is based on the principle of social insurance, with an important role for employers. In 1883 he introduced health insurance and in 1884 accident insurance, followed by old age and disability pensions in 1889. Benefit schemes are related to previous earnings and occupation and the benefit system is a middle way between more socialist and residual models of welfare. The schemes are earnings related, and are concerned with maintaining one's standard of living if one has to exit the labour market. It embraces the principle of subsidiarity, which advocates that the state should only intervene as a last resort once individual and family resources are inadequate. The state, employers and trade unions are viewed as partners.

Scholarship on welfare regimes and models of welfare have focused on the Bismarckian model. Titmuss (1974), in his three-pronged model of welfare, referred to the industrial-achievement model, a system in which entitlements are earned based on contributory payments associated with one's employment. Esping-Andersen (1990: 24) refers to the social insurance model, which

> is a form of class politics. It sought, in fact, to achieve two simultaneous results in terms of stratification. The first was to consolidate divisions among wage-earners by legislating distinct programs for different class and status groups, each with its own conspicuously unique set of rights and privileges which was designed to accentuate the individual's appropriate station in life. The second objective was to tie the loyalties of the individual directly to the monarch or the central state authority. It allowed for a privileged welfare provision for the civil service.

Beveridgian is a term used to describe a particular model of welfare which emerged after the publication of *Social Insurance and Allied Services* (The Beveridge Report; Beveridge, 1942). It was the blueprint for the modern British welfare state and is commonly referred to by the name of its author William Beveridge (1879–1963), who has been described as the founding father of the welfare state. The Committee on Social Insurance and Allied Services was established in June 1941 by the British Minister of Labour to inquire into the social security system. During the Second World War an interest in welfare reform developed alongside a concern that the current system was inefficient, as a number of government departments were engaged in the administration of welfare.

The Beveridge Report proposed a 'cradle to the grave' system for all British citizens. It formed the basis of the Labour Government's (1945–51) programme for reform. It presented proposals for a national health service, family allowance, full employment and a comprehensive system of social insurance. It was seen as progress against the *five giants* of Want, Ignorance, Squalor, Idleness and Disease. It was based on three guiding principles: blending of experience of the past, comprehensive social planning, and cooperation between voluntary and public action and between the individual and the state. It designed a social insurance scheme which would provide a safety net in times when earning was interrupted, and for special events such as childbirth, marriage and death. It proposed flat rate contributions and benefits, simplification of administrative responsibility, and comprehensive coverage. It proposed guiding principles for social insurance policy. In times of sickness, retirement, unemployment and widowhood, benefits would be paid to those who had contributed. The report advocated a male-breadwinner model (Lewis, 1993: 61), which assumed the husband would participate in the labour market and earn a family wage and the wife/mother would be a carer/dependent. Colwill refers to the 'remarkably enduring influence of Beveridge Report' and 'its spectacularly successful construction of womanhood in particular' (Colwill, 1994: 53).

Further reading

Esping-Andersen, G. (1990) *The Three Worlds of Welfare Capitalism*. Cambridge, UK: Polity Press.
Harris, J. (1977) *William Beveridge, a Biography*. Oxford: Clarendon Press.

SOCIAL JUSTICE

Related entries: Citizenship; Equality; Needs

Justice is a term that is used in common discourse, usually understood as fairness; it is often discussed in relation to the judicial process. Social justice is a broader term and has received considerable attention by social policy scholars. Sen (2009: 2) suggests that 'central to the idea of justice, is that we can have a strong sense of injustice on many different grounds, and yet not agree on one particular ground as being the dominant reason for the diagnosis of injustice'.

Sen traces the historical interest in justice pointing to two different approaches. The first he associates with Hobbes, Rousseau, Locke and Kant, which concentrated on the institutional arrangements in society, which he refers to as 'transcendental injustice' (Sen, 2009: 5). This is the social contract approach. The comparative approaches concerned with social realization he associates with Adam Smith, the Marquis de Condorcet, Jeremy Bentham, Mary Wollstonecraft, Karl Marx and John Stuart Mill, and these approaches were concerned with the removal of injustice as it existed.

Sen is concerned with injustice. 'Injustices relate often enough to hardy social divisions, linked with divisions of class, gender, rank, location, religion, community and other established barriers' (Sen, 2009: 389). Sen is also concerned with global justice, and global democracy. His focus is on social realizations, what actually happens, and on comparative issues of enhancement of justice. He draws on social choice theory and concentrates on capabilities. The focus is on a person's ability and freedom to do or be something.

Sen (2009) argues that we are moved to action by the idea of remedial injustices and a sense of manifest injustices and suggests that what animates us about justice and injustice is central to a theory of justice. He draws on non-western beliefs, Indian intellectual history and western thought and suggests that justice is concerned with fairness, responsibility, duty, goodness and rightness. Understanding involves reasoning and perceptions and feelings which we must take them into account without being overwhelmed by them. Assessing ethical and political concepts such as justice and injustice involves reasoning. Critical assessment of the grounds on which judgements about justice are based involve concepts of freedoms, capabilities, resources, happiness and well-being. He acknowledges the special relevance of diverse considerations that figure under the general headings of equality and liberty and the evident connection between pursuing justice and seeking democracy. He suggests that the principles of justice are defined not in terms of institutions, but rather in terms of lives and freedoms of the people involved. Institutions play a significant role in the pursuit of justice along with the determinants of individual and social behaviour and an appropriate choice of institutions has a critically important place in the enterprise of enhancing justice. Democracy has to be judged not only by institutions but by the extent to which different voices from diverse sections of the people can be heard.

The Commission on Social Justice presents four principles of social justice, based on a basic belief in the intrinsic worth of every human being: the foundation of a free society is the equal worth of all its citizens; as a right of citizenship everyone should be able to meet their basic needs; the right to self-respect and personal autonomy demands the widest possible spread of opportunities; and not all inequalities are unjust, but unjust inequalities should be reduced and, where possible, eliminated (Commission on Social Justice, 1994: 16). The Commission decided that there is a concept of 'social justice' linked to equality, sometimes to need, entitlement, merit and desert. The Commission suggests that justice is perceived to have something to do with equality, but asks equality for what, and argues that not all inequalities are unjust.

Loizou (1997) suggests that social justice is related to equality. It is associated with both rights and liberty. What makes a policy just rather than unjust? What makes distribution of resources just rather than unjust? Does it always mean equality of distribution? What do we mean when we speak of equality? Spicker (2008: 88) outlines two perceptions of justice: Platonic and Aristotelian. Platonic justice, associated with Rawls, is what reasonable people should do. The Aristotelian view sees justice in terms of proportion: corrective justice is when punishment fits the crime, and distributive justice is when people have resources in proportion to accepted criteria, such as desert or needs. Nozick (1974) in *Anarchy State and Utopia* was against social policy striving for equality, for example through taxation, as continual interference in people's lives to redistribute will undermine liberty.

Rawls (1971) views justice as fairness. He imagines a hypothetical scenario in which a group of self-interested rational actors are under a *veil of ignorance*, that is, they do not know their own identity. Thus, in striving for the 'original position', no personal agendas will be pursued. The intention is that individuals will arrive at principles of justice which favour no group, and this is genuine equal opportunity: all interpretations of justice will be considered and some inequality will be accepted as promoting the interests of all. In relation to the distribution of limited resources, inequalities must benefit the weakest and negotiators will ensure that access to jobs is genuinely open to all.

Rawls presents two principles of justice. First, each person is to have an equal right to the most extensive total system of equal basic liberties compatible with a similar system of liberty for all. Second, social and economic inequalities are to be arranged so that they are both (1) to the greatest benefit of the least advantaged, and (2) attached to offices and positions open to all under conditions of fair equality.

Regarding the second principle, the greatest benefit to the least advantaged, if this delivers more resources then the poorest will not resent the richest and this will ensure social cohesion. There will be a balance between free market and government regulation of economy.

Further reading

Rawls, J. (1971) *A Theory of Justice*. London: Sage.
Sen, A. (2009) *The Idea of Justice*. London: Allen Lane.
Loizou, A. (1997) 'Social Justice and Social Policy', in Lavalette, M. and Pratt, A. (eds.), *Social Policy: A Conceptual and Theoretical Introduction*. London: Sage, pp. 163–181.

SOCIAL POLICY

Related entries: Social administration

Social Policy is an academic subject. It is one of the social sciences. It has been described as a field of study rather than as a discipline. It originated in Britain at the end of the nineteen century in line with an increased concern with social problems as a result of industrialization and urbanization.

Social Administration, as it was initially called, was first taught in the London School of Economics (LSE), where the first Department of Social Administration was established in 1912. It was associated with Sidney and Beatrice Webb and the Fabian Society. The focus of Social Administration was on description. In the wake of the Second World War and the development of the British welfare state, Social Policy as a field of study developed. It was associated with Richard Titmuss, who was the first Professor of Social Administration in LSE from 1950 to 1973. He viewed Social Administration as normative, that it is concerned with values: what 'ought to' happen. He developed models to help understand how policies are formulated: 'The purpose of model building is not to admire the architecture of the building but to help us see some order in all the disorder and confusion of facts, systems and choices concerning certain areas of our economic and social life' (Titmuss, 1974: 30).

During the 1970s a more critical stance emerged which viewed social administration from a structural position. This new stance was associated with Ramesh Mishra, who built on Titmuss's model building, arguing that 'models are prescriptions regarding social policy and incorporate both normative and explanatory propositions derived from wider social theories and philosophies' (Mishra, 1977: 23). Mishra's work was prophetic when he identified that models would help to develop a large body of concepts related to welfare and work which would be cumulative, would provide meaning and relevance and would

> provide an excellent vantage point; a point of departure as well as return – from
> which to examine normative and explanatory theories and a point of departure in

that they provide meaning for wider explorations, e.g. the nature of social justice, the locus of power in modern society, which otherwise remain somewhat abstract and remote from the concerns of social administration (this seems to be the case at present); a point of return in that wider normative and positive explorations, in turn, help evaluate the policy models themselves and in this way inform social choice and policy decisions.

(Mishra, 1977: 24)

Scholarship on models of welfare gathered momentum in the 1970s. Policies involve action. They are designed, formulated, implemented and evaluated. These are the focus of Social Policy as a subject. Such provision can be organized by the state, private, voluntary and informal sectors. This is known as the mixed economy of welfare or welfare pluralism. It is concerned with substantive areas best classified by Paul Spicker (2008: 1) as 'the big five': housing, health, social welfare, education and the personal social services. Social policy is designed, formulated, implemented and evaluated.

Further reading

Mishra, R. (1977) *Society and Social Policy: Theories and Practice of Welfare*. London: Macmillan.
Spicker, P. (2008) *Social Policy Themes and Approaches*, 2nd edn. Bristol: Policy Press.
Titmuss, R. (1974) *Social Policy: An Introduction*. London: Allen & Unwin.

STIGMA

> Related entries: Deserving/Undeserving; Means testing; Selectivity; Social exclusion

Stigma is something that is felt. It is a human response to a specific situation. Reisman (2001: 91) defines stigma as 'a loss of self-respect and personal dignity, a sense of guilt, of shame, of personal fault and failure. It means the sensation of second-class citizenship that results from self-discrimination'.

Robert Page (1984) explains that references to stigma were commonplace in the 1970s, both generally and in the media. The same can be said today; for example, we often hear people saying that they cannot get employment because they live in a certain area, and that there is a stigma attached to certain addresses or to a personal attribute such as sexual orientation or disability.

According to Page (1984) the term can be applied to any 'discredited' person, place, group, activity or occupation. However, Page says that the concept needs to be clarified. He refers to Titmuss (1967), who said the concept of stigma is as elusive as any other concept. Page presents a comprehensive overview of how the concept of stigma has been used in social science literature. Stigma is an emotional response to the behaviour of others. It is experienced by those who appear to breach norms. Page explains that stigma is a term used to refer to any attribute that is deeply discrediting and incongruous with our perceptions of what a given type of individual should be. He explains that the word originated from the Greek word for 'tattoo-mark', a brand made with a hot iron to show if people were devoted to a life of prayer or a life of criminality. It is an invisible mark or stain.

Page suggests that in the 1970s stigma was more likely to be associated with inferior forms of physical appearance, conduct or ethnicity. He says that stigma is generally associated with 'major norm infractions'. He draws on the scholarship of Erving Goffman (1963) in *Stigma: Notes on the Management of Spoiled Identity*; Goffman identified 'three grossly different' types of stigma: abominations of the body, which relates to any physical deformities or blemishes of individual character, including weak will; domineering or dishonest behaviour; and tribal stigma, carried through lineage.

Goffman identifies two ways in which stigma can be 'carried': discredited or discreditable. Discredited is when people assume their stigma is already apparent because it is visible to others, for example skin colour or wheelchair use. Discreditable is when a person assumes that their stigma is neither known about by those present nor immediately perceptible to them, for example sexual orientation or hearing loss. Whether people's stigmas are discredited or discreditable will determine the level of blame placed on them by others.

Page presents a taxonomy of stigma: *felt stigma* occurs when all individuals who carry stigmas are likely to experience feelings of stigma; *stigma by association* occurs when one is judged in relation to a certain reference point, for example a lone woman walking through a red light district may be perceived as a sex worker; *courtesy stigma* occurs when one is stigmatized by association with another discredited person, for example the child of a criminal. Finally, Page refers to stigma *of excellence*, which occurs when one stands out from the crowd as a result of excelling, for example 'a nerd' or a 'non-drinker'.

Page discusses the different responses to stigmatization. One response to stigma may include acceptance, for example an alcoholic may respond by seeking treatment. Another response may be rejection, for example when one becomes politicized and becomes involved in a social movement. Spicker (2008) suggests that consumer participation can reduce stigma and can enable people to express grievances and improve self-esteem.

In relation to social policy, stigma has a long history, going back to the Poor Law, when a distinction was made between deserving and undeserving. Socially constructed terms reflecting stigmatization, such as 'sturdy beggars', emerged at that time. Institutions such as Magdalene homes gave rise to such stigmatization, labelling women as penitents and offenders.

Titmuss (1967) was one of the collectivist theorists who referred to the association between selectivist (residual) payments and stigma. He favoured a collectivist response, arguing that universal, non-stigmatizing services are superior. On the other hand, residual welfare can lead to poor-quality services for poor people, in which deterrence is central and the most effective instrument, stigma, is used to induce a sense of personal fault and personal failure. Titmuss suggests that this too has repercussions for staff recruitment and is reflected in the quality of the service. He was opposed to the administration of residual services, for example the means test, arguing its goal was to keep people out, and not in.

Titmuss (1967) highlighted the relationship between social policy and stigma. He explored the effects of stigma on the take-up of means-tested benefits, the experiences of stigma resulting from social service provisions, public attitudes towards the social services, public attitudes towards the poor and welfare recipients, and the private provision of welfare and stigma.

Page (1971) suggests that the very existence of private welfare devalues public provision. Selection procedures most commonly used in the private services used criteria which stigmatized people by excluding 'bad risks'. Page explores the relationship between stigma and other welfare concepts and explores the social control function of stigma in society.

Robert Pinker perceives stigma as having a social control function and soberingly suggests that:

> the imposition of stigma is the commonest form of violence used in democratic societies. It is slow, unobtrusive and genteel in its effect. It is a highly sophisticated form of violence in so far as it is rarely associated with physical threats or attack. It can best be compared with forms of psychological torture in which the victim is broken psychically and physically but left to all outward appearances unmarked.
>
> (Pinker, 1971: 175)

Pinker agues that all studies of social welfare institutions ought to include an exploration of human sensibilities. He looks at social services as a system of social exchange in terms of their status-enhancing and stigmatizing propensities. He views social services as representing a compromise between compassion and indifference. They also reflect our dispositions to remember and forget our social obligations. He suggests that systems of unilateral exchange are less stigmatizing than bilateral exchange. People raised in a capitalist society in which competition is valued may be humiliated by any unilateral exchange when they are the recipients.

Titmuss's concern was to find ways of redistributing resources without stigma. Titmuss (1967: 121) refers to the 'stigma of the means test'. He argues: 'It is a regrettable but human fact that money (and the lack of it) is linked to personal and family self-respect'. In addition, he says that 'separate discriminatory services for poor people have always tended to be poor quality services' (*ibid.*). This is in the context of a residual system in which welfare was viewed as a burden. The primary purpose of the system and the method of discrimination was, therefore, deterrence (it was also an effective rationing device). 'To this end, the most effective instrument was to induce among recipients (children as well as adults) a sense of personal fault, of personal failure, even if the benefit was wholly or partially a compensation for disservices inflicted by society' (Titmuss, 1967: 122).

Further reading

Goffman, E. (1963) *Stigma: Notes on the Management of Spoiled Identity*. London: Prentice Hall.

Page, R. (1984) *Stigma: Concepts in Social Policy Two*. London: Routledge and Kegan Paul.
Pinker, R. (1971) *Social Theory and Social Policy*. London: Heinemann.
Reisman, D. (2001), 'Stigma' in Reisman, D., *Richard Titmuss: Welfare and Society*, 2nd edn. London: Palgrave, pp. 91–97.

STRATIFICATION

> Related entries: Social divisions

Stratification indicates a hierarchical situation. This is a result of social divisions in which one individual or group/category of people is perceived as superior to another. Giddens (2006: 295) defines social stratification as 'inequalities that exist between individuals and groups within human societies. Often we think of stratification in terms of assets or property; however, it can also occur because of other attributes, such as gender, age, religious affiliation or military rank'. Giddens explains that this can guarantee differential rewards and 'stratification can most simply be defined as structured inequalities between different groupings of people' (Giddens, 2006: 296).

Welfare systems are systems of stratification. Esping-Andersen (1990: 23) suggests that the welfare state is actively involved in ordering social relations. He suggests that welfare systems aid the maintenance of inequality and, therefore, welfare systems stratify. Although they provide welfare benefits they also produce inequality and this plays out differently in different welfare regimes.

Esping-Andersen examines the role of welfare regimes in stratifying citizens. He reveals the different levels of stratification produced by different welfare systems in different countries. He says that the effect of the state in redistributing resources to create equality in countries such as France and Germany is minuscule, whereas in some countries, for example Sweden, the state is a major player in creating equality through redistribution. He argues that increased equality in Sweden is because of welfare state intervention. Esping-Andersen reviews studies from the 1980s which look at how government policies reduce or eliminate poverty and inequality among vulnerable groups in society. In particular, he looks at income maintenance schemes to see how these produce inequality. He notes that in some countries the provision of income maintenance through state pensions reinforces old status divisions. In particular, he is talking about countries which have very generous benefits attached to employment in the civil service. On the other hand, Esping-Andersen says that some countries use income maintenance payments to nurture individualism and self-reliance, by targeting state funds only at the very needy, whereas those better off provide for their own welfare.

Esping-Andersen looks at stratification in conservative, liberal and social democratic regimes. He concludes that welfare states stratify in different ways and the differences in how they do this are related to the different conservative, liberal and social democratic, and historical legacies which exist in each country. As regards how the welfare state stratifies, the clustering patterns found by Esping-Andersen in his study of eighteen countries are remarkably similar to those identified for decommodification. Unlike with decommodification, Esping-Andersen is not looking for an overall country score of stratification. Instead, he wants to see how prevalent the characteristics associated with conservative, liberal and social democratic stratification are in each country.

Orloff (1993) in her writing on welfare regimes broadens the concept of stratification to consider the effects of social provision by the state on gender relations. She explores how state dealings with labour, both paid and unpaid, act as a stratifying factor (Orloff, 1993: 32).

Further reading

Esping-Andersen, G. (1990) *The Three Worlds of Welfare Capitalism*. Cambridge, UK: Polity Press.
Orloff, A.S. (1993) 'Gender and the Social Rights of Citizenship: The Comparative Analysis of Gender Relations and Welfare States', *American Sociological Review*, 58: 303–328.

SUSTAINABLE DEVELOPMENT

Related entries: Environmentalism; Ideology

Sustainable development as a concept was introduced by The World Commission on Environment and Development Report (WCED, 1987), known as the Brundtland Report. It introduces the three pillars of society to be economic, social and environmental. It states that sustainable development 'meets the needs of the present without compromising the ability of future generations to meet their own needs' (WCED, 1987: 43). It is concerned with equity, within and between generations, and it focuses on participation in decision making. The Brundtland Report refers to the environment as 'where we all live' and development as 'what we all do in attempting to improve our lot within that abode' (WCED, 1987: xi). It states 'each nation will have to work out its own policy objectives' (WCED, 1987: 40).

Brundtland argued that security must be sought through change which recognizes not only the need for economic development to meet human need but also the imperative to halt environmental destruction, which involves maximum community participation, empowerment and local activism. Agenda 21, a blueprint for sustainable development for the twenty-first century, was signed at the United Nations Conference on Environment and Development held in Rio de Janeiro in 1992. Local Agenda 21 involves the engagement and empowerment of local communities in working towards sustainable development. It is where local communities should be able to participate in decision making on their future and in determining what changes need to be made at a local level to work towards sustainable development. Fitzpatrick (2011b) explores the idea of sustainability. He suggests it

> is a 'portal', an entrance into a series of debates. Its meaning and implications both can and should imply a degree of openness just as the contestability of other

principles – liberty, democracy, equality – does not stop societies from valuing and trying to embody them; indeed, a wide degree of disagreement may be essential to any society claiming to *be* free, democratic or equal. It is the same with sustainability. The necessity of acting rapidly and meeting important targets should not be used to justify an illiberal, moralistic, intolerant, authoritarian approach. The principle of sustainability is, then, not an inflexible reference point and is certainly not shorthand for a 'green utopia'.

(Fitzpatrick, 2011b: 8)

Baker acknowledges the complexity of defining sustainability. She explains how 'the focus of analysis shifted from that of ecology to that of society' (Baker, 2006: 7). Baker argues that:

promoting sustainable development is about steering societal change at the interface between: the social; this relates to human mores and values, relationships and institutions. The economic: this concerns the allocation and distribution of scarce resources. The ecological: this involves the contribution of both the economic and the social and their effect on the environment and its resources.

(*ibid.*)

Fitzpatrick (2011b: 7) indicates that there is a disjunction between

what we demand of the world and what the world is capable of supplying (resources) and absorbing (pollution). If the demands we make are significantly larger than the planet's 'coping capacity' then ours is an unsustainable existence. Sustainability therefore implies reducing human demands and/or increasing the coping capacity of the earth so that this disjunction is repaired.

He argues that sustainability is multidimensional:

It implies slowing the rate of growth of emissions, halting and stabilising emissions so that global warming levels off and then reducing emissions so that global warming itself eventually reverses towards a level which can be maintained and which is not detrimental to humans, animals, future generations or to the very ecosystem itself. And sustainability is also concerned with preserving a certain stock of non-renewable natural resources and replenishing the stock of renewables.

(*ibid.*)

Stiglitz and colleagues (2009) suggest that sustainability involves the future and its assessment involves many assumptions and normative choices. This is further complicated by the fact that at least some aspects of environmental sustainability (notably climate change) are affected by interactions between the socio-economic and environmental models followed by different countries. They recommend that sustainability assessment requires a well-identified dashboard of indicators and argue that 'the assessment of sustainability is complementary to the question of current well-being or economic performance, and must be examined separately' (Stiglitz *et al.*, 2009: 36).

149

Further reading

Baker, S. (2006) *Sustainable Development*. Abingdon, UK: Routledge.
Fitzpatrick, T. (2011b) *Understanding the Environment and Social Policy*. Bristol: Policy Press.
Stiglitz, J., Sen, A. and Fitoussi, J. (2009) *Report by the Commission on the Measurement of Economic Performance and Social Progress*. Available at www.stiglitz-sen-fitoussi.fr
WCED (World Commission on Environment and Development) (1987) *Our Common Future*. Oxford: Oxford University Press.

THEORY

Related entries: Ideology; Social administration; Social policy

O'Brien and Penna (1998) suggest that we all hold theories about how the world works, with different levels of complexity: 'They are generalisations about what exists in the world around us and how the components of that world fit together into patterns . . . they generalize across actual situations our expectations and suppositions about the reasons why certain patterns exist and how we should deal with them' (O'Brien and Penna, 1998: 3). They define theory as 'a dimension of action in so far as it gives direction and meaning to what we do' (*ibid.*).

Lister (2010: 3) suggests that theory helps us make sense of the world, make connections between different social phenomena and policies, place specific issues and policies in a wider context, question assumptions underlying policies and adopt a more critical stance.

Fitzpatrick (2011a) on welfare theory writes about its use in enabling us to achieve both transcendence and immanence. It enables us 'to transcend our immediate contexts, to look beyond the particular, the apparent, the visible; we understand the social world by trying to look at it from the outside' (Fitzpatrick, 2011a: 3). With regard to 'immanence', Fitzpatrick suggests that 'rather than transcending our contexts, theorizing enables us to delve into those contexts still further: we understand the world by looking at it from the inside' (Fitzpatrick, 2011a: 4).

O'Brien and Penna (1998) suggest that to understand social policy we need to be conscious of theory in two senses. They differentiate between a theory of social welfare and a social theory of welfare. The former is concerned with the distribution of resources and opportunities; social patterns and access, participation, exclusion and support; and contributions to, and undermining of, individual and collective well-being. On the other hand, a social theory of welfare is concerned with how the organization of social relations (exclusions, centralizations, marginalizations, liberations and oppressions) comes to express particular patterns. What are the social forces and struggles that come to underpin those exclusions, inclusions and distributions? This, they say, is the distinction between normative theory and social theory. The second type of theory, they argue, points to interconnections between welfare, economic and social change, and O'Brien and Penna are concerned with this type of theory in their book. They are interested in the role of the state in economic and social affairs and this depends on the ideology held (which will be reflected in perceptions regarding the private market, the role of family and the distribution of resources within society).

Further reading

Fitzpatrick, T. (2011a) *Welfare Theory: An Introduction to the Theoretical Debates in Social Policy*, 2nd edn. London: Palgrave Macmillan.
Lister, R. (2010) *Understanding Theories and Concepts in Social Policy*. Bristol: Policy Press.
O'Brien, M. and Penna, S. (1998) *Theorising Welfare: Enlightenment and Modern Society*. London: Blackwell.

UNIVERSALITY

Related entries: Citizenship; Needs; Selectivity; Stigma

Universality is a strategy of redistribution. It is concerned with non-means-tested benefits, based on rights as opposed to needs, and is generally perceived as less stigmatizing than selectivist (means-tested) payments.

One of the aims of universality is to make

> services available and accessible to the whole population in such ways as would not involve users in any humiliating loss of status, dignity or self-respect. There should be no sense of inferiority, pauperism, shame or stigma in the use of a publicly provided service; no attribution that one was being or becoming a public burden. Hence the emphasis on the social rights of all citizens to use or not use as responsible people the services made available by the community in respect of certain needs which the private market and the family were unable or unwilling to provide universally. If these services were not provided for everybody they would either not be available at all or only for those who could afford them, and for others on such terms as would involve the infliction of a sense of inferiority and stigma.

According to Titmuss, 'avoidance of stigma was not, of course, the only reason for the development of the twin concepts of social rights and universalism'. Titmuss suggests 'welfare was summoned to prevent waste' and points to four of the universalist social services: retirement pensions, the health service, unemployment insurance and school meals. Titmuss suggests that although the concept appears simple the practice is 'immensely complex'. Titmuss provides an analytical framework to investigate universal strategies. There are three central issues: what is the nature of the entitlement to use (legal, contractual, contributory, functional, discretionary or professionally determined); who is entitled and on what conditions (individual/family characteristics, group, territorial, social-biological, variable, arbitrary, discretionary); what methods (financial, administrative) are employed in the determination of the access, utilization, allocation and payment? Titmuss says that then we have to reflect on the nature of the service or benefit and the functions they aim to fulfil. Lister (2008: 238) remarks that 'totally universal, unconditional citizenship benefits are rare'.

Reddin (1978) completed a comprehensive study of universalist and selectivist payments on behalf of the National Economic and Social Council (NESC). It addressed the role of the citizen as taxpayer and the citizen as recipient. Reddin suggests the attractions of universality and selectivity can be understood only in the context of a specific time, a specific context, and any discussion of universality and selectivity must involve a discussion of sources of finance, forms of finance, utilization (how much/ by whom), sense of time, how long financing will take and how long benefit will be paid/received. This involves evaluating the impact of policy, measuring the outcome of policy choices and avoiding presumptions that events subsequent to a policy act are necessarily its consequences. He argues that there is a need to acknowledge unintended consequences, for example underutilization, identification and the claiming process (by agencies, by self) income and the unit to be tested, and issues associated with dependants.

Reddin identifies four important dimensions of redistributive strategies: (1) what benefits are provided; (2) to whom are they directed; (3) to what extent are they used by those at whom they are directed; and (4) who pays and how do they pay? He discusses whether there is a distributional incentive and the effects of the way in which costs are met and for how long. He is concerned with changes that occur over time for those who pay and those who receive and with how those who pay judge those who benefit and how those who benefit judge those who pay.

Further reading

Lister, R. (2008) 'Citizenship and Access to Welfare', in Alcock, P., May, M. and Rowlingson, K. (eds.), *The Student's Companion to Social Policy*. Oxford: Blackwell, pp. 234–240.
Reddin, M. (1978) *Universality and Selectivity: Strategies in Social Policy*. Dublin: NESC.
Reisman, D. (2001) *Richard Titmuss: Welfare and Society*, 2nd edn. London: Palgrave.
Titmuss, R. (1967) Lecture delivered at the *British National Conference on Social Welfare*, London, April 1967, and published in *Proceedings of the Conference*. This extract from Titmuss, R. (1968) *Commitment to Welfare*. London: Allen & Unwin, pp. 128–137.

WAGES

Related entries: Capitalism; Occupational welfare

Wages is money paid for labour. *Minimum wage* is when legislation exists guaranteeing workers a certain amount per hour. It can be controversial, with some seeing it as an obstacle to employment growth and others seeing it as an important protection for workers. Minimum wage is the lowest hourly, daily or monthly remuneration that employers may legally pay to workers. Although minimum wage laws are in effect in many jurisdictions, there are differences of opinion about the benefits and drawbacks of a minimum wage. Supporters of minimum wage argue that it improves the standard of living of workers and reduces poverty. Opponents say that it increases unemployment and forces employers to raise the prices of their products. It can lead to unemployment if employers relocate to areas where labour is cheaper.

Eighteen European countries have some kind of statutory national minimum wage (in a similar way to non-European countries, such as Canada, Japan and the USA). This group is made up of nine of the 'old' EU 15 Member States (Luxembourg and Portugal also have statutory national minimum wages) and all of the 10 new Member States, apart from Cyprus, which has a statutory minimum wage for a few specific occupations only. Whereas France, Greece, Portugal, Spain and the Benelux countries have a long tradition of protecting pay at the bottom of the labour market in this way, Ireland and the UK introduced national minimum wage systems only in the late 1990s. In Austria, Denmark, Finland, Germany, Italy and Sweden – the remaining six 'old' EU Member States – as well as in Norway and Cyprus, collective agreements are the main mechanism used for regulating low pay.

Wages for housework was a campaign associated with Selma James and Mariarosa Dalla Costa. They launched the *domestic labour debate* by spelling out how housework and other caring work women do outside the market is central to the market economy. In 1972 James founded the International Wages for Housework Campaign, which demands money from the state for the unwaged work in the home and in the community.

Further reading

James, S. and Della Costa, M. (1972) *The Power of Women and the Subversion of the Community*. Bristol: Falling Wall Press.

WELFARE REGIMES

> **Related entries: Comparative social policy; Models of welfare; Welfare state**

Welfare regimes is a term that has become widespread in social policy scholarship since 1990. Esping-Andersen (1990: 32) argued 'when we focus on the principles embedded in welfare states, we discover distinct regime-clusters, not merely variations of "more" or "less" around a common denominator'. Orloff (2010: 253) refers to regime types or worlds of welfare capitalism 'in which variation was conceptualized as qualitative and multi-dimensional, resulting in clusters of countries with similar characteristics; these shifts were often also historicizing-emphasizing conjectures, sequencing, turning points, and path dependency'.

A vast scholarship on families, regimes and clusters has developed. Arts and Gelissen (2010: 569) state: 'we can identify patterns (or "worlds" or "regimes" or "families") through which to identify groups of welfare states that share similar features persisting over time'. They give a succinct overview of scholarship on welfare regimes since Esping-Andersen's classic text. They suggest that since then 'a voluminous literature focusing on the construction of welfare state models has emerged' (Arts and Gelissen, 2010: 572). They identify in the alternative typologies four criticisms of Esping-Andersen's work: his neglect of the gender dimension; the misspecification of the Mediterranean welfare states; the labelling of the Antipodean welfare states as liberal; and finally the failure to recognize the contribution of employers to welfare state development. They present an overview of scholars who have questioned the empirical robustness of welfare state models (Arts and Gelissen, 2010: 575–576). Arts and Gelissen question whether welfare regimes in the developing world can be classified into regime types and they focus some attention on Asia, Latin America and Eastern Europe.

Castles and Mitchell (1993) identify four families of nations. These are: an English-speaking family of nations including Australia, Canada, Ireland, New Zealand, the United Kingdom and the United States; a Continental family of nations consisting of Austria, Belgium, France, Germany, Italy and the Netherlands; a Scandinavian family of nations consisting of Denmark, Finland, Norway and Sweden; and a southern family of nations comprising Greece, Portugal and Spain. Castles (2010a) further interrogates differences between English-speaking nations.

The Nordic countries are studied by Kautto (2010), explaining that after the Second World War Scandinavian countries were seen as a third way between state socialism and unregulated capitalism. Kautto asks if the Nordic model ever existed, and if so what are its characteristics, are its features and outcomes desirable and, if it still exists, can it survive?

Ferrera (2010) explores literature on the southern European countries. Looking at Spain, Portugal, Greece and Italy, he reviews scholarship which has tried to classify these particular states as a family. He suggests that in the latter half of the twentieth century those countries have become modernized and 'have gradually "caught up" with the more advanced European countries and are now fully part of the group of rich and stable democracies' (Ferrera, 2010: 627). However, in the light of the current economic recession this may prove to change. Gal (2010) refers to the extended family of welfare states, in which he includes Cyprus, Greece, Israel, Italy, Malta, Spain, Portugal and Turkey.

Huber and Bogliaccini (2010) discuss the origins and development of Latin American welfare states and investigate more recent reforms, exploring why some regimes are more effective than others and consider evidence on the impact of programmes in different countries. Peng and Wong (2010) explore the development of welfare regimes in East Asia and look at scholarship on the economic success there. They focus on common global challenges for welfare regimes throughout the world.

Further reading

Castles, F. (2010a) 'The English-Speaking Countries', in Castles, F., Leibfried, S., Lewis, J., Obinger, H. and Pierson, C. (eds.), *The Oxford Handbook of the Welfare State*. Oxford: Oxford University Press, pp. 630–642.

Ferrera, M. (2010) 'The Southern European Countries', in Castles, F., Leibfried, S., Lewis, J., Obinger, H. and Pierson, C. (eds.), *The Oxford Handbook of the Welfare State*. Oxford: Oxford University Press, pp. 616–629.

Gal, J. (2010) 'Is There an Extended Family of Mediterranean Welfare States?', *Journal of European Social Policy*, 20(4): 283–300.

Huber, E. and Bogliaccini, J. (2010) 'Latin America', in Castles, F., Leibfried, S., Lewis, J., Obinger, H. and Pierson, C. (eds.), *The Oxford Handbook of the Welfare State*. Oxford: Oxford University Press, pp. 644–655.

Kautto, M. (2010) 'The Nordic Countries', in Castles, F., Leibfried, S., Lewis, J., Obinger, H. and Pierson, C. (eds.), *The Oxford Handbook of the Welfare State*. Oxford: Oxford University Press, pp. 586–600.

Peng, I. and Wong, J. (2010) 'East Asia', in Castles, F., Leibfried, S., Lewis, J., Obinger, H. and Pierson, C. (eds.), *The Oxford Handbook of the Welfare State*. Oxford: Oxford University Press, pp. 656–670.

Powell, M. and Barrientos, A. (2004) 'Welfare Regimes and the Welfare Mix', *European Journal of Political Research* 43: 83–105.

WELFARE STATE

Related entries: Capitalism; Globalization; Social administration; Social policy; Welfare regimes

---

The welfare state is a term used widely but often without definition. Titmuss (1962: 49) states that 'The welfare state has evolved as a particular manifestation of western democratic societies', and he attributes the term to William Temple, Archbishop of Canterbury, in 1941. He indicates that it was founded in wartime debate in the Atlantic Charter and the Four Freedoms: freedom of speech, freedom of religion, freedom from want and freedom from fear. Although all welfare states are welfare systems, not all welfare systems are welfare states. This is because there is generally a mixed economy of welfare or welfare pluralism.

Briggs defines a welfare state as:

> a state in which organised power is deliberately used (through politics and administration) in an effort to modify the play of market forces in at least three directions – first, by guaranteeing individuals and families a minimum income irrespective of the market value of their work or their property; second, by narrowing the extent of insecurity by enabling individuals and families to meet certain 'social contingencies' (for example, sickness, old age and unemployment) which lead otherwise to individual and family crises; and third, by ensuring that all citizens without distinction of status or class are offered the best standards available in relation to a certain agreed range of social services.
>
> (Briggs, 2000: 180)

Briggs differentiates between a welfare state and a social state 'in which communal resources are employed to abate poverty and to assist those in distress'. The welfare state goes a step further in that 'it is concerned not merely with abatement of class differences or the needs of scheduled groups but with equality of treatment and the aspirations of citizens as voters with equal shares of electoral power' (Briggs, 2000: 18).

Kuhlne and Sander (2010: 67) trace the historical development of welfare states in an international context. They suggest that the emergence of welfare states reflect an increased acceptance of collective responsibility for social problems.

Flora and Alber (1981) present a historical comparison of twelve European countries and show that social insurance for industrial accidents was introduced first, with unemployment insurance introduced last. Thirty-two countries had schemes for industrial accident by the end of the First World War and eighteen had some kind of sickness insurance. Germany (1883), Norway (1909), the UK (1911) and the Netherlands (1913) were pioneers of compulsory schemes. After the First World War more state intervention was accepted (less liberal). In the inter-war years, state social insurance and protection was extended in terms of the scope of risks and coverage of the population and increase in compulsory provision. Social security principles were increasingly part of social and economic policies after the First World War and there was a shift from relief to rights. Rights as important in avoiding class conflict was a rationale. Along with a growing labour movement came social rights as an aspect of democracy. Social policy issues shaped election campaigns and the state increasingly took on the role of protector and provider.

The Great Depression led to more reforms with more groups compulsorily covered and for broader risks. The International Labour Organization (ILO) in 1919 (www.ilo.org) spread the idea of minimum social standards, created as part of the Treaty of Versailles, in the belief that through justice peace could be accomplished. The First World War led to the diffusion, expansion and consolidation of social insurance schemes. The ILO provided international best practice and was a storehouse for statistics, documentation and legislation.

Mishra (1984: 6) refers to the foundations of the British post-war welfare state based on the two pillars of Keynesianism economics and the Beveridge model of social insurance. The former encouraged state intervention to ensure a high level of economic activity, the economic component of the welfare state, and the social component was the Beveridge notion of social insurance.

Further reading

Kuhlne, S. and Sander, A. (2010) 'The Emergence of the Welfare State', in Castles, F., Leibfried, S., Lewis, J., Obinger, H. and Pierson, C. (eds.) *The Oxford Handbook of the Welfare State*. Oxford: Oxford University Press, pp. 61–80.

Titmuss, R. (1962) 'The Welfare State: Images and Realities. Lecture at the University of California (1962)', in Alcock, P., Glennerster, H., Oakley, A. and Sinfield, A. (eds.) (2001), *Welfare and Wellbeing: Richard Titmuss's Contribution to Social Policy*. Bristol: Policy Press, pp. 49–58.

WELFARE/WELL-BEING

> Related entries: Health; Quality of life

Welfare is generally used in a positive sense as if it is understood that welfare is worth promoting. It can refer to individuals or groups. Welfare is often the focus of social policy. 'There are few words used as inconsistently as welfare' (Deacon, 2002: 4). It can be used in connection with other concepts, for example state, regime, provision. It is linked with ideological beliefs about who is responsible for welfare.

Richard Titmuss (1967) defines welfare as all publicly provided and subsidized services, statutory, occupational and fiscal. Fitzpatrick (2011a: 1) uses welfare and well-being interchangeably, referring to 'faring well' and 'being well'. He suggests that, unlike happiness, welfare is concerned with a more long-term condition, a general state associated with security. This can be in relation to security of income, employment or housing and provides a certain confidence that the security is sustainable over time. It implies a foreknowledge that one's circumstances are not going to decline for the foreseeable future. Fitzpatrick indicates that many social policy commentators equate welfare with need fulfilment.

There is an extensive literature on well-being across a range of disciplines. In the UK an index of child well-being has been drawn up by the UK government (http://www.communities.gov.uk/publications/communities/childwellbeing 2009).

Shah and Marks (2004: 2) state that well-being is 'more than just happiness. As well as feeling satisfied and happy, well-being means developing as a person, being fulfilled, and making a contribution to the community'. They continue: 'one of the key aims of a democratic government is to promote the good life; a flourishing society where citizens are happy, healthy, capable, and engaged, in other works with high levels of well-being' (Shah and Marks, 2004: 4).

Stiglitz and colleagues (2009: 21) recognize that although Gross Domestic Product (GDP) is the most widely used measure of economic activity it measures market production and has erroneously been treated as if it were a measure of economic well-being. They argue that conflating the two can lead to misleading indications about how well-off people are, and can entail the wrong policy decisions. They suggest that a multidimensional definition of well-being is necessary and should include the following dimensions, which should be considered simultaneously. These are material living standards (income, consumption and wealth); health; education; personal activities including work; political voice and governance; social connections and relationships; environment (present and future conditions); and insecurity, of an economic as well as a physical nature (Stiglitz *et al.*, 2010: 14). They conclude that 'all these dimensions shape people's well-being, and yet many of them are missed by conventional income measures' (Stiglitz *et al.*, 2010: 15). They suggest that both objective and subjective dimensions of well-being are important.

The National Economic and Social Council (NESC) offers the following definition of well-being:

a person's well-being relates to their physical, social and mental state. It requires that basic needs are met, that people have a sense of purpose, and that they feel able to achieve important goals, to participate in society and to live the lives they value and have reason to value. People's well-being is enhanced by conditions that include financial and personal security, meaningful and rewarding work, supportive personal relationships, strong and inclusive communities, good health, a healthy and attractive environment, and values of democracy and social justice. Public policy's role is to bring about these conditions by placing the individual at the centre of policy development and delivery, by assessing the risks facing him/her, and ensuring the supports are available to address those risks at key stages in his/her life.

(NESC, 2009: xiv)

In applying this definition, NESC (2009: xiv) focuses on six domains of well-being, on which a certain amount of data are available. These are economic resources, work and participation, relationships and care, community and environment, health, and democracy and values. All of these domains are interconnected and are important for a person's well-being. The emphasis given to each may depend on an individual's particular circumstances or the situation in which they find themselves.

NESC (2009: xix) suggests there are a number of lessons which have emerged from the review of well-being, summarized as follows.

First of all, at the most fundamental level having a level of income to meet basic needs matters. This level of income is contingent both on the standard of living in the society within which one is living, as well as the distribution of income, as people compare their income levels with those around them. It is also known that although loss of income can lead to a reduction in well-being in the short term, people do readjust to their new financial circumstances.

NESC (2009: xx) suggests

the fundamental elements which contribute to long-term well-being include participation in meaningful activity, along with affectionate and caring relationships, a secure, safe and attractive environment, good social relations, and good health. The context matters and the situations within which people find themselves can contribute to or detract from their well-being. These situations include their socio-economic circumstances and the values of the society within which they live. The operation of democracy, trustworthy institutions, standards of transparency and openness, acceptance and support for diversity, and principles of equality have been found to be conducive to well-being.

NESC (2009: xxi) outlines a 'well-being test' based on a developmental perspective. It suggests that by focusing on *capability* we are paying attention to what an individual can do rather than what they cannot do. Thus, we would focus on the developmental potential of all people from an early age: from pre-education, through the education system and into life-long learning.

It is concerned with *agency* as an important component of well-being, acknowledging the importance of empowering people and the importance of people having a purpose in life. They also recognize the importance of relationships for people. In empowering people and taking into account their views, appropriate and tailored services can be provided, with the individual also taking responsibility for their needs in conjunction with service providers. NESC (2009) reviews in considerable detail the philosophical approaches to well-being.

The capabilities approach advocated by Amartya Sen is informed by the eudaimonic concept of well-being. Sen's basic proposition is that we should evaluate development and progress as 'the expansion of the "capabilities" of people to lead the kind of lives they value – and have reason to value' (Sen, 1999: 18). Sen also draws on Adam Smith's analysis of 'necessities' and 'conditions of living', emphasizing in particular the ability to 'appear in public without shame' in relation to the society within which one is living (Sen, 1999: 73). Sen acknowledges that, although income and wealth are important, 'leading the kinds of lives we have reason to value' requires much more, and he focuses on the development and expansion of the 'capabilities' of people:

> without ignoring the importance of economic growth, we must look beyond it . . . attention is thus paid to the expansion of 'capabilities' . . . these capabilities can be enhanced by public policy, but also, on the other side, the direction of public policy can be influenced by the effective use of participatory capabilities by the public. The *two-way relationship* is central.
>
> (Sen, 1999: 18, italics in original)

Further reading

Stiglitz, J., Sen, A. and Fitoussi, J. (2009) *Report by the Commission on the Measurement of Economic Performance and Social Progress*. Available at http://www.stiglitz-sen-fitoussi.fr, www. communities.gov.uk/publications/communities/childwellbeing2009

NESC (National Economic and Social Council) (2009) *Well-Being Matters: A Social Report for Ireland*. Report Number: 119 volumes 1 and 2. Dublin: NESC.

WORK–LIFE BALANCE

Related entries: Care; Gender; Labour

Work–life balance refers to striving for a balance between 'work' as in paid work, or a career, and, on the other hand, 'life', referring to personal, private relationships and activities. It is associated with more flexible work patterns, including flexi-time and flexi-place. It is a concept employed by the European Commission.

EurLIFE is an interactive database on quality of life in Europe developed by the European Foundation for Living and Working Conditions (Eurofound). It collates data drawn from surveys and other published sources on the amount of time individuals spend on family activities, sports, social activities, cultural activities and relaxation.

It provides comparisons between countries on issues relating to the employment situation, living and working conditions, family and community life, health and housing in twenty-eight countries in Europe.

In relation to the reconciliation of work and family life, the survey finds increasing support for more flexible working time arrangements. The European Company Survey provides data on why and how companies make use of a broad variety of working time arrangements, such as full- and part-time work, overtime, flexi-time, shift work, phased and early retirement and childcare leave arrangements (http://www.eurofound.europa.eu/areas/industrialrelations/dictionary/definitions/WORKLIFEBA).

Every five years, Eurofound conducts a survey to study working conditions in Europe; the European Working Conditions Fieldwork for the fifth EWCS (European Working Conditions Survey) took place from January to June 2010, with almost 44,000 workers interviewed in the EU27, Norway, Croatia, the former Yugoslav Republic of Macedonia, Turkey, Albania, Montenegro and Kosovo. It found that almost one fifth of European workers are having difficulties achieving a satisfactory work–life balance, a slight decrease since 2000. It showed that although work–life balance continues to be a key element of the European Employment Strategy in facilitating individuals' entering and remaining in the workforce and in facilitating greater gender equality, there is a rise in the number of households in which both partners work and this has shifted work–life balance higher up the agenda, this being reflected also in the organization of the workplace. Overall, 18 per cent of workers in the EU27 are not satisfied with their work–life balance, a marginal decrease since 2000. Although men are most likely to experience problems with their work–life balance in the middle of their careers (between the ages of 30 and 49), women are less likely to experience dissatisfaction, but experience it on a constant, ongoing basis over the course of their careers. Given that women still do most household and caring work, this may seem somewhat surprising. However, many more women than men adapt their working lives to facilitate domestic demands by engaging in more flexible work. This may reduce the conflict they experience from two opposing sets of demands.

Further reading

http://www.eurofound.europa.eu/areas/industrialrelations/dictionary/definitions/
    WORKLIFEBA

BIBLIOGRAPHY

Abel-Smith, B. and Townsend, P. (1965) *The Poor and the Poorest*. London: Bell.

Ahmed, A.I. (2007) 'Consensual Poverty in Britain, Sweden and Bangladesh: A Comparative Study', *Bangladesh e–Journal of Sociology*, 4(2): 56–77.

Alber, J. (1995) 'A Framework for the Study of the Social Services', *Journal of European Social Policy*, 5(2): 131–149.

Alcock, C., Payne, S. and Sullivan, M. (2000) *Introducing Social Policy*. Harlow: Prentice Hall.

Alcock, P., Glennester, H., Oakley, A. and Sinfield, A. (2001) *Welfare and Wellbeing, Richard Titmuss's Contribution to Social Policy*. Bristol: Policy Press.

Alcock, C., Daly, G. and Griggs, E. (2008a) *Introducing Social Policy*, 2nd edn. Edinburgh: Pearson.

Alcock, P., May, M. and Rowlingson, K. (2008b) *The Student's Companion to Social Policy*, 3rd edn. Oxford: Blackwell.

Anderies, J.M., Folke, C., Ostrom, E. and Walker, B. (2012) *Aligning Key Concepts for Global Change Policy: Robustness, Resilience, and Sustainability*. CSID Working Paper Series No. CSID–2012–002, Center for the Study of Institutional Diversity, Arizona State University, Tempe, AZ. Available at http://hdl.handle.net/10535/8063

Arts, W.A. and Gelissen, J. (2010) 'Models of the Welfare State', in Castles, F., Leibfried, S., Lewis, J., Obinger, H. and Pierson, C. (eds.), *The Oxford Handbook of the Welfare State*. Oxford: Oxford University Press, pp. 569–584.

Bahle, T., Pfeifer, M. and Wendt, C. (2010) 'Social Assistance', in Castles, F., Leibfried, S., Lewis, J., Obinger, H. and Pierson, C. (eds.), *The Oxford Handbook of the Welfare State*. Oxford: Oxford University Press, pp. 448–461.

Baker, J., Lynch, K., Cantillon, S. and Walsh J. (2004) *Equality from Theory to Action*. London: Palgrave.

Baker, S. (2006) *Sustainable Development*. Abingdon, UK: Routledge.

Bambra, C. (2005a) 'Health Status and the Worlds of Welfare', *Social Policy & Society*, 5(1): 53–62.

Bambra, C. (2005b) 'Cash versus Services: "Worlds of Welfare" and the Decommodification of Cash Benefits and Health Services', *Journal of Social Policy*, 34(2): 195–213.

Banton, M. (1993) *Racial and Ethnic Competition*. Cambridge, UK: Cambridge University Press.

Baptiste, I. (2001) 'Educating Lone Wolves: Pedagogical Implications of Human Capital Theory', *Adult Education Quarterly*, 51: 184–201.

Barnes, C. (2011) 'Understanding Disability and the Importance of Design for All', *Journal of Accessibility and Design for All*, 1(1): 54–79.

Barrett, M. (1980) *Women's Oppression Today: The Marxist/Feminist Encounter*. London: Verso.

Barrett, M. and McIntosh, M. (1982) *The Anti-social Family*. London: Verso.

Barrett, M. and McIntosh, M. (1991) *The Anti-social Family*. London: Verso.

Barth, F. (ed.) (1969) *Ethnic Groups and Boundaries: The Social Organisation of Cultural Difference*. London: Allen & Unwin.

Bartlett, W. (1991) *Quasi-markets and Contracts: A Market and Hierarchies Perspective on NHS Reform*. Bristol: School for Advanced Urban Studies.

Basic Income Studies, http://www.degruyter.com/view/j/bis

Bayley, M. (1973) *Mental Handicap and Community Care*. London: Routledge and Kegan Paul.

Beasley, C. (1999) *What Is Feminism? An Introduction to Feminist Theory*. London: Sage.

Beasley, C. (2005) *Gender and Sexuality*. London: Sage.

Beck, U. (1992) *Risk Society: Towards a New Modernity*. London: Sage.

Beck, W., van der Maesen, L. Thomése and Walker, A. (2001) *Social Quality: A Vision for Europe*. The Hague: Kluwer Law International.

Becker, G.S. (1975) *Human Capital: A Theoretical and Empirical Analysis, with Special Reference to Education*, 2nd edn. New York: Columbia University Press.

Becker, G.S. (1991) *Treatise on the Family*, 2nd edn. Cambridge, MA: Harvard University Press.

Beveridge, W. (1942) *Social Insurance and Allied Services* (Beveridge Report). London: HMSO.

Blakemore, K. (1998) *Social Policy and Introduction*. Buckingham: Open University Press.

Bloch, A. (2008) 'Migrants and Asylum-Seekers', in Alcock, P., May M. and Rowlingson, K. (eds.), *The Student's Companion to Social Policy*. Oxford: Blackwell, pp. 410–417.

Blumkin, T., Margalioth, Y. and Sadka, E. (2010) *Taxing Children: The Re-distributive Role of Child Benefits – Revisited*. CESIFO Working Paper No. 2970. Available at http://www.cesifo-group.org/wpt

Bochel, H., Bochel, C., Page, R. and Sykes, R. (2009) *Social Policy: Themes, Issues and Debates*, 2nd edn. Harlow: Pearson.

Booth, C. (1889–91) *Life and Labour of the People*, 1st edn, 2 vols.

Booth, C. (1892–7) *Life and Labour of the People in London*, 2nd edn, 9 vols.

Booth, C. (1902–3) *Life and Labour of the People in London*, 3rd edn, 17 vols.

Bosanquet, N. (1983) *After the New Right*. London: Heinemann.

Bradshaw, J. (1972) 'The Concept of Social Need', *New Society*, 30: 640–643.

Briggs, A. (2000) 'The Welfare State in Historical Perspective', in Pierson, C. and Castles, F.G. (eds.), *The Welfare State Reader*. Cambridge, UK: Polity Press, pp. 16–29.

Budig, M.J., Misra, J. and Böckmann, I. (2012) 'The Motherhood Penalty in Cross-National Perspective: The Importance of Work–Family Policies and Cultural Attitudes', *Social Politics*, 19(2): 163–193.

Burchardt, T. and Vizard, P. (2009) *Research Report 18: Developing an Equality Measurement Framework: A List of Substantive Freedoms for Adults and Children*. Centre for Analysis of Social Exclusion, London School of Economics. Available at http://www.equalityhuman-rights.com

Burchardt, T., Le Grand, J. and Piachaud, D. (2002) 'Introduction', in Hills, J., Le Grand, J. and Piachaud, D. (eds.), *Understanding Social Exclusion*. Oxford: Oxford University Press, pp. 1–12.

Burstrum, B., Whitehead, M., Clayton, S. and Fritzell, S. (2010) 'Health Inequalities between Lone and Couple Mothers and Policy under Different Welfare Regimes: The Example of Italy, Sweden and Britain', *Social Science and Medicine*, 70(6): 912–920.

Byrne, D. (2005) *Social Exclusion*. Milton Keynes: Open University Press.

Callister, P. (2005) 'Ethnicity Measures, Intermarriage and Social Policy', *Social Policy Journal of New Zealand Te Puna Whakaaro*. Available at http://www.msd.govt.nz/about-msd-and-our-work/publications-resources/journals-and-magazines/social-policyjournal/spj23/index.html

Carabine, J. (1996a) 'Heterosexuality and Social Policy', in Richardson, D. (ed.), *Theorising Heterosexuality*. Milton Keynes: Open University Press, pp. 55–74.

Carabine, J. (1996b) 'Constructing Women: Women's Sexuality and Social Policy', in Taylor, D. (ed.), *Critical Social Policy*. London: Sage, pp. 113–126.

Carabine, J. (1996c) 'Empowering Sexualities', in Humphries, B. (ed.), *Critical Perspectives on Empowerment*. London: Venture Press, pp. 17–34.

Carabine, J. (2000) 'Constituting Welfare Subjects through Poverty and Sexuality', in Lewis, G., Gewirtz, S. and Clarke, J. (eds.), *Rethinking Social Policy*. London: Sage, pp. 78–93.

Carabine, J. (ed.) (2004) *Sexualities: Personal Lives and Social Policy*. Bristol: Policy Press.

Castles, F. (2010a) 'The English-Speaking Countries', in Castles, F., Leibfried, S., Lewis, J., Obinger, H. and Pierson, C. (eds.), *The Oxford Handbook of the Welfare State*. Oxford: Oxford University Press, pp. 630–642.

Castles, F. (2010b) 'Black Swans and Elephants on the Move: The Impact of Emergencies on the Welfare State', *Journal of European Social Policy*, 20: 91–101.

Castles, F. and Mitchell, D. (1993) 'Worlds of Welfare and Families of Nations', in Castles, F.G. (ed.), *Families of Nations: Patterns of Public Policy in Western Democracies*. Aldershot, UK: Dartmouth, pp. 93–128.

Castles, S. and Schierup, C. (2010) 'Migration and Ethnic Minorities', in Castles, F., Leibfried, S., Lewis J., Obinger, H. and Pierson, C. (eds.), *The Oxford Handbook of the Welfare State*. Oxford: Oxford University Press, pp. 278–291.

Castles, F., Leibfried, S., Lewis, J., Obinger, H. and Pierson, C. (eds.) (2010) *The Oxford Handbook of the Welfare State*. Oxford: Oxford University Press.

Chodorow, N. (1978) *The Reproduction of Mothering*. Berkeley: University of California Press.

Clasen, J. (2004) 'Defining Comparative Social Policy', in Kennett, P. (ed.), *A Handbook of Comparative Social Policy*. Cheltenham: Edward Elgar, pp. 91–102.

Coffey, A. (2004) 'Social Policy and the Body', in *Reconceptualising Social Policy, Sociological Perspectives on Contemporary Social Policy*. Maidenhead: Open University Press, pp. 77–94.

Colebatch, H.K. (2002) *Policy*, 2nd edn. Buckingham: Open University Press.

Collard, D. (1978) *Altruism and Economy: A Study in Non-selfish Economics*. Oxford: Martin Robertson.

Collier, R.B. and Collier, D. (1991) *Shaping the Political Arena: Critical Junctures, the Labour Movement and Regime Dynamics in Latin America*. Princeton, NJ: Princeton University Press.

Colwill, J. (1994) 'Beveridge, Women and the Welfare State', *Critical Social Policy*, 41: 53–78.

Commission on Social Justice (1994) *Social Justice Strategies for National Renewal*. London: Institute for Policy Renewal.

Connell, R.W. (1995) *Masculinities*. Cambridge, UK: Polity Press.

Coote, A. and Franklin, J. (2009) *Green Well Fair: Three Economies for Social Justice*. London: New Economics Foundation.

Croft, S. and Beresford, P. (1996) 'The Politics of Participation', in Taylor, D. (ed.), *Critical Social Policy*. London: Sage, pp. 175–198.

Crossley, N. (2002) *Making Sense of Social Movements*. Buckingham: Open University Press.

Daly, M. (1978) *Gyn/Ecology: The Metaethics of Radical Feminism*. Boston: Beacon Press.

Daly, M. (2010) 'Families versus State and Market', in Castles, F., Leibfried, S., Lewis, J., Obinger, H. and Pierson, C. (eds.), *The Oxford Handbook of the Welfare State*. Oxford: Oxford University Press, pp. 139–151.

Daly, M. (2011) 'What Adult Worker Model? A Critical Look at Recent Social Policy Reform in Europe from a Gender and Family Perspective', *Social Politics*, 18(1): 1–23.

Daly, M. and Rake, K. (2003) *Gender and the Welfare State in Europe and the USA*. Cambridge, UK: Polity Press.

De Wispelaere, J. and Stirton, L. (2004) 'The Many Faces of Universal Basic Income', *Political Quarterly*, 75(3): 266–274.

Deacon, A. (2002) *Perspectives on Welfare: Ideas, Ideologies and Policy Debates*. Buckingham: Open University Press.

Deacon, A. and Mann, K. (1999) 'Agency, Modernity and Social Policy', *Journal of Social Policy*, 28(3): 413–435.

Deacon, B., Hulse, M. and Stubbs, P. (1997) *Global Social Policy: International Organisations and the Future of Welfare*. London: Sage.

Dean, H. (2000) 'Managing Risk by Controlling Behaviour: Social Security Administration and the Erosion of Welfare Citizenship', in Taylor-Gooby, P. (ed.), *Risk, Trust and Welfare*. London: Macmillan, pp. 71–92.

Dean, H. (2009) 'Critiquing Capabilities', *Critical Social Policy*, 29(2): 261–278.

Dean, H. (2010) *Understanding Human Need*. Bristol: Policy Press.

DFID (Department for International Development) (2005) *Reducing Poverty by Tackling Social Exclusion: A DFID Policy Paper*. London: DFID.

DHSS (Department of Health and Social Security) (1980) *Inequalities in Health: Report of a Research Working Group* (Black Report). London: DHSS.

Donnison, D., Chapman, V., Meacher, M., Sears, A. and Urwin, K. (1970) *Social Policy and Administration Studies in the Development of Social Services at the Local Level*, 3rd edn. London: Allen & Unwin.

Doran, C.F. (1980) 'Modes, Mechanisms, and Turning Points: Perspectives on the Transformation of the International System', *International Political Science Review*, 1(1): 35–61.

Dower, N. (2003) *An Introduction to Global Citizenship*. Edinburgh: Edinburgh University Press.

Doyal, L. and Gough, I. (1991) *A Theory of Human Need*. London: Macmillan.

Drake, R.F. (1999) *Understanding Disability Policies*. London: Macmillan.

Dunleavy, P. and O'Leary, B. (1987) *Theories of the State: The Politics of Liberal Democracy*. Basingstoke, UK: Macmillan.

Dworkin, G. (1981) *Pornography: Men Possessing Women*. London: Plume.

Dworkin, G. (1988) *The Theory and Practice of Autonomy*. Cambridge: Cambridge University Press.

Dwyer, P. (2003) *Understanding Social Citizenship*, 2nd edn. Bristol: Policy Press.

Dyer, J.D. and Minton McGuinness, T. (1996) 'Resilience: Analysis of the Concept', *Archives of Psychiatric Nursing*, 10(5): 276–282.

Eardley, T., Bradshaw, J., Ditch, J., Gough, I. and Whiteford, P. (1996) *Social Assistance in OECD Countries: Synthesis Report*, Research Report 46. London. HMSO: Department of Social Security. Available at http://research.dwp.gov.uk/aasd/asd5/rrepo46.pdf

Ebbinghaus, B. (2005) *Can Path Dependence Explain Institutional Change?* Cologne: Max-Planck-Institut fuer Gesellschaftsforschung.

Edwards, J. (1987) *Positive Discrimination: Social Justice and Social Policy*. London: Tavistock.

Edwards, R. and Glover, J. (eds.) (2001) *Risk and Citizenship: Key Issues in Welfare*. London: Sage.

Ehrenreich, B. and Hochschild, A. (eds.) (2003) *Global Woman: Nannies, Maids and Sex Workers in the New Economy*. London: Granta.

Ellis, K. and Dean, H. (eds.) (1999) *Social Policy and the Body*. Basingstoke, UK: Macmillan.

Esping-Andersen, G. (1990) *The Three Worlds of Welfare Capitalism*. Cambridge, UK: Polity Press.

Esping-Andersen, G. (ed.) (1996) *Welfare States in Transition: National Adaptations of Global Economies*. London: Sage.

Esping-Andersen, G. (1999) *Social Foundations of Post-industrial Economics*. Oxford: Oxford University Press.

Esping-Andersen, G. (2002) 'A New Gender Contract', in Esping-Andersen, G., Gallie, D., Hemerijck, A. and Myles, J. (eds.), *Why We Need a New Welfare State*. Oxford: Oxford University Press, pp. 68–95.

Esping-Andersen, G., Gallie, D., Hemerijck, A. and Myles, J. (eds.) (2002) *Why We Need a New Welfare State*. Oxford: Oxford University Press.

Etzioni, A. (1996) *The New Golden Rule: Community and Morality in a Democratic Society*. New York: Basic Books.

European Commission (1992) *Towards a Europe of Solidarity: Intensifying the Fight against Social Exclusion, Fostering Integration.* Communication from the Commission. COM(92) 542 final, 23 December.

European Commission (1997) *European Employment Strategy.* Brussels: European Commission.

European Commission (2007) *Towards Common Principles of Flexicurity: More and Better Jobs through Flexibility and Security,* COM(2007) 359 final. Brussels: European Commission. Available at http://europa.eu/employment_social/social_inclusion/docs/2007/study_lone_parents_en.pdf

European Commission (2012) *Strategy towards the Eradication of Trafficking in Human Beings (2012–2016).* Brussels: European Commission.

European Foundation for the Improvement of Living and Working Conditions (2009) *Second European Quality of Life Survey.* Dublin: EFILWC.

European Foundation for the Improvement of Living and Working Conditions (2010) *Flexicurity Perspectives and Practice.* Dublin: Eurofound.

Fagnani, J. (2007) 'Family Policies in France and Germany: Sisters or Distant Cousins?', *Community Work and Family* 10(1): 39–56.

Fahey, T., Nolan, B. and Whelan, C.T. (2003) *Monitoring Quality of Life in Europe.* Dublin: European Foundation for the Improvement of Living and Working Conditions.

Fahey, T., Russell, H. and Whelan, C.T. (eds.) (2008) *Quality of Life in Ireland: Social Impact of Economic Boom.* New York: Springer.

Falkingham, J. and Baschieri, A. (2009) 'Gender and Poverty: How Misleading Is the Unitary Model of Household Resources?', in Yeates, N. and Holden, C. (eds.), *The Global Social Policy Reader.* Bristol: Policy Press, pp. 123–128.

Fanning, B. (2012) *Racism and Social Change in the Republic of Ireland,* 2nd edn. Manchester: Manchester University Press.

Feld, L.P. and Schneider, F. (2010) 'Survey on the Shadow Economy and Undeclared Earnings in OECD Countries', *German Economic Review* 11(2): 109–149.

Ferguson, I., Lavalette, M. and Mooney, G. (2002) *Rethinking Welfare: A Critical Perspective.* London: Sage.

Ferrera, M. (2010) 'The Southern European Countries', in Castles, F., Leibfried, S., Lewis, J., Obinger, H. and Pierson, C. (eds.), *The Oxford Handbook of the Welfare State.* Oxford: Oxford University Press, pp. 616–629.

Fine-Davis, M. (2005) 'Work–Life Balance of Irish Parents: A Cross-National Comparative Study', in Boucher, G. and Collins, G. (eds.), *The New World of Work: Labour Markets in Contemporary Ireland.* Dublin: Liffey Press, pp. 17–41.

Firestone, S. (1979) *The Dialectic of Sex: The Case for Feminist Revolution.* London: Bantam.

Fitzpatrick, T. (2011a) *Welfare Theory: An Introduction to the Theoretical Debates in Social Policy,* 2nd edn. London: Palgrave Macmillan.

Fitzpatrick, T. (2011b) *Understanding the Environment and Social Policy.* Bristol: Policy Press.

Fitzpatrick, T. and Cahill, M. (2002) *Environment and Welfare: Towards a Green Social Policy.* London: Palgrave Macmillan.

Flora, P. and Alber, J. (1981) 'Modernization, Democratization, and the Development of Welfare States in Western Europe', in Flora, P. and Heidenheimer, A.J. (eds.), *The Development of Welfare States in Europe and America.* London: Transaction, pp. 37–80.

Forder, A. (1974) *Concepts in Social Administration: A Framework for Analysis.* London: Routledge & Kegan Paul.

Foucault, M. (1977) *Discipline and Punish: The Birth of the Prison,* translated by Sheridan, A. London: Allen Lane.

Foucault, M. (1979) *The History of Sexuality – Volume 1: An Introduction,* translated by Hurly, R. Harmondsworth, UK: Penguin.

Fraser, N. (1989) *Unruly Practices*. Cambridge, UK: Polity Press.

Fraser, N. (1995) 'From Redistribution to Recognition? Dilemmas of Justice in a "Post-socialist" Age', *New Left Review*, 212: 68–92.

Friedman, M. (1962) *Capitalism and Freedom*. Chicago: Chicago University Press.

Friedman, M. (1976) *Price Theory: A Provisional Text*, 2nd edn. Chicago: Aldine Publishing.

Friedman, M. (1997) 'Autonomy and Social Relationships: Rethinking the Feminist Critique', in Meyers, D.T. (ed.), *Feminists Rethink the Self*. Boulder, CO: Westview Press, pp. 40–61.

Friedman, M. and Friedman, R. (1980) *Free to Choose*. London: Secker & Warburg.

Gal, J. (1998) 'Categorical Benefits in Welfare States: Findings from Great Britain and Israel', *International Social Security Review*, 1: 73–101.

Gal, J. (2010) 'Is There an Extended Family of Mediterranean Welfare States?', *Journal of European Social Policy*, 20(4): 283–300.

George, V. and Wilding, P. (1994) *Welfare and Ideology*. London: Harvester Wheatsheaf.

George, V. and Wilding, P. (2009) 'Globalization and Human Welfare: Why Is There a Need for a Global Social Policy?' in Yeates, N. and Holden, C. (eds.), *The Global Social Policy Reader*. Bristol: Policy Press, pp. 27–34.

Giddens, A. (1976) *New Rules of Sociological Method: A Positive Critique of Interpretive Sociologies*. London: Hutchinson.

Giddens, A. (1998a) 'Risk and Responsibility', *Modern Law Review*, 62(1): 1–10.

Giddens, A. (1998b) 'Risk Society: The Context of British Politics', in Franklin, J. (ed.), *The Politics of Risk Society*. Cambridge, UK: Polity Press, pp. 23–44.

Giddens, A. (1999) *BBC Reith Lectures*. BBC Radio 4, London. Available at http://www.bbc.co.uk/radio4/features/the-reith-lectures/transcripts/1990/

Giddens, A. (2006) *Sociology*, 5th edn. Cambridge, UK: Polity Press.

Gilligan, C. (1982) *In a Different Voice: Psychological Theory and Women's Development*. London: Harvard University Press.

Ginsburg, N. (1979) *Class, Capital and Social Policy*. London: Macmillan.

Ginsburg, N. (1992) *Divisions of Welfare: A Critical Introduction to Comparative Social Policy*. London: Sage.

Glendinning, C. and Millar, J. (1992) *Women and Poverty in Britain in the 1990s*. London: Harvester Wheatsheaf.

Glendinning, C. and Arksey, H. (2008) 'Informal Care', in Alcock, P., May, M. and Rowlingson, K. (eds.), *The Student's Companion to Social Policy*. Oxford: Blackwell, pp. 219–225.

Goffman, E. (1963) *Stigma: Notes on the Management of Spoiled Identity*. London: Prentice Hall.

Goldberg, S. (1979) *Male Dominance: The Inevitability of Patriarchy*. London: Abacus Sphere.

Goodin, R.E. and Rein, M. (2001) 'Regimes or Pillars: Alternative Welfare State Logics and Dynamics', *Public Administration*, 79(4): 769–801.

Gordon, D. (2010) 'Concepts of Poverty and Deprivation', in Walker, A., Gordon, D., Levitas, R., Phillimore, P., Phillipson, C., Salomon, M.E. and Yeates, N. (eds.), *The Peter Townsend Reader*. Bristol: Policy Press, pp. 191–213.

Gough, I. (1979) *The Political Economy of the Welfare State*. London: Macmillan.

Gough, I., Bradshaw, J., Ditch, J., Eardley, T. and Whiteford, P. (1997) 'Social Assistance in OECD Countries', *Journal of European Social Policy*, 7(1): 17–43.

Grahame, H. (1983) 'Caring, a Labour of Love', in Finch, J. and Groves, D. (eds.), *A Labour of Love*. London: Routledge & Kegan Paul, pp. 13–30.

Greer, S.L. (2008) 'Choosing Paths in European Health Services Policy: A Political Analysis of a Critical Juncture', *Journal of European Social Policy* 18(3): 219–231.

Greve, B. (2007) *Occupational Welfare: Winners and Losers*. Cheltenham: Edward Elgar.

Harris, J. (1977) *William Beveridge, a Biography*. Oxford: Clarendon Press.

Hartmann, H. (1982) 'Capitalism, Patriarchy and Job Segregation by Sex', in Giddens, A. and Held, D. (eds.), *Classes, Power and Conflict*. London: Macmillan, pp. 446–469.

Haux, T. (2011) 'Activating Lone Parents: An Evidence-based Policy Appraisal of Welfare-to-Work Reform in Britain', *Social Policy and Society*, 11(1): 1–14.

Hayek, F. (1949) *Individualism and Economic Order*. London: Routledge & Kegan Paul.

Hayek, F. (1972) *Law, Legislation and Liberty, Volume 1*. London: Routledge & Kegan Paul.

Hayek, F. (1976) *Law, Legislation and Liberty, Volume 2*. London: Routledge & Kegan Paul.

Hayek, F. (1979) *Law, Legislation and Liberty, Volume 3*. London: Routledge & Kegan Paul.

Hays, S. (1994) 'Structure and Agency and the Sticky Problem of Culture', *Sociological Theory*, 12(1): 57–72.

Hearn, J. (2010) 'Reflecting on Men and Social Policy: Contemporary Critical Debates and Implications for Social Policy', *Critical Social Policy*, 30(2): 165–188.

Hearn, J., Nordberg, M., Andersson, K., Balkmar, D., Gottzén, L., Klinth, R., Pringle, K. and Sandberg, L. (2012) 'Hegemonic Masculinity and Beyond: 40 Years of Research in Sweden', *Men and Masculinities*, 15: 31–55.

Heywood, A. (2007) *Political Ideologies: An Introduction*, 4th edn. London: Palgrave Macmillan.

Hill, M. (2009) *The Policy Process in the Modern State*, 5th edn. Harlow: Pearson.

Hills, J. (2008) 'The Distribution of Welfare', in Alcock, P., May, M. and Rowlingson, K. (eds.), *The Student's Companion to Social Policy*, 3rd edn. Oxford: Blackwell, pp. 139–148.

Hinrichs, K. (2001) 'Elephants on the Move: Patterns of Public Pension Reform in OECD Countries', in Liebfried, S. (ed.), *Welfare State Futures*. Cambridge, UK: Cambridge University Press, pp. 77–102.

Hinrichs, K. and Lynch, J.F. (2010) 'Old-Age Pensions', in Castles, F., Leibfried, S., Lewis, J., Obinger, H. and Pierson, C. (eds.), *The Oxford Handbook of the Welfare State*. Oxford: Oxford University Press, pp. 353–366.

Hochschild, A.R. (2000) 'Global Care Chains and Emotional Surplus Value', in Hutton, W. and Giddens, A. (eds.), *On the Edge: Living with Global Capitalism*. London: Jonathan Cape, pp. 130–146.

Holden, C. (2008) 'Commercial Welfare', in Alcock, P., May, M. and Rowlingson, K. (eds.), *The Student's Companion to Social Policy*. Oxford: Blackwell, pp. 196–202.

Holmes, M. (2007) *What Is Gender? Sociological Approaches*. London: Sage.

Huber, E. and Bogliaccini, J. (2010) 'Latin America', in Castles, F., Leibfried, S., Lewis, J., Obinger, H. and Pierson, C. (eds.), *The Oxford Handbook of the Welfare State*. Oxford: Oxford University Press, pp. 644–655.

Huby, M. (2002) *Social Policy and the Environment*. Buckingham: Open University Press.

ILC (International Labour Conference) (2002) *Provisional Record: The Informal Economy (General Discussion)*, Committee on the Informal Economy, 90th Session, Geneva, June, paragraph 3. Available at http://www.ilo.org/public/english/standards/relm/ilc/ilc90/pdf/pr-25.pdf

ILO (International Labour Organization) (1942) *Approaches to Social Security*. Montreal: ILO.

ILO (1973) *Resolutions Concerning an Integrated System of Wages: Statistics Adopted by the 12th International Conference of Labour Statisticians*, October, paragraph 8. Geneva: ILO.

ILO (2010) *Constitution of the International Labour Organisation and Selected Texts*. Geneva: ILO.

ILO (2012) *Global Estimate of Forced Labour*, International Labour Organization Special Action Programme to Combat Forced Labour (SAP–FL). Geneva: ILO.

IOM (International Organization for Migration) (2004) *IOM Glossary on Migration*, International Migration Law Series No. 25. Available at http://www.iom.int/jahia/Jahia/about-migration/key-migration-terms/lang/en#Immigration

James, S. and Della Costa, M. (1972) *The Power of Women and the Subversion of the Community*. Bristol: Falling Wall Press.

Johnson, N. (1999) *Mixed Economies of Welfare, a Comparative Perspective*. London: Prentice Hall.

Kahn, R. (2012) *Topic Guide on Social Exclusion*. International Development Department, University of Birmingham.

Kautto, M. (2010) 'The Nordic Countries', in Castles, F., Leibfried, S., Lewis, J., Obinger, H. and Pierson, C. (eds.), *The Oxford Handbook of the Welfare State*. Oxford: Oxford University Press, pp. 586–600.

Keenan, M. (2010) *Child Sexual Abuse and the Catholic Church: Gender, Power and Organizational Culture*. Oxford: Oxford University Press.

Kelly, E., McGuinness, S. and O'Connell, P.J. (2011) *What Can Active Labour Market Policies Do?* Renewal Series Paper 1, Economic and Social Research Institute, Dublin.

Kemshall, H. (2002) *Risk, Social Policy and Welfare*. Buckingham: Open University Press.

Kendall, J. (2008) 'Voluntary Welfare', in Alcock, P., May, M. and Rowlingson, K. (eds.), *The Student's Companion to Social Policy*. Oxford: Blackwell, pp. 212–218.

Kennedy, P. (2002) *Maternity in Ireland: A Woman-Centred Perspective*. Dublin: Liffey Press.

Kennedy, P. and Einasto, H. (2010) 'Changes and Continuities in Maternity Policies: Comparison of Maternity Legislation in Ireland and Estonia', *European Societies*, 12(2): 187–207.

Kenworthy, L. (2010) 'Labour Market Activation', in Castles, F., Leibfried, S., Lewis, J., Obinger, H. and Pierson, C. (eds.), *The Oxford Handbook of the Welfare State*. Oxford: Oxford University Press, pp. 435–447.

Keynes, J.M. (1936) *The General Theory of Employment, Interest and Money*.

Kirby, P. (2004) 'Globalisation', in Fanning, B., Kennedy, P., Kiely, G. and Quin, S. (eds.), *Theorising Irish Social Policy*. Dublin: UCD Press, pp. 23–41.

Kjeldstad, R. (2001) 'Gender Policies and Gender Equality', in Kautto, M., Fritzell, J., Hvinden, B., Kvist, J. and Uusitalo, H. (eds.), *Nordic Welfare States in the European Context*. London: Routledge, pp. 79–93.

Klein, R. (1993) 'O'Goffe's Tale, or What Can We Learn from the Success of the Capitalist Welfare States?', in Jones, C. (ed.), *New Perspectives on the Welfare State in Europe*. London: Routledge, pp. 6–15.

Knill, C. (2005) 'Introduction: Cross-National Policy Convergence: Concepts, Approaches and Explanatory Factors', Journal of European Public Policy, 12(5): 764–774.

Korpi, W. (1983) *The Democratic Class Struggle*. London: Routledge & Kegan Paul.

Kuhlne, S. and Sander, A. (2010) 'The Emergence of the Welfare State', in Castles, F., Leibfried, S., Lewis, J., Obinger, H. and Pierson, C. (eds.) *The Oxford Handbook of the Welfare State*. Oxford: Oxford University Press, pp. 61–80.

Land, H. (1980) 'The Family Wage', *Feminist Review*, 6: 55–77.

Land, H. (2008) 'Altruism, Reciprocity, and Obligation', in Alcock, P., May, M. and Rowlingson, K. (eds.), *The Student's Companion to Social Policy*, 3rd edn. Oxford: Blackwell, pp. 50–57.

Lasch, C. (1977) *Haven in a Heartless World: The Family Besieged*. London: Norton.

Law, I. (2010) *Racism and Ethnicity: Global Debates, Dilemmas, Directions*. Harlow: Pearson.

Le Grand, J. (1982) *The Strategy of Equality*. London: Allen & Unwin.

Le Grand, J. (1997) 'Knights, Knaves or Pawns? Human Behaviour and Social Policy', *Journal of Social Policy*, 26: 149–169.

Lebow, R.N. (2000/2001) 'Contingency, Catalysts, and International System Change', *Political Science Quarterly*, 115(4): 591–616.

Leibfried, S. and Mau, S. (eds.) (2008) *Welfare States: Construction, Deconstruction and Reconstruction. Volume I: Analytical Approaches*. Cheltenham: Edward Elgar.

Leibfried, S. and Mau, S. (eds.) (2008) *Welfare States: Construction, Deconstruction and Reconstruction. Volume II: Varieties and Transformations.* Cheltenham: Edward Elgar.

Leibfried, S. and Mau, S. (eds.) (2008) *Welfare States: Construction, Deconstruction and Reconstruction. Volume III: Legitimation, Achievement and Integration.* Cheltenham: Edward Elgar.

Leira, A. (1992) *Welfare States and Working Mothers.* Cambridge: Cambridge University Press.

Leisering, L. (2003) 'Government and the Life Course', in Mortimer, J.T. and Shanahan, M.J. (eds.), *Handbook of the Life Course.* New York: Academic Publishers.

Lenoir, R. (1974) *Les Exclus.* Paris: Editions du Seuil.

Lessenich, S. (2005) '"Frozen Landscapes" Revisited: Path Creation in the European Social Mode', *Social Policy & Society* 4(4): 345–356.

Levitas, R. (2005) *The Inclusive Society,* 2nd edn. Basingstoke, UK: Palgrave.

Lewis, G., Gewirtz, S. and Clarke, J. (eds.) (2000) *Rethinking Social Policy.* London: Sage.

Lewis, J. (1992) 'Gender and the Development of Welfare Regimes', *Journal of European Social Policy,* 2(3): 159–173.

Lewis, J. (ed.) (1993) *Women and Social Policies in Europe: Work, Family and the State.* New York: Edward Elgar.

Lewis, J. (2001) 'The Decline of the Male Breadwinner Model: Implications for Work and Care', *Social Politics,* 8(2): 152–169.

Lieberman, R. (2002) 'Political Institutions and the Politics of Race in the Development of the Modern Welfare State', in Rothstein, B. and Steinmo, S. (eds.), *Restructuring the Welfare State: Political Institutions and Policy Change.* New York: Palgrave, pp. 102–128.

Lippert, O. and Walker, M. (eds.) (1997) *The Underground Economy: Global Evidences of Its Size and Impact.* Vancouver: Fraser Institute.

Lipsky, M. (1980) *Street Level Bureaucracy.* New York: Russell Sage Foundation.

Lister, R. (ed.) (1996) *Charles Murray and the Underclass: The Developing Debate.* London: IEA Health and Welfare Unit.

Lister, R. (1997) *Citizenship: Feminist Perspectives.* London: Macmillan.

Lister, R. (2003) *Citizenship: Feminist Perspectives,* 2nd edn. New York: New York University Press.

Lister, R. (2004) *Poverty.* Cambridge, UK: Polity Press.

Lister, R. (2008) 'Citizenship and Access to Welfare', in Alcock, P., May, M. and Rowlingson, K. (eds.), *The Student's Companion to Social Policy.* Oxford: Blackwell, pp. 234–240.

Lister, R. (2010) *Understanding Theories and Concepts in Social Policy.* Bristol: Policy Press.

Lister, R., Williams, F., Anttonen, A., Bussemaker, J., Gerhard, U., Heinen, J., Johansson, S., Leira, A., Siim, B., Tobias, C. and Gavanas, A. (2007) *Gendering Citizenship in Western Europe: New Challenges for Citizenship Research in a Cross-National Context.* Bristol: Policy Press.

Loizou, A. (1997) 'Social Justice and Social Policy', in Lavalette, M. and Pratt, A. (eds.), *Social Policy: A Conceptual and Theoretical Introduction.* London: Sage, pp. 163–181.

Lowi, T.A. (1972) 'Four Systems of Policy, Politics and Choice', *Public Administration Review,* 32: 298–310.

Lukes, S. (1974) *Power: A Radical View.* London: Macmillan.

Luthar, S.S. and Zigler, E. (1991) 'Vulnerability and Competence: A Review of Research on Resilience in Childhood', *American Journal of Orthopsychiatry,* 61: 6–22.

Luthar, S.S., Cicchetti, D. and Becker, B. (2000) 'The Construct of Resilience: A Critical Evaluation and Guidelines for Future Work', *Child Development,* 71(3): 543–562.

Lynch, K. and McLaughlin, E. (1995) 'Caring Labour and Love Labour', in Clancy, P., Drudy, S., Lynch, K. and O'Dowd, L. (eds.), *Irish Society: Sociological Perspectives.* Dublin: Institute of Public Administration, pp. 250–292.

McIntosh, M. (1981) 'Feminism and Social Policy', *Critical Social Policy*, 1: 32–42.

McIntosh, M. (1996) 'Feminism and Social Policy', in Taylor, D. (ed.), *Critical Social Policy, A Reader*. London: Sage, pp. 13–26.

Mack, J. and Lansley, S. (1985) *Poor Britain*. London: Allen & Unwin.

McKay, S. and Rowlingson, K. (2008) 'Social Security and Income Maintenance', in Alcock, P., May, M. and Rowlingson, K. (eds.), *Companion to Social Policy*, 3rd edn. Oxford: Basil Blackwell, pp. 303–310.

MacPherson, S. and Silburn, R. (1998) 'The Meaning and Measurement of Poverty', in Dixon, J. and Macarov, A. (eds.), *Poverty: A Persistent Global Reality*. London: Routledge, pp. 1–19.

Marshall, A. (1890/1930) *Principles of Economics*, 8th edn. London: Macmillan.

Marshall, T.H. (1950) *Citizenship and Social Class*. Cambridge, UK: Cambridge University Press.

Marx, K. (1867/1976) *Capital, Volume 1* (ed. by Mandel, E.). Harmondsworth, UK: Penguin.

Marx, K. (1894/1981) *Capital, Volume 3* (ed. by Mandel, E.). Harmondsworth, UK: Penguin.

Maslow, A.H. (1943) 'A Theory of Human Motivation', *Psychological Review*, 50: 370–396.

May, M. (2007) 'Occupational Welfare', in Powell, M. (ed.), *Understanding the Mixed Economy of Welfare*. Bristol: Policy Press, pp. 149–176.

May, M. (2008) 'Occupational Welfare', in Alcock, P. May, M. and Rowlingson, K. (eds.), *The Student's Companion to Social Policy*. Oxford: Blackwell, pp. 203–211.

Mayo, M. (2008) 'The Role of Comparative Study in Social Policy', in Alcock, P. May, M. and Rowlingson, K. (eds.), *The Student's Companion to Social Policy*, 3rd edn. Oxford: Blackwell, pp. 421–429.

Meyers, D.T. (1997) *Feminists Rethink the Self*. Boulder, CO: Westview Press.

Mill, J.S. (1859/1956) *On Liberty* (ed. by Shields, C.). New York: Macmillan.

Millar, J. (1989) *Poverty and the Lone Parent: The Challenge to Social Policy*. Aldershot, UK: Avebury.

Millar, J. and Ridge, T. (2001) *Families, Poverty, Work and Care: A Review of Literature on Lone Parents and Low Income Couple Families with Children*. Department for Work and Pensions Research Report No. 153. Leeds: Centre for Disability Studies.

Millar, J. and Rowlingson, K. (eds.) (2001) *Lone Parents, Employment and Social Policy: Cross-National Comparisons*. Bristol: Policy Press.

Mincer, J. (1958) 'Investment in Human Capital and Personal Income Distribution', *Journal of Political Economy*, 66(4): 281–302.

Mishra, R. (1977) *Society and Social Policy: Theories and Practice of Welfare*. London: Macmillan.

Mishra, R. (1981) *Society and Social Policy: Theories and Practice of Welfare*, 2nd edn. London: Macmillan.

Mishra, R. (1984) *The Welfare State in Crisis*. London: Harvester Press.

Mishra, R. (1986) 'Social Policy and the Discipline of Social Administration', *Social Policy and Administration*, 20(1): 28–38.

Mishra, R. (1990) *The Welfare State in Capitalist Society*. London: Harvester Wheatsheaf.

Mishra, R. (1999) *Globalization and the Welfare State*. London: Edward Elgar.

Mooney, G. (2000) 'Class and Social Policy', in Lewis, G., Gewirtz, S. and Clarke, J. (eds.), *Rethinking Social Policy*. Basingstoke, UK: Open University Press, pp. 156–170.

Moran, M. (1999) *Governing the Health Care State: A Comparative Study of the United Kingdom, the United States and Germany*. Manchester: Manchester University Press.

Moran, M. (2000) 'Understanding the Welfare State: The Case of Health Care', *British Journal of Politics and International Relations*, 2(2): 135–160.

Morris, J. (1991) *Pride against Prejudice: Transforming Attitudes towards Disability*. London: Women's Press.

Morris, J. (2011) 'Rethinking Disability Policy', York: Joseph Rowntree Foundation, 15 November. Available at http://www.jrf.org.uk/publications/rethinking-disability-policy

Morrisens, A. and Sainsbury, D. (2005) 'Migrants, Social Rights, Ethnicity, and Welfare Regimes', *Journal of Social Policy*, 34(4): 637–660.

Murray, C. (1990) *The Emerging British Underclass*. London: IEA Health and Welfare Unit.

Murray, C. (1994) *Underclass: The Crisis Deepens*. London: IEA Health and Welfare Unit.

Myrdal, G. (1963) *Challenge to Affluence*. New York: Random House.

NESC (National Economic and Social Council) (2009) *Well-Being Matters: A Social Report for Ireland*. Report Number: 119 volumes 1 and 2. Dublin: NESC.

NESF (National Economic and Social Forum) (1996) *Equality Proofing Issues*. Forum Report Number 10, February. Available at www.nesf.ie

Nolan, B. and Whelan, C. (1996) *Resources, Deprivation and Poverty*. Oxford: Clarendon Press.

Nozick, R. (1974) *Anarchy, State and Utopia*. New York: Basic Books.

Nussbaum, M. (2011) *Creating Capabilities: The Human Development Approach*. Cambridge, MA: Harvard University Press.

OAU (1969) Convention governing the specific aspects of refugee problems in Africa adopted by the Assembly of Heads of State and Government at its Sixth Ordinary Session. United Nations, Treaty Series No. 14691.

O'Brien, M. and Penna, S. (1998) *Theorising Welfare: Enlightenment and Modern Society*. London: Blackwell.

O'Connor, J. (1973) *The Fiscal Crisis of the State*. New York: St. Martin's Press.

O'Connor, J. (1993) 'Gender, Class and Citizenship in the Comparative Analysis of Welfare State Regimes: Theoretical and Methodological Issues', *British Journal of Sociology*, 44(3): 501–518.

O'Connor, J.S., Orloff, A.S. and Shaver, S. (1999) *States, Markets, Families: Gender, Liberalism and Social Policy in Australia, Canada, Great Britain and the United States*. Cambridge, UK: Cambridge University Press.

OECD (Organisation for Economic Co-operation and Development) (1981) *The Welfare State in Crisis*. Paris: OECD.

OECD (1987) *Financing and Delivering Health Care: A Comparative Analysis of OECD Countries*, Social Policy Studies No. 4, OECD, Paris.

OECD (1994) *Jobs Strategy*. Paris: OECD.

OECD (2007) *OECD Employment Outlook*, Chapter 5. Paris: OECD.

OECD (2008) *The Distribution of Household Income in OECD Countries: What Are Its Main Features? Growing Up Unequal?* Available at http://www.oecd.org/els/social/inequality

Offe, C. (1984) *The Contradictions of the Welfare State*. London: Hutchinson.

Oliver, M. (1981) 'A New Model of the Social Work Role in Relation to Disability', in Campling, J. (ed.), *The Handicapped Person: A New Perspective for Social Workers*. London: RADAR, pp. 19–32.

Oliver, M. (1990) *The Politics of Disablement*. London: Macmillan.

Oliver, M. (1996) *Understanding Disability: From Theory to Practice*. London: Palgrave.

Oliver, M. and Barnes, C. (2009) 'Disabled People, the Welfare State and a Welfare Society', in Oliver, M., *Understanding Disability: From Theory to Practice*. Basingstoke, UK: Palgrave Macmillan.

Orloff, A.S. (1993) 'Gender and the Social Rights of Citizenship: The Comparative Analysis of Gender Relations and Welfare States', *American Sociological Review*, 58: 303–328.

Orloff, A.S. (2010) 'Gender', in Castles, F. Leibfried, S., Lewis, J., Obinger, H. and Pierson, C. (eds.), *The Oxford Handbook of the Welfare State*. Oxford: Oxford University Press, pp. 252–264.

Orloff, A.S. and Skocpol, T. (1984) 'Why Not Equal Protection? Explaining the Politics of Public Social Spending in Britain, 1900–1911, and the United States, 1880s–1920', *American Sociological Review*, 49(6): 720–750.

Orshansky, M. (1965) 'Counting the Poor: Another Look at the Poverty Portfolio', *Social Security Bulletin*, 51: 1–4.

Page, R. (1984) *Stigma: Concepts in Social Policy Two*. London: Routledge and Kegan Paul.

Pahl, J. (1990) 'Household Spending, Personal Spending and the Control of Money in Marriage', *Sociology*, 24(1): 119–138.

Parker, J. (1975) *Social Policy and Citizenship*. London: Macmillan.

Pascall, G. (1986) *Social Policy: A Feminist Analysis*. London: Tavistock Publications.

Pascall, G. (2012) *Gender Equality in the Welfare State?* Bristol: Policy Press.

Payne, G. (2000) *Social Divisions*. Hampshire: Palgrave.

Pearce, D. (1990) 'Welfare Is Not for Women', in Gordon, L. (ed.), *Women, the State and Welfare*. Madison: University of Wisconsin Press, pp. 265–279.

Peng, I. and Wong, J. (2010) 'East Asia', in Castles, F., Leibfried, S., Lewis, J., Obinger, H. and Pierson, C. (eds.), *The Oxford Handbook of the Welfare State*. Oxford: Oxford University Press, pp. 656–670.

Pfau-Effinger, B. (2005) 'Culture and Welfare State Policies: Reflections on a Complex Interrelation', *Journal of Social Policy*, 34(1): 3–20.

Phoenix, A. (2000) 'Constructing Gendered and Racialized Identities: Young Men, Masculinities and Educational Policies', in Lewis, G., Gewirtz, S. and Clarke, J. (eds.), *Rethinking Social Policy*. London: Sage, pp. 94–110.

Pierson, C. (2006) *Beyond the Welfare State*, 3rd edn. Cambridge, UK: Polity Press.

Pierson, P. (ed.) (2001) *The New Politics of the Welfare State*. Oxford: Oxford University Press.

Pierson, P. (2004) *Politics in Time, History, Institutions and Social Analysis*. Princeton, NJ: Princeton University Press.

Pilcher, J. and Whelehan, I. (2004) *50 Key Concepts in Gender Studies*. London: Sage.

Pinker, R. (1971) *Social Theory and Social Policy*. London: Heinemann.

Pinker, R. (1999) 'Do Poverty Definitions Matter?', in Gordon, D. and Spicker, D. (eds.), *The International Glossary on Poverty*. London: Zed Books, pp. 1–5.

Platt, L. (2008) '"Race" and Social Welfare', in Alcock, P., May, M. and Rowlingson, K. (eds.), *The Student's Companion to Social Policy*, 3rd edn. Oxford: Blackwell, pp. 369–377.

Plummer, K. (2003) 'Intimate Citizenship and Sexual Storytelling', in Weeks, J., Holland, J. and Waites, M. (eds.), *Sexualities and Society: A Reader*. Cambridge, UK: Polity Press, pp. 33–42.

Powell, M. and Barrientos, A. (2004) 'Welfare Regimes and the Welfare Mix', *European Journal of Political Research* 43: 83–105.

Priestly, M. (2010) 'Disability', in Castles, F., Leibfried, S., Lewis, J., Obinger, H. and Pierson, C. (eds.), *The Oxford Handbook of the Welfare State*. Oxford: Oxford University Press, pp. 406–419.

Rafferty, Y. (2008) 'The Impact of Trafficking on Children: Psychological and Social Policy Perspectives', *Journal of Society for Research in Child Development*, 2(1): pp. 13–18.

Rambaldini-Gooding, D. (2012) *The Trafficking of Women into Ireland: A Model of Best Practice in Service Provision*. Unpublished PhD thesis, School of Applied Social Science, University College Dublin.

Ransome, P. (2010) *Social Theory for Beginners*. Bristol: Policy Press.

Rawls, J. (1971) *A Theory of Justice*. London: Sage.

Raz, J. (1986) *The Morality of Freedom*. Oxford: Oxford University Press.

Reddin, M. (1978) *Universality and Selectivity: Strategies in Social Policy*. Dublin: NESC.

Reibling, N. (2010) 'Healthcare Systems in Europe: Towards an Incorporation of Patient Access', *Journal of European Social Policy*, 20: 5–18.

Reisman, D. (2001) *Richard Titmuss: Welfare and Society*, 2nd edn. London: Palgrave.

Rich, A. (1977) *Of Woman Born: Motherhood as Experience and Institution*. London: Virago.

Richardson, D. (ed.) (1996) *Theorising Heterosexuality*. Milton Keynes: Open University Press.

Richardson, D. (1997) 'Sexuality and Feminism', in Robinson, V. and Richardson, D. (eds.), *Introducing Women's Studies*, 2nd edn. London: Macmillan, pp. 152–174.

Richardson, D. (2000) 'Constructing Sexual Citizenship: Theorizing Sexual Rights', *Critical Social Policy*, 20: 105–135.

Rieger, E. and Leibfried, S. (2003) *Limits to Globalization*. London: Polity Press.

Robinson, V. and Richardson, D. (eds.) (1997) *Introducing Women's Studies*, 2nd edn. London: Macmillan.

Room, G. (2008a) 'Social Policy in Europe: Paradigms of Change', *Journal of European Social Policy*, 18: 345–352.

Room, G. (2008b) 'The International and Comparative Analysis of Social Exclusion: European Perspectives', in Kennet, P. (ed.), *A Handbook of Comparative Social Policy*. Cheltenham: Edward Elgar, pp. 341–354.

Rowntree, S. (1901) *Poverty: A Study of Town Life*. London: Macmillan.

Rowntree, S. (1941) *Poverty and Progress*. London: Longmans Green.

Rowntree, S. (2000) *Poverty: A Study of Town Life*, centennial edn. Bristol: Policy Press.

Rowntree, S. and Lavers, G.R. (1951) *Poverty and the Welfare State: A Third Social Survey of York Dealing Only with Economic Questions*. London: Longmans Green.

Sainsbury, D. (1994) *Gendering Welfare States*. Sage: London.

Sainsbury, D. (1996) *Gender Equality and Welfare States*. Cambridge, UK: Cambridge University Press.

Sainsbury, D. (ed.) (1999) *Gender and Welfare State Regimes*. Oxford: Oxford University Press.

Saunders, P. (2010) 'Inequality and Poverty', in Castles, F., Leibfried, S., Lewis, J., Obinger, H. and Pierson, C. (eds.), *The Oxford Handbook of the Welfare State*. Oxford: Oxford University Press, pp. 526–538.

Schmitter, P. (1974) 'Still the Century of Corporatism', *Review of Politics*, 36: 85–131.

Schultz, T. (1963) *The Economic Value of Education*. New York: Columbia University Press.

Scrivens, E. (1980) 'Towards a Theory of Rationing', in Leaper, R. (ed.), *Health, Wealth and Housing*. Oxford: Blackwell, pp. 223–239.

Sen, A. (1985) *Commodities and Capabilities*. Amsterdam: Elsevier Science Publishers.

Sen, A. (1991) *Poverty and Famines: An Essay on Entitlement and Deprivation*. Oxford: Clarendon Press.

Sen, A. (1999) *Development as Freedom*. Oxford: Oxford University Press.

Sen, A. (2000) *Social Exclusion: Concept, Application and Scrutiny*. Social Development Papers No. 1, Office of Environment and Social Development. Manila: Asian Development Bank.

Sen, A. (2009) *The Idea of Justice*. London: Allen Lane.

Sewell, W.H. (1992) 'A Theory of Structure: Duality, Agency and Transformation', *American Journal of Sociology*, 98(1): 1–29.

Shah, H. and Marks, N. (2004) *A Well-Being Manifesto for a Flourishing Society*. London: New Economics Foundation.

Shakespeare, T. (2000) 'The Social Relations of Care', in Lewis, G., Gewirtz, S. and Clarke, J. (eds.), *Rethinking Social Policy*. London: Sage, pp. 52–65.

Sharkey, P. (2000) *The Essentials of Community Care: A Guide for Practitioners*. London: Macmillan.

Shildrick, M. (2004) 'Silencing Sexuality: The Regulation of the Disabled Body', in Carabine, J. (ed.), *Sexualities, Personal Lives and Social Policy*. Milton Keynes: Open University Press, pp. 123–157.

Shils, E. (1957) 'Primordial, Personal, Sacred and Civil Ties', *British Journal of Sociology*, 8(2): 130–145.

Shuttleworth, R., Wedgwood, N. and Wilson, N.J. (2012) 'The Dilemma of Disabled Masculinity', *Men and Masculinities*, 15(2): 174–194.

Smith, A. (1776/1976) *An Inquiry into the Nature and Causes of the Wealth of Nations* (ed. by Campbell, R.H. and Skinner, A.S.). Oxford: Clarendon Press.

Smith, B.C. (1976) *Policy Making in British Government*. London: Martin Robertson.

Spicker, P. (2007) *The Idea of Poverty*. Bristol: Policy Press.

Spicker, P. (2008) *Social Policy Themes and Approaches*, 2nd edn. Bristol: Policy Press.

Spicker, P. and Gordon, D. (eds.) (1999) *Poverty: An International Glossary*. London: Zed Books.

Spicker, P., Álvarez Leguizamón, S. and Gordon, D. (eds.) (2007) *Poverty: An International Glossary*, 2nd edn. London: Zed Books.

Stephens, J.D. (2010) 'Social Rights of Citizenship', in Castles, F., Leibfried, S., Lewis, J., Obinger, H. and Pierson, C. (eds.), *The Oxford Handbook of the Welfare State*. Oxford: Oxford University Press, pp. 511–525.

Stiglitz, J. (2002) *Globalization and Its Discontents*. London: Penguin.

Stiglitz, J., Sen, A. and Fitoussi, J. (2009) *Report by the Commission on the Measurement of Economic Performance and Social Progress*. Available at http://www.stiglitz-sen-fitoussi.fr, www.communities.gov.uk/publications/communities/childwellbeing2009

Sutherland, H. (2005) 'Women, Men and the Redistribution of Income', *Fiscal Studies*, 18(1): 1–22.

Swank, D. (2010) 'Globalization', in Castles, F. and Leibfried, S., Lewis, J., Obinger, H. and Pierson, C. (eds.), *The Oxford Handbook of the Welfare State*. Oxford: Oxford University Press, pp. 318–330.

Sykes, B. (2010) 'Globalization and Social Policy', in Alcock, P., May, M. and Rowlingson, K. (eds.), *The Student's Companion to Social Policy*, 3rd edn. Oxford: Blackwell, pp. 430–437.

Taleb, N.N. (2007) *The Black Swan: The Impact of the Highly Improbable*. London: Penguin.

Taylor, D. (ed.) (1996) *Critical Social Policy: A Reader*. London: Sage.

Taylor-Gooby, P. (1991) 'Welfare State Regimes and Welfare Citizenship', *Journal of Social Policy*, 1(20): 93–105.

Taylor-Gooby, P. (2000) 'Risk and Welfare', in Taylor-Gooby, P. (ed.), *Risk, Trust and Welfare*. London: Palgrave, pp. 1–28.

Taylor-Gooby, P. (2004) 'New Risks and Social Change', in Taylor-Gooby, P. (ed.), *New Risks, New Welfare: The Transformation of the European Welfare State*. Oxford: Oxford University Press, pp. 1–28.

Tiemann, S. (1993) *Opinion on Social Exclusion*, Official Journal of the European Communities, J 93/C352/13.

Titmuss, R. (1962) 'The Welfare State: Images and Realities. Lecture at the University of California (1962)', in Alcock, P., Glennerster, H., Oakley, A. and Sinfield, A. (eds.) (2001), *Welfare and Wellbeing: Richard Titmuss's Contribution to Social Policy*. Bristol: Policy Press, pp. 49–58.

Titmuss, R. (1963) *Essays on the Welfare State*. London: Allen & Unwin.

Titmuss, R. (1967) 'Welfare State and Welfare Society', in Alcock, P., Glennester, H., Oakley, A. and Sinfield, A. (eds.), *Welfare and Wellbeing: Richard Titmuss's Contribution to Social Policy*. Bristol: Policy Press, pp. 113–124.

Titmuss, R. (1968) *Commitment to Welfare*. London: Allen & Unwin.

Titmuss, R. (1970) *The Gift Relationship*. London: Allen & Unwin.

Titmuss, R. (1974) *Social Policy: An Introduction*. London: Allen & Unwin.

Titmuss, R. (1976) *Essays on the Welfare State*, 3rd edn. London: Allen & Unwin.

Titmuss, R., Abel-Smith, B. and Titmuss, K. (1987) *The Philosophy of Richard Titmuss: Selected Writings of Richard M. Titmuss*. London: Allen & Unwin.

Titmuss, R. (2001) 'The Social Division of Welfare: Some Reflections on the Search for Equity, Lecture at the University of Birmingham in honour of Eleanor Rathbone (1955)', in Alcock, P., Glennester, H., Oakley, A. and Sinfield, A. (eds.), *Welfare and Wellbeing: Richard Titmuss's Contribution to Social Policy*. Bristol: Policy Press, pp. 59–70.

Townsend, P. (1979) *Poverty in the United Kingdom*. Harmondsworth, UK: Penguin.

Tronto, J. (1993) *Moral Boundaries: A Political Argument for an Ethics of Care*. New York: Routledge.

Turner, B.S. (2008) *The Body and Society*, 3rd edn. London: Sage.

Twigg, J. (2000a) 'Social Policy and the Body', in Lewis, G., Gewirtz, S. and Clarke, J. (eds.), *Rethinking Social Policy*. London: Sage, pp. 127–140.

Twigg, J. (2000b) *Bathing: The Body and Community Care*. London: Routledge.

Twigg, J. (2002) 'The Body in Social Policy: Mapping a Territory', *Journal of Social Policy*, 31(3): 421–439.

Twigg, J. (2006) *The Body in Health and Social Care*. London: Palgrave Macmillan.

Twigg, J. and Atkin, K. (1994) *Carers Perceived: Policy and Practice in Informal Care*. Buckingham: Open University Press.

UN DESA (United Nations Department of Economic and Social Affairs) (2008) *Trends in International Migrant Stock: The 2008 Revision*. Available at http://esa.un.org/migration/index.asp?panel=1

UNDP (United Nations Development Programme) (2005) *International Co-operation at a Crossroads: Aid, Trade and Security in an Unequal World*. New York: UNDP.

UNHCR (United Nations High Commissioner for Refugees) (1984) *Cartagena Declaration on Refugees, Colloquium on the International Protection of Refugees in Central America, Mexico and Panama*, 22 November. Available at: http://www. unhcr.org/refworld/docid/3ae6b36ec.html

United Nations (2000) *United Nations Convention on Transnational Organized Crime and the Protocol to Prevent, Suppress and Punish Trafficking in Persons, Especially Women and Children*. Adopted and opened for signature, ratification and accession by General Assembly resolution 55/25, 15 November. Available at: http://www2.ohchr.org/english/law/protocoltraffic.htm

United Nations (2002) *International Migration*. New York: United Nations.

United Nations (2005) Article 25 of the UN Convention on the Rights of Persons with Disabilities (CRPD). New York: United Nations.

Van Berkel, R. (2009) 'The Provision of Income Protection and Activation Services for the Unemployed in "Active" Welfare States: An International Comparison', *Journal of Social Policy*, 39(1): 17–34.

Van Berkel, R., De Graaf, W. and Sirovátka, T. (eds.) (2011) *The Governance of Active Welfare States in Europe*. London: Palgrave Macmillan.

Viebrock, E. and Clasen, J. (2009) 'Flexicurity and Welfare Reform: A Review', *Socio-economic Review*, 7: 305–331.

Volkomer, W. (2007) *American Government*, 11th edn. New York: Pearson.

Walby, S. (1990) *Theorizing Patriarchy*. London: Blackwell.

Walby, S. (2012) 'Sen and the Measurement of Justice and Capabilities: A Problem in Theory and Practice', *Theory, Culture & Society*, 29(1): 99–118.

Walsh, F. (2003) 'Family Resilience: A Framework for Clinical Practice', *Family Process*, 42(1): pp. 1–18.

Walsh, F. and McGoldrick, M. (eds.) (1991) *Living beyond Loss*. New York: W.W. Norton.

Watson, S. (2000) 'Foucault and Social Policy', in Lewis, G., Gewirtz, S. and Clarke, J. (eds.), *Rethinking Social Policy*. London: Sage, pp. 66–77.

WCED (World Commission on Environment and Development) (1987) *Our Common Future*. Oxford: Oxford University Press.

Weeks, J. (1986) *Sexuality*. London: Ellis Horwood.

Weeks, J. (1996) 'The Idea of a Sexual Community', *Soundings*, 2: 71–84.

Weeks, J. (1998) 'The Sexual Citizen', *Theory, Culture & Society*, 15(3): 35–52.

Weeks, J. (2001) 'Live and Let Love? Reflections on the Unfinished Sexual Revolution of Our Times', in Edwards, R. and Glover, J. (eds.), *Risk and Citizenship: Key Issues in Welfare*. London: Routledge, pp. 48–63.

Weeks, J., Holland, J. and Waites, M. (eds.) (2003) *Sexualities and Society: A Reader*. Cambridge, UK: Polity Press.

WHO (World Health Organization) (2001) *International Classification of Functioning, Disability and Health*. Geneva: WHO.

WHO (1946) Preamble to the Constitution of the World Health Organization as adopted by the International Health Conference, New York, 19–22 June 1946; signed on 22 July 1946 by the representatives of 61 States (Official Records of the World Health Organization, no. 2) and entered into force on 7 April 1948.

WHO (2011) *World Report on Disability*. Geneva: WHO.

Wilensky, H.L. (1975) *The Welfare State and Equality: Structural and Ideological Roots of Public Expenditures*. Berkeley: University of California Press.

Wilhagen, T. and Tros, F. (2004) 'The Concept of Flexicurity: A New Approach to Regulating Employment and Labour Markets', *Transfer: European Review of Labour and Research*, 10(2): 166–186.

Williams, F. (1989) *Social Policy: A Critical Introduction, Issues of Race, Gender and Class*. Cambridge, UK: Polity Press.

Williams, F. (1997) 'Feminism and Social Policy', in Robinson, V. and Richardson, D. (eds.), *Introducing Women's Studies*. London: Macmillan, pp. 258–281.

Williams, F. (1999) 'Good Enough Principles for Welfare', *Journal of Social Policy*, 28(4): 667–687.

Williams, F. (2000) 'Principles of Recognition and Respect in Welfare', in Lewis, G., Gewirtz, S. and Clarke, J. (eds.), *Rethinking Social Policy*. London: Open University Press, pp. 338–352.

Wilson, E. (1977) *Women and the Welfare State*. London: Tavistock Publications.

Wispelaere, J. and Stirton, L. (2004) 'The Many Faces of Universal Basic Income', *Political Quarterly*, 75(3): 266–274.

Wittgenstein, L. (1953) *Philosophical Investigations*, translated by Anscombe, G.E.M. New York: Macmillan.

World Bank (2011) *Learning for All: Investing in People's Knowledge and Skills to Promote Development*. World Bank Group Education Strategy 2020.1. Washington: International Bank for Reconstruction and Development/World Bank.

Yeates, N. (2001) *Globalization and Social Policy*. London: Sage.

Yeates, N. (ed.) (2008) *Understanding Global Social Policy*. Bristol: Policy Press.

Yeates, N. and Holden, C. (eds.) (2009) *The Global Social Policy Reader*. Bristol: Policy Press.

INDEX